Lifelong Engagement in Sport and Physical Activity

Sport and physical activity should now be understood as lifelong activity, beginning in childhood, and accessible to participants of all levels of ability. This book offers an overview of some of the core concerns underlying lifelong engagement in sport and physical activity, encompassing every age and phase of engagement. The book explores key models of engagement from around the world, as well as specific areas of research that will help the reader understand this important topic.

In adopting a lifespan approach, the book pays particular attention to sport and physical activity during childhood and adolescence as well as transitions into adulthood, the developmental periods when participation in sport and physical activity are most likely to decline. Understanding more about participation during these early years is important for sustaining participation during adulthood. The book also addresses issues relating to sport and physical activity during adulthood, across a range of different populations, while a final section examines sport and physical activity among older adults, an often overlooked, but growing segment of society in this context.

Lifelong Engagement in Sport and Physical Activity is important reading for undergraduate and postgraduate students in teacher education, sport and coaching science, and for health promoters, coaches, teachers and relevant bodies and organisations in sport and education.

This book is published in partnership with ICSSPE, and is part of the Perspectives series.

Nicholas L. Holt is an Associate Professor in the Faculty of Physical Education and Recreation at the University of Alberta, Canada, where he directs the Child and Adolescent Sport and Activity laboratory. He is also the Associate Editor of *The Sport Psychologist* journal and recently edited a book titled *Positive Youth Development through Sport* (Routledge, 2007).

Margaret Talbot is President of the International Council of Sport Science and Physical Education (ICSSPE) and Principal of Margaret Talbot Consulting. She is currently leading a team of experts developing a twenty-first century physical education curriculum for schools in Egypt; and is Physical Education Champion for SportsXtra. Professor Talbot was appointed Officer of the Order of the British Empire (OBE) for services to physical education and sport in 1993.

Perspectives
The Multidisciplinary Series of Physical Education
and Sport Science

By publishing Perspectives, ICSSPE aims to facilitate the application of sport science results to practical areas of sport by integrating the various sport science branches. In each volume of Perspectives, expert contributions from different disciplines address a specific physical education or sport science theme, which has been identified by a group of leading international experts.

Published by ICSSPE – www.icsspe.org

School Sport and Competition
Edited by Steve Bailey

Physical Activity and Ageing
Edited by Steve Bailey

The Business of Sport
Edited by Darlene Kluka and Guido Schilling

Sport and Information Technology
Edited by Gretchen Ghent and Darlene Kluka

Health Enhancing Physical Activity
Edited by Pekka Oja and Jan Borms

Aspects of Sport Governance
Edited by Darlene Kluka, William Stier Jr. and Guido Schilling

Sport for Persons with a Disability
Edited by Colin Higgs and Yves Vanlandewijck

Talent Identification and Development
The search for sporting excellence
Edited by Richard Fisher and Richard Bailey

Published by Routledge – www.routledge.com/sport

Children, Obesity and Exercise
Edited by Andrew Hills, Neil King and Nuala Byrne

Lifelong Engagement in Sport and Physical Activity
Participation and performance across the lifespan
Edited by Nicholas L. Holt and Margaret Talbot

Lifelong Engagement in Sport and Physical Activity

Participation and performance
across the lifespan

Edited by
Nicholas L. Holt and Margaret Talbot

ICSSPE

Routledge
Taylor & Francis Group

LONDON AND NEW YORK

First published 2011
by Routledge
2 Park Square, Milton Park, Abingdon, Oxon OX14 4RN

Simultaneously published in the USA and Canada
by Routledge
711 Third Avenue, New York, NY 10017

Routledge is an imprint of the Taylor & Francis Group, an informa business

First issued in paperback 2013

© 2011 ICSSPE ICSSPE

British Library Cataloguing in Publication Data
A catalogue record for this book is available from the British Library

Library of Congress Cataloging in Publication Data
A catalog record for this book has been requested

ISBN: 978-0-415-67589-5 (hbk)
ISBN: 978-0-415-85790-1 (pbk)
ISBN: 978-0-203-80718-7 (ebk)

Typeset in Times New Roman by Swales & Willis Ltd, Exeter, Devon

Contents

About ICSSPE

The International Council of Sport Science and Physical Education (ICSSPE) was founded in Paris, France, in 1958. It is an international umbrella organisation that disseminates and promotes findings from sport science and highlights their practical application in cultural and educational contexts.

The organisation has a membership of approximately 300 national and international governmental and non-governmental organisations, federations and institutes of sport, sport science and physical education that cooperate in a multi- or interdisciplinary setting on an international level. The organisation provides worldwide scientific knowledge and practical experiences in many different disciplines.

ICSSPE works towards achieving a higher awareness of human values inherent in sport, physical activity and physical education worldwide. There are three primary objectives, namely to encourage international cooperation, to facilitate differentiation in sport science whilst promoting the integration of various branches, and to make scientific knowledge available.

The current working programme of ICSSPE emphasises the importance of healthy living across the lifespan and the continuum of human performance/development, ethics and professionalisation, and quality physical education. This programme, decided upon by ICSSPE members, is translated into practice through the working channels of:

- Science, by analysing and initiating research across all disciplines using the knowledge and experience of expert organisations and scientific institutions;
- Service, by facilitating the exchange of information among members and partners by organising conferences, meetings and seminars and designing publications; and
- Advocacy, by acting as a voice for sport science and physical education and encouraging international initiatives to promote and improve the position of physical education and sport science as a strong partner for the development of human society.

To support cooperation across disciplines and to assist practitioners and administrators by providing research based information, ICSSPE focuses on the development of multi- and interdisciplinary publications. Perspectives, the multi-disciplinary series of ICSSPE, has been developed to disseminate information to all interested organisations and institutions and to integrate the various sport science disciplines. By doing so, the organisation facilitates the application of research results to practical areas of sport. In each volume of this series, expert contributions address current and relevant themes.

Previous titles of the series include: *Talent Identification and Development – The Search for Sporting Excellence*; *Children, Obesity and Exercise – Prevention*; *Treatment and Management of Childhood and Adolescent Obesity*; and *Sport for Persons with a Disability*.

The motivation for this volume, the tenth within the Perspectives series, has its origin in the emphasis that is placed on health and lifelong participation in physical activity by many scientists, governments, international non-governmental and governmental organisations, particularly in the health and sport sectors, on both national and international levels. Although there is much research based evidence available, the political will to implement structural change that leads to lifelong engagement in sport and physical activity can still be strengthened in many countries. This statement is made despite the growing number of pre-school activities in many countries, a variety of activity programmes developed by the health sector and a growing number of master's programmes in different sports. With this publication, ICSSPE delivers information from different countries for students, academics, politicians and administrators working in this, and related, fields.

In line with ICSSPE's working programme, the publication analyses participation and performance in sport as well as in physical activity in different periods across the human lifespan including childhood and adolescence, adulthood and late adulthood. The relationship between performance and participation especially continues to be an unsolved issue for decision-makers.

The publication documents how different concepts of sport, such as high-performance sport, sport for all, adapted physical activities, as well as physical activity, can contribute to different fields of human and societal development.

Contributors

Len Almond
Dr Len Almond is Visiting Professor at St. Mary's University College in Twickenham, London. He is also the Foundation Director of the British Heart Foundation National Centre for Physical Activity at Loughborough University where he coordinates the Older Adults programmes with Bob Laventure. Len is also the chairperson of the National Coalition for Active Ageing.

Richard Bailey
Richard Bailey is a writer and researcher on education and sport. A former teacher in both primary and secondary schools and a teacher trainer, he has been a Professor at Canterbury, Roehampton and most recently, Birmingham Universities. Richard has undertaken funded research in every continent of the world. He works with UNESCO as Expert Adviser for Physical Education, the World Health Organisation, the European Union, and many similar agencies. He has carried out research on behalf of the English and Scottish governments, as well as numerous educational and sports agencies. In 2004 he was selected by delegates from more than 200 countries to act as Rapporteur for UNESCO's Athens Declaration. He is author of more than 100 publications, including books, academic and professional articles and monographs. Recent books include the *Routledge Physical Education Reader*, the *Sage Handbook of the Philosophy of Education*, *The Philosophy of Education: An Introduction* (Continuum) and *Physical Education for Learning* (Continuum).

Dave Collins
Dave Collins is Professor of Coaching and Performance at the University of Central Lancashire and Director of Grey Matters Consultants. Previously, as Performance Director of UK Athletics, Dave directed the programme which progressed the team from twenty-fourth to fifth (World then Olympic); twenty-first to third (World Indoors); and twelfth to first (European Team). Dave has over 90 peer review publications and 25 books/book chapters published. He has worked with more than 60 World or Olympic medallists plus professional sports teams, dancers, musicians and executives in business and public service. Current research interests include performer and coach development, cognitive expertise and the

promotion of peak performance across different challenge environments. As a performer, Dave was excessively average at low skill sports such as rugby, American football, martial arts and outdoor pursuits. He has coached rugby to national level. Dave is a Fellow of the Society of Martial Arts and the British Association of Sport and Exercise Sciences, and an Associate Fellow of the British Psychological Society.

Paul De Knop

Paul De Knop, PhD Physical Education and Master in Sports Sociology and Sports Management from the University of Leicester (UK), is Professor in the Faculty of Physical Education of Vrije Universiteit Brussel, where he teaches in the areas of sport, leisure and physical education from a socio-pedagogical perspective. His research interests include youth and sport, sport and ethnic minorities, sport and tourism, sport management, quality in sport and sport policy.

Paul's research relates to, amongst other things, benchmarking of top-level sport success, top-level sport students at the university, competencies of sport managers, sport policy strategic plans, ethical and qualitative aspects of youth sport and evaluation of physical education programmes.

Lars-Magnus Engström

Lars-Magnus Engström, Professor Emeritus from Stockholm University, Sweden, has studied sport habits of children, young people and adults in various projects since the end of the 1960s. Central issues have been how, and under which conditions, knowledge, skills and values within leisure culture are communicated. His research focuses on the importance of sports, fitness activities and outdoor life for the development of personal identity and lifestyle. He is one of the founders of the European College of Sport Sciences (ECSS) and has published around 50 scientific articles in Swedish journals, 25 articles in international journals/publications and 20 books or major reports. Lars-Magnus is currently connected to the Swedish School of Sport and Health Sciences in Stockholm.

Elizabeth A. Fallon

Elizabeth A. Fallon is an Assistant Professor in the Department of Kinesiology at Kansas State University where she co-directs the Physical Activity and Public Health Laboratory. Her research maintains two primary focus areas pertaining to the positive effects of physical activity for the prevention and treatment of obesity and chronic diseases: (1) testing health behaviour theory related to physical activity initiation and maintenance; and (2) the promotion of physical activity among women and minorities.

Paul A. Ford

Paul A. Ford is Director of Olympic and Paralympic Partnership Operations at the University of East London. He is a BASES Accredited Physiologist (Scientific Support) who has worked with several elite athletes and professional sports teams within the UK. Currently, Paul is helping to coordinate the delivery of

Games-time training centres for several Olympic and Paralympic teams for the London 2012 Games, including the United States Olympic Committee. Paul specialises in paediatric research on the effects of growth and maturation upon athletic performance. His doctoral research was focused on physical activity and health-related outcomes in children, specifically the 'Effects of brisk walking on children aged 5–11 years old'.

Nicholas L. Holt

Nicholas Holt is an Associate Professor in the Faculty of Physical Education and Recreation at the University of Alberta, where he directs the Child and Adolescent Sport and Activity laboratory. His research focuses on psychosocial dimensions of youth sport and physical activity participation. He is particularly interested in the roles of parents and coaches along with peer interactions. His research is funded by the Social Sciences and Humanities Research Council of Canada and the Canadian Institutes of Health Research. He is the Associate Editor of *The Sport Psychologist* journal and recently edited a book titled *Positive Youth Development through Sport* (Routledge, 2007).

Marijke Hopman-Rock

Professor Marijke Hopman-Rock is working at TNO (Netherlands Organisation for Applied Scientific Research) in Leiden and is a Professor in physical activity and health of older persons at the VU University Medical Centre in Amsterdam. She is also on the management team of the Body@Work Research Center on Physical Activity, Work and Health. Her professional background is Biology, Psychology (statistics) and Epidemiology (PhD). As a part-time professor in Amsterdam, she guides several PhD students. She is also founding (past) chair of the European Network for Action on Ageing and Physical Activity (EUNAAPA) and associate partner in several European Union projects in the area of physical activity (PA). She is Associate Editor of the *Journal of Aging and Physical Activity* and *BMC Public Health* and is also in the board of other journals, including the Human Kinetics journal, *Active Aging Today*. In this publication, first issued in 2009, Marijke writes columns about Reach and Adoption of PA programmes for older persons as this journal is aimed at health professionals working in the area of PA and aging. During her career at TNO, she has written more than 60 peer reviewed articles and numerous reports and book chapters. In the past, she was Head of the Department of PA and Health at TNO and programme manager in the same area; Vice-president of the EGREPA (European Group for Research in Elderly and PA) and co-chair of the Aging interest group of the American College of Sport and Exercise Medicine (ACSM).

Clare Hume

Clare Hume, BAppSc (Hons), PhD, is National Heart Foundation of Australia Post-doctoral research fellow at the Centre for Physical Activity and Nutrition Research in the School of Exercise and Nutrition Sciences, Deakin University, Australia. Her research interests are primarily concerned with children's and adolescents' physical activity, and particularly physical and social environmental influences on behaviour. Her research has included measuring whether factors in the physical and social environment, both at home and in the neighbourhood, are associated with children's physical activity. Her particular interest relates to understanding whether these factors influence children's active transport and independent mobility. In addition, Clare's research focuses on intervention strategies targeting physical activity and sedentary behaviours among children. This includes the development and refinement of intervention strategies, which aim to promote increased physical activity and reduced sedentary behaviours among children, both in the family and school settings.

Maryam Koushkie Jahromi
Maryam Koushkie Jahromi is an Assistant Professor in the Department of Physical Education and Sport Sciences, School of Education and Psychology at the Shiraz University, in Iran, where she teaches and directs many researchers. She holds a PhD in exercise physiology and her research focuses on physiological dimensions of women's sport and physical activity participation. She is particularly interested in Muslim women in sport from social and cultural aspects. She is an executive board member of the International Association of Physical Education and Sport for Girls and Women (IAPESGW) and in 1998 was the awarded best student in her PhD entrance exam of exercise physiology. She has published books and articles nationally and internationally and presented congress speeches in several countries including Canada, China, South Africa and Saudi Arabia. She has been a referee and scientific board member of a number of national and international conferences.

Camilla J. Knight
Camilla J. Knight is a PhD student in the Faculty of Physical Education and Recreation at the University of Alberta. She is completing her PhD under the supervision of Dr Nick Holt in the Child and Adolescent Sport and Activity Research Laboratory. Her research interests are concerned with the psycho-social experiences of children in sport, particularly focused upon the influence of parents. Recent studies have examined athletes' preferences for parental behaviours at youth sport competitions, coaches' perceptions of parental involvement in youth sport and understanding the experiences of parents involved in youth sport. Camilla has produced a number of parent education materials, including parental dos and don'ts lists, a parental behaviour leaflet and presentations. She has also consulted with various tennis organisations in Canada and the UK, providing recommendations for improving parental involvement in junior tennis.

Áine MacNamara
Áine MacNamara is a Senior Lecturer in Elite Performance at the Institute of Coaching and Performance at the University of Central Lancashire. The Institute for Coaching and Performance is focused on developing providers of, and the systems employed in, the enhancement of performance. Áine is currently researching

talent development processes across different performance domains, with a particular interest in the role that psychological characteristics play in the realisation of potential.

Howard L. Nixon II

Howard L. Nixon is Professor of Sociology and former Chair of the Department of Sociology, Anthropology and Criminal Justice at Towson University in Baltimore, Maryland. His primary teaching interests are the sociology of sport, organisational deviance and the sociology of higher education, and his research and writing in recent years have focused on commercial aspects of college athletics, disability sports and pain and injury in sports. His most recent book, *Sport in a Changing World* (Paradigm, 2008), examines the dynamics of commercialised sports in a global context. He has had various roles in the North American Society for the Sociology of Sport (NASSS) and he currently serves on the editorial board of its journal, the *Sociology of Sport Journal*.

Gemma Pearce

Gemma Pearce (MSc) is a Doctoral Researcher in the School of Sport and Exercise Sciences at the University of Birmingham. Her areas of research focus around life transitions, body image concerns and health. She previously worked as a research methods specialist with Richard Bailey at Roehampton University, after doing an MSc in Sport and Exercise Psychology at Chichester University. Recent publications and presentations have focused on children's perceptions of health and play, research methods and literature reviews, self-presentational concerns, elite athletes' attitudes towards doping, gifted and talented education and player pathways in sport.

Anke Reints

Anke Reints, Master in Developmental Psychology from the Universiteit Utrecht and Sport Psychology from the Universiteit van Amsterdam, is currently finalising her PhD on career development and transitions of elite athletes at the Vrije Universiteit Brussel. In 2008, she conducted research on the provision of career support services worldwide for the International Olympic Committee (IOC). Anke presented at several international congresses on the career development of and career support services for talented and elite athletes. Finally, as a sport psychology consultant, Anke has worked with several talented tennis players within elite sport schools.

Jo Salmon

Jo Salmon, BA, BBSc (Hons), PhD, is National Heart Foundation and sanofi-aventis Career Development Award Fellow in the Centre for Physical Activity and Nutrition Research at the School of Exercise and Nutrition Sciences, Deakin University, Australia.

Jo's programme of research focuses on the behavioural epidemiology of children's and adults' physical activity and sedentary behaviour. She is interested in the assessment of these behaviours; in understanding the individual, social and environmental factors that influence participation; and the development of strategies to promote physical activity and reduce sedentary time among children and adults.

Recent research includes the development and validation of instruments to assess physical activity and sedentary behaviour among children; descriptive studies of influences on child and youth physical activity and sedentary behaviour; and examination of the effectiveness of strategies to reduce children's sitting time and promote physical activity at school and at home.

Maarten Stiggelbout

Maarten Stiggelbout received his MSc degree in 1990. He then went to TUFTs University in Boston where he visited the post-doctoral course in Epidemiology (by Kenneth Rothman and Lemeshaw). Since completing his university degree, he worked for a range of organisations: The Dutch Ministry of Welfare, Public Health and Culture from 1990 to 1992, where he carried out two freelance projects: (1) the organisation and reporting of an invitational expert meeting 'Sports, Physical Activity and Health'; and (2) the inventory of scientific research in sports in the Netherlands; The Netherlands Institute of Sports and Health from 1992 to 1995 as Consultant for Physical Activity and Health, and project leader for the development of a database on exercise programmes for the elderly and people with chronic diseases; TNO Prevention and Health, Department of Physical Activity and Health, from 1995 until 2005 as a researcher in the field of physical activity, sport and e-health, monitoring physical activity and health, as well as offering consultancy and research on governmental policy; and the Netherlands Institute for Health Promotion (NIGZ), from mid-2005 to the present. Maarten is currently Senior Advisor with Specialty Healthy Lifestyle. He is involved in the development and implementation of healthy lifestyle programmes, i.e. Woerden Active/Local Active, Scoring for Health, and he is also advisor to the National Action Plan Sports and Physical Activity for the NISB. He completed his thesis on More Exercise for Seniors in 2008, on which his chapter in this book is based and relates to.

Margaret Talbot, PhD OBE FRSA

Margaret Talbot is President of the International Council of Sport Science and Physical Education (ICSSPE) and Principal of Margaret Talbot Consulting. Previous employment includes Chief Executive, Association for Physical Education (United Kingdom (UK)); Chief Executive, Central Council of Physical Recreation, the umbrella organisation for English and UK non-governmental sport organisations; and Carnegie Research Professor and Head of Sport, Leeds Metropolitan University. She is a lifelong researcher, advocate and activist for equity in sport and physical education and has continually fought to defend and promote the statutory entitlement to physical education, which is the cornerstone of its status and development in the UK. She is currently leading a team of experts developing a twenty-first century physical education curriculum for schools in

Egypt; and is Physical Education Champion for SportsXtra, a company supporting the delivery of physical education and physical activity, mainly in primary schools.

Professor Talbot was appointed Officer of the Order of the British Empire (OBE) for services to physical education and sport in 1993.

Martin Toms

Dr Martin Toms is a Senior Lecturer in Coaching and Sport Education in the Department of Sport Pedagogy at the University of Birmingham. He is a former professional cricket coach and amateur player and has spent some years researching the coaching experiences of young performers at grassroots level in the UK. His areas of research and teaching include the sociological aspects of participant and talent development and grassroots youth sports participation. In addition he is also interested in the influence of the family and other socio-cultural factors in the sports participation process. He works closely with organisations and National Governing Bodies such as The Professional Golfers' Association (PGA), and was responsible for developing the partnership programmes between the University and the PGA. He is currently co-editor of the *European Journal of Sport and Society* and is involved in a Europe-wide Da Vinci funded project investigating occupational standards in sport.

Paul Wylleman

Paul Wylleman, PhD Psychology, is Professor in the Faculties of Physical Education and Physiotherapy and of Psychology and Educational Sciences at the Vrije Universiteit Brussel where he teaches sport psychology, mental support provision across the athletic career and lifestyle management for elite athletes. He is Head of the Department Topsport and Study, which provides support services to elite student-athletes. Paul has published articles, chapters and books and has been a keynote speaker at international congresses as well as at meetings of the IOC, European Olympic Committees (EOC) and national Olympic Committees on the topics of, amongst others, career and lifestyle management of elite (young) athletes, the quality of sport psychology support service/providers and mental skills of elite athletes and coaches. Paul Wylleman coordinated the project Career Support Services for Elite Sport Federations and is a sport psychology consultant to the Belgian Olympic Committee and elite sport federations.

Bradley W. Young

Bradley W. Young, PhD, is an Assistant Professor in the School of Human Kinetics in the Faculty of Health Sciences at the University of Ottawa. His research considers the psycho-social aspects of participation in sport across the lifespan, and investigates how such participation relates to issues of successful aging and the retention of skilled sport performance. He is specifically interested in identifying the various agents and groups in the social environment of aging athletes that facilitate prolonged sport commitment and motivation. He examines topics such as perceived barriers to lifelong sport activity, as well as benefits from such participation among middle-aged and older persons, in order to inform strategies for promoting Masters Sport and Seniors Games programmes. His research is funded by the Social Sciences and Humanities Research Council of Canada, in concert with Sport Canada.

Editors' introduction

Margaret Talbot and Nicholas L. Holt

This collection represents the mission and core values of the International Council of Sport Science and Physical Education (ICSSPE) – the promotion of the role of physical activity and sport; and multi-disciplinary insights gained from different countries and cultures. It also demonstrates what the ICSSPE 'Perspectives' series is about, by celebrating the respective contributions of a range of sciences and the unique capacity for reflective theory and practice that multi-disciplinary approaches provide. The chapters in this edited collection, both individually and collectively, show that sport and exercise sciences cannot afford to ignore the influence of context and culture, or to confine study to any one theoretical or applied framework.

The theme of the book – lifelong engagement in sport and physical activity – is challenging, especially so because the choice has been to include both participation and performance sport as foci; and to offer two chapters which focus on specific groups – Muslim women and people with disabilities. These chapters enrich and extend the scope of the collection, but also show the difficulties of including sufficient research across heterogeneous populations. While the contributions come from eight countries and four continents, the editors are acutely aware of the omission of material from Africa, Central and East Asia and Latin America. Forthcoming editions in the 'Perspectives' series will attempt to redress this.

A further challenge was to secure research which represents the whole life span. Tracking lifelong engagement is notoriously difficult, not least because of the scarcity of longitudinal research, mainly because of the expense, as well as the problems involved in maintaining contact with research populations over a number of years. Since almost all the chapters provide 'snapshots' of the role of sport and/or physical activity in people's lives, at different stages of their lives, within particular cultures and among particular cohorts, it is not possible to claim representativeness of the findings, although there is an extent of verification across the different chapters from different countries. Engström's chapter alone describes tracking a cohort of children through their youth and into middle age. The task for researchers wishing to explore life span processes more accurately appears to be to persuade those undertaking large scale longitudinal research projects that participants' relationships with sport and physical activity are important enough to the overall survey data to include in the successive moments of data capture across the years. This would also have the advantage of ensuring that people's engagement in physical activity and sport is seen within the overall contexts of their lives and life stages; and that life transitions can be seen against the backgrounds in which they occur. To achieve this, grant-making agencies will need to commit to long-term funding; and universities and other research agencies will need to accept that outcomes from longitudinal research will be deferred, sometimes for decades.

These accounts, however, do show, very clearly, that sport and physical activity are capable of making hugely positive and significant contributions throughout people's lives, whether they participate at recreational or performance level, or seek to improve health and fitness or avoid morbidity; and that this is true of people from all walks of life and at all ages and life stages. Here are opportunities to break myths and challenge stereotypes related to ageism and life stageism, gender, ability, culture and religion.

Scoping the book across the life span has been ambitious, and has exposed the scarcity of longitudinal research that effectively tracks engagement in sport and physical activity across people's lives. It is possible that some significant insights could be gained by retrospective approaches, such as life histories, which are commonly used in other social sciences, in evaluating the influence of (for example) education (Goodson and Sikes, 2001); and of health crises and illness upon family lives and individuals' careers (Moss and Goldstein, 1986). Some attempts were made in the United Kingdom, during the 1980s and 1990s, to assess the potential of such approaches for research into leisure and recreation behaviour, including people's uses of physical activity and sport as recovery after traumatic life events (see Hedges, 1986; Talbot, 1997, 1998). It is regrettable that the rich data and theoretical explorations of sport and recreation participation which are available in published leisure journals and books have apparently not been visible to sport psychologists and researchers into exercise participation and adherence, since much of this work is directly relevant to their enquiries. This is yet another argument for multi-disciplinary approaches.

It has to be acknowledged that multi-disciplinary approaches, while providing multi-dimensional, more holistic views of human experience and the dynamics of their lives, do pose tough challenges, which must be recognised and addressed. The sheer enormity of the task, in searching for and using published work in several disciplines and fields of study, is one factor. More daunting, however, is the need for enormous commitment, when researchers are moving out of areas which are familiar to them, and over which they have a level of mastery, into research and writing which is unfamiliar and often threatening: this truly does represent a move from one's comfort zone, and requires the building of trustful relationships between collaborating researchers. The benefits when this can be achieved are clear, as is shown in Chapter 4, which offers a rich range of insights through collaboration by six authors who between them span social and health science approaches, applied to sport, physical activity and exercise.

There is the further challenge of varying terminology. Even before meeting the potential misunderstandings between differential use of the same language in different countries and cultures, different sport and exercise sciences and physical education employ different terms, often related to the primary purpose of whether the experience is related to analysis of participation, learning, performance sport or health benefit. The notion of 'exercise adherence' is central to health promotion, but less relevant to researchers of life stage participation. There remains little work on the constant and changing meanings of physical activity and sport to those engaged in it, as their lives and circumstances evolve. This perhaps is related to the dearth of longitudinal research available, but possibly also is a reflection of distinctive concepts and constructs related to different disciplines and fields of study. The crucial importance of conceptual clarity in all research, but especially multi-disciplinary research, is very apparent.

The clustering of research around particular stages of the life span, too, is worthy of remark. It is not surprising that so much research has been focused upon the phases of childhood and adolescence, given the dramatic and fundamental changes that take place during this period of young people's lives. This period is also assumed to lay down the basis for future life. Yet the evidence for this in the research, as is noted by several of the authors in this collection, is sparse. This is not to say that there *are* no relationships between childhood, adolescence and adulthood habits of physical activity and sport – just that there is little evidence to demonstrate them. This is another function of the lack of research which successfully tracks experiences between these stages, and it offers a rich potential research agenda.

The focus on childhood and adolescence is possibly also explainable by recognising the extent to which social problem definition focuses on adolescence – the period during which the behaviour of young people, especially young men, becomes problematic for older people. The state policy deployment of physical activity and sport in providing what society sees as positive alternatives to anti-social, unhealthy or deviant behaviour, is universal, across cultures and state systems. This, too, helps to explain why there has been so much research attention to this life stage. Similarly, the interest of physical education in identifying the impact of school and curriculum programmes on children's and young people's participation, gives further impetus to and extends the work on the sporting and physical activity behaviour of this age range and life stage. There are several references by the contributing authors in this collection, which highlight the vital importance of children's and young people's experiences of physical education at school, and their influence on later engagement.

However, other life stages are relatively neglected; and sound data on physical activity, including physical play, during the early years of childhood, and its interaction with later engagement, is very rare. The physical and social changes associated with the early years are arguably even greater and more rapid than those experienced during adolescence, yet little attention has been focused on this stage. Researchers appear to share the reluctance of actors to work with children! Yet even young children are capable of articulating what is important to them, about their experiences and learning. The contributions of early-years specialists and childhood kinesiologists are urgently needed to shed light on this. The inclusion of emerging approaches like the development of physical literacy (see Whitehead,

2010) could help to provide some continuity and coherence of thinking about the way individuals learn, adapt and deploy their physical capacities at different stages of their lives and in different circumstances; and could make a very special contribution to knowledge about the early years. This emphasises the need for inclusion of insights from physical education and pedagogy, in examination of physical activity and sport across the life span.

Given the reported power of the length and quality of educational experience and achievement in physical education and sport on the later engagement of young people and adults, it is surprising that so little attention has been focused on the role of higher education, especially since the percentage of young people accessing higher education is increasing in countries across the world; and the length of time spent in full-time education in many countries is also increasing. The international commitment to ensuring better access to education for children and young people in those countries where access is limited, especially for girls, as represented by the United Nations Millennium Goals, provides a policy background for international, longitudinal tracking of the relationships between education, physical education and engagement in physical activity and sport.

Similarly, the data from leisure studies has demonstrated the power of the influence of life events on individuals' participation and performance in physical activity and sport – life events like bereavement, life partnerships beginning or breaking up, marriage, and the birth of children and parenthood. Since the influence of parents is so important for children's participation, this is a serious omission. There appear to be few references to these in this collection, other than in Chapter 5, which refers to them as cited in the biographies of internationally successful sportspeople. This omission is partly explained by the dearth of study on the dynamics of adult engagement – and also illustrates the challenges of dealing with a life stage which is so much longer than those of younger people, and hence with a very wide range of heterogeneity. But the chapters which focus on adult engagement show that, just as 'drop-out' is a central issue when studying the sporting and activity behaviour of young people, and of the careers of performance level athletes, so is drop-out a central issue for people at all stages of their lives, including adults and older people. 'Drop-out' is often constructed as problematic, or even deviant, yet it is actually typical, and is not confined to young people. This has huge implications for sport policy, and especially for the assumption that club membership is the panacea to ensuring lifelong participation. Rather, it points to the need for focus on providing opportunities throughout the life span, for both drop-out and re-engagement in physical activity and sport, in contexts and experiences which are meaningful and fit into individuals' needs as they change.

One change which is little represented in sport sociology, with the exception of athlete retirement, is that of occupational retirement. Strong relationships have been drawn between community engagement (including recreational or sporting participation and volunteering) and health and well-being; the vital importance of sociability in older people's lives is well established. But the multi-dimensional approaches required to track these relationships have rarely been included in the sport sciences, and traditionally, little attention has been focused on women's experiences, or on the interactions between older people and other age groups. Given the fact of an ageing population in Northern Europe and North America, and state concern to minimise costs associated with morbidity among elderly people, these relationships are likely to become a focal area for policy-related research. There are three chapters in this collection on aspects of older people's lives, each of which offers a different perspective, from different countries and cultures, and with a range of policy implications.

This collection provides a wealth of data and insights into experiences and processes of physical activity and sport at different stages of life. This introduction has identified some of the gaps and opportunities for further work and innovative approaches and collaborations. Each chapter is extensively referenced, so that scholars and researchers can follow up specific issues and interests. The collection shows the value of interaction between researchers, practitioners and policymakers – another central part of the ICSSPE's mission. Most exciting of all is the realisation that multi-disciplinary work can be further enriched, by considering which pedagogies of practice are most appropriate in delivering the policy objectives of physical activity and sport, across the life span.

Margaret Talbot and Nicholas L. Holt

References

Goodson, I. F. and Sikes, P. (2001). *Life History Research in Educational Settings: Learning from Lives*, Buckingham, Open University Press.

Hedges, B. (1986). *Personal Leisure Histories*, London, Sports Council/Social Science Research Council.

Moss, L. and Goldstein, H. (Eds). (1986). *The Recall Method in Social Surveys*, University of London Institute of Education, Studies in Education (new series) 9.

Talbot, M. (1997). The Use of Time Profiles in Researching the Relationships Between Time and Context in Women's Sport and Leisure. In G. Clarke and B. Humberstone (Eds). *Researching Critically Women's Sport, Leisure and Physical Education*, Brighton, Falmer Press.

Talbot, M. (1998). It Means a Lot to Me: A Life History Approach to Understanding the Place and Meaning of Physical Education and Sport through Women's Lives and Leisure. In Nabilah Abdelrahman (Ed). *Woman and Child: Future Vision from Sport's Perspective*, University of Alexandria, pp. 85–97.

Whitehead, M. (2010). *Physical Literacy Throughout the Lifecourse*, London, Routledge.

Part I

Sport and physical activity during childhood and adolescence

1 Sport participation during childhood and adolescence

Camilla J. Knight and Nicholas L. Holt

Introduction

The last two decades have been characterised by rapid technological advances that have dramatically altered the landscape of young people's leisure time activities. Children and adolescents in contemporary society have unprecedented access to televisions, computers, games consoles, mobile phones and a world of opportunities through the Internet (Pew Internet and American Life Project, 2003). Given the availability of so many activities, along with declining rates of physical activity participation, researchers and practitioners have become increasingly concerned with keeping young people physically active and socially engaged. One way to achieve this is through participation in sport. In this chapter, we explore the current trends in youth sport participation, specifically identifying the types of sporting opportunities that are available and the rates of young people engaging in sport across a number of countries. We examine motives for participating in sport and suggest means to enhance sporting experiences. Our ultimate aim is to provide a developmental overview of youth sport participation from a broadly international perspective.

In Canada, sport has been defined as a regulated form of physical activity organised as a contest between two or more participants for the purpose of determining a winner by fair and ethical means. Such contests may be in the form of a game, match, race or other type of competitive event. Sport requires neuromuscular skills and a high degree of difficulty, risk and effort (Sport Canada, 2009). Although this definition is useful, youth sport is an 'umbrella term' that refers to a range of activities, varying in terms of adult involvement, level and intensity of competition and reasons for participation (Brustad *et al.*, 2008; Ryba and Kashope Wright, 2010). For instance, youth sport may refer to highly structured programmes, run by a professional coach, that focus on deliberately developing young people's physical skills, technique and tactical understanding. Youth sport may also refer to recreational sports clubs run by volunteers or organised by young people themselves, focused on providing opportunities to play, with the development of skills and tactics occurring incidentally (Coakley, 2009). In recent years, the term youth sport has become synonymous with organised, adult-structured competitive experiences (Seefeldt and Ewing, 1996). Furthermore, as youth sport has become more organised, it has also become increasingly privatised and subject to adult control (Coakley, 2009).

Sport and youth development

In 1978, the United Nations Educational, Scientific and Cultural Organisation (UNESCO) deemed participation in sport to be an essential right of all human beings, recognising the benefits sport participation can have on individuals' physical, social and psychological development. However, the idea of using sport participation to promote development is not something that arose in the 1970s. In the 1920s, when sporting activities started to become a common part of young people's daily lives, reasons for involvement were often centred around the concept of 'muscular Christianity' which involved developing well grounded, physically strong, 'Christian' boys who would be successful contributors to society (Woods, 2007). In this way, youth sport was seen as a breeding ground for successful military personnel and businessmen in society (Coakley, 2009). Young people often engaged in sport through mass participation, in games that had little structure, rules or regulation (Weiss *et al.*, 2008). Nowadays, youth sport continues to be promoted within society, but for varying reasons. Some see youth sport as a breeding ground for tomorrow's sporting champions, while others (especially researchers and policy-makers) increasingly view sport as a vehicle for healthy physical and psychological development (Holt and Knight, in press).

Numerous benefits have been associated with sport participation. Sport provides young people with opportunities to socialise with peers and adults (Weiss *et al.*, 2007). The face-to-face interactions that occur in sport are laden with emotion and provide a forum that cannot be matched by electronic forms of communication. Through sporting interactions, young people have the chance to acquire communication skills, learn to work alongside others, demonstrate empathy and develop lifelong friendships (Fraser-Thomas *et al.*, 2005). Sport involvement can also provide young people with opportunities to experience success, demonstrate competence and become better educated in physical literacy (Ewing *et al.*, 2002). Perhaps most importantly within our current society, sport participation may be one contributing factor in slowing the increase in the number of young people who are overweight or obese (Brustad *et al.*, 2008).

Organisation of youth sport

The organisation of youth sport varies across countries and sport type (Brettschneider and Naul, 2004). Children who participate in sports such as football in North America are likely to access the majority of their training and games through high school teams because of the well-developed high school football structure. In contrast, track and field athletes from African nations may be involved in sport externally to school, developing their skills initially through sport clubs. This again contrasts with countries such as China, where children may be selected by the state to attend specific schools to train for certain sports (Syed, 2010).

Somewhat similarly, in Sweden (and a number of other countries), children who show high potential in different sports are selected to attend sports schools, where they are provided with the highest level of training facilities and coaches along-side flexible school schedules (Radtke and Coalter, 2007).

Beyond school and club access, the most highly skilled athletes may be selected to play on regional or national representative teams, compete at events such as the Youth Olympics, or age group international competitions (Judge *et al.*, 2009). In some sports, there are also opportunities for the most highly skilled athletes to be part of youth development programmes associated with professional sport teams. This is particularly evident in soccer, where 'promising' young athletes are selected for academies in the hope they will eventually join a club's professional team (English Football Association, 2003). If the sporting landscape was not com-plicated enough, some young people, particularly in individual sports such as ten-nis and gymnastics, may even begin their professional sporting careers while they are still in mid-adolescence.

Sport participation trends

Whereas physical activity trends among young people have been relatively well documented, less attention has been given to youth sport participation rates (Brettschneider and Naul, 2004). Nonetheless, based on the available data, it appears that somewhere between 50 and 70 per cent of young people participate in at least one sporting activity. For example, a recent study of Australian Young People indicated that 63 per cent of children (aged 5–14 years) participated in organised sport within the previous year (Australian Bureau of Statistics, 2009). The 2002 health survey in the United Kingdom (UK) identified that 59 per cent of boys and 55 per cent of girls (aged 2–15 years) participated in sports on a weekly basis (Stamatakis, 2002). Canadian statistics indicated that in 2005, 51 per cent of children and adolescents regularly participated in sport (Clark, 2008) and data from the United States (US) showed that 54 per cent of all high school students participated in sport during 2006–2007 (Sabo and Veliz, 2008). Similar participa-tion rates have been identified in Asian and African populations. A national survey in Singapore indicated that 67 per cent of 15–19-year-olds participated in sport at least once a week (Singapore Sports Council, 2001). In Japan, the rate of sport par-ticipation among 10–14-year-olds appeared to peak in 2006 at around 90 per cent (Japanese Statistics Bureau, 2006). Data from 2001 showed that 63 per cent of 13–18-year-olds South Africans participated in sport (Sport and Recreation South Africa, 2009).

Youth sport participation appears to be increasing in a number of countries (Brettschneider and Naul, 2004; Sabo and Veliz, 2008). For example, data from the UK from 1994 to 2002 indicated a steady increase in sport participation among young people during and outside school hours (Sport England, 2003). Participation rates in the US also appear to have increased by 8.6 per cent in the last nine years (National Sporting Goods Association, 2009). Increased sport participation rates have been illustrated in Australia between 2003 and 2009 – from 68.6 per cent to 69.6 per cent in boys and 64.3 per cent to 66.9 per cent in girls (Australian Bureau of Statistics, 2009), and in South Africa between 1998 and 2001 (Sport and Recreation South Africa, 2009). Further, there has been an increase in membership of sports clubs by Swedish and Finnish young people in the last decade (Brettschneider and Naul, 2004). Reasons for this increasing participation in sport may relate to the growing popularity of extreme or alternative sports (National Sporting Goods Association, 2009), increased provision of sporting opportunities for females (Coakley, 2009) and greater commitment to providing opportunities for sport participation among underserved young people in developing nations (Sport and Recreation South Africa, 2005).

However, although data indicates an increase in sport participation in a number of countries, in other countries participation rates appear to have decreased (Sabo and Veliz, 2008). For example, data from Canada has shown a slight decrease in sport participation rates among young people between 1992 and 2005, from 49 per cent to 45 per cent in females and 66 per cent to 56 per cent in males (Clark, 2008). Similarly, in Japan there appears to have been a decrease in sport participation between 2001 and 2006 (Japanese Statistics Bureau, 2006). In general, it appears that during the progression from childhood to adolescence, sport participation decreases (e.g., Australian Bureau of Statistics, 2009; Japanese Statistics Bureau, 2006). This may be because adolescents are able to make their own decisions regarding their use of time and other organised activities, school, or spending time with peers, may replace sport participation (Olds *et al.*, 2004).

Some caution must be used when drawing conclusions from the data reported above. One issue in measuring sport participation rates is that definitions of sport vary across countries (Olds *et al.*, 2004), as do measures of 'participation'. In some surveys, questions refer to participation in sport once in the last year, whereas in others, participants are asked to record sport participation in the last month or week. If respondents are asked to report if they had played sport in the previous year, one would expect relatively higher sport participation rates to be reported compared to measures of participation in the previous week or month. Further, some studies include sport that occurred during school hours, whereas others do not. Sport involvement out of school hours is likely to be more indicative of regular commitment to youth sport. Standardised measurements, definitions of youth sport and regular surveys are required to ensure researchers and policy-makers have a detailed and accurate knowledge of sport participation rates internationally. This is an important area for future research.

Inequalities in sport participation

Sport participation continues to be lower among young females compared to young males. This trend is apparent across a range of countries, including Japan, Australia, US, UK, South Africa and Canada (Australian Bureau of Statistics, 2009; Clark, 2008; Japanese Statistics Bureau, 2006; National Sporting Goods Association, 2009; Sport England, 2003; Sport and Recreation South Africa, 2009). There appears to be a greater likelihood that children from higher socioeconomic

(SES) families have access to sport than children from lower SES families (Clark, 2008; Sport England, 2003). Children from two-parent families seem to be more involved in youth sport than children from single-parent families (Australian Bureau of Statistics, 2009). Finally, although there have been strides towards equal access to participation in youth sport among different ethnicities, more young people from ethnic minority groups continue to have limited access to sport (Sport and Recreation South Africa, 2009).

Sport participation pathways

A number of models depicting pathways of sport participation have been presented in the literature (e.g., Bloom, 1985; Wylleman and Lavallee, 2004). One of the most popular approaches is the Developmental Model of Sport Participation (Côté, 1999; Côté and Hay, 2002; Côté *et al.*, 2007). This model identifies three distinct stages young people may progress through during their sporting lives: sampling, specialising and investment. During the sampling stage (aged approximately 8–12 years), children try out a range of sports, with the support of their parents. Sporting involvement focuses on fun, play-based activities, with limited competition. As athletes progress (early- to mid-adolescence), they enter the specialising stage. During this stage, young people commit to one or two sports. There is an increasing focus upon developing technical and tactical skills and young people are often heavily involved in competition. Finally, athletes enter the investment stage during mid- to late adolescence. It is at this stage that athletes fully commit to one sport with the desire of becoming elite athletes. Intensive training and competition characterise the investment stage as athletes attempt to become the best they can be in their chosen sport (Côté *et al.*, 2007).

However, not all athletes progress through these three stages in the sampling–specialising–investment progression. For example, some children and adolescents may 'fast track' through the sampling stage and enter the specialising and investment stages earlier than the traditional route. This pathway, termed early specialisation, appears to have become more common in recent years (Côté, 2009). It provides individuals with the opportunity to specialise in one sport at an earlier age in the hopes of becoming an elite athlete. However, early specialisation pathways have been associated with high rates of injuries, a lack of enjoyment and dropout (Côté *et al.*, 2007; Law *et al.*, 2007).

Participation motivation and attrition

Understanding what motivates children and adolescents to participate in sport may provide useful information that can be used to maintain or even increase sport participation rates (Weiss and Williams, 2004). As McArdle and Duda (2002, p. 410) explained, 'There is a need to gain insight into the nature and determinants of young athletes' motivational processes. Only with such knowledge can we try and "set the stage" for an optimal encounter among all these youngsters who take the chance and give sport "a go"'.

The three most consistent reasons for young people's participation in sport are: (1) to develop and display physical competence, such as physical fitness and enhanced technical skills; (2) to gain social acceptance and approval from peers and adults; and (3) to have enjoyable experiences, such as fun and excitement (Weiss and Williams, 2004). For example, Klint and Weiss (1986) examined US gymnasts' motives for continuing or dropping out of gymnastics. Competitive gymnasts' motives for participation included feeling competent, fitness and the challenge of gymnastics. Recreational gymnasts were motivated by fitness and fun. Other studies have identified similar motives for young people's sport participation in Australia (Longhurst and Spink, 1987) and Scandinavia (Wold and Kannas, 1993).

Researchers have also examined young people's reasons for withdrawing from sport. Gould (1987) asked young athletes why they had withdrawn from sport. The most common reasons cited were lack of fun, too much time, an overemphasis on winning, other interests, issues with the coach and a lack of playing time. Similarly, Gould *et al.* (1982) asked youth swimmers to report their motives for participation, and, if they had left the sport, their reasons for dropping out. Younger participants were more concerned with their social status, encouragement from others and their relationship with their coach (all affiliation type motives), while older participants were more interested in developing their skills and experiencing the excitement and challenges associated with swimming (competence and excitement focused motives). In summary, these data suggest that when children's and adolescents' reasons for participating in sport are not being fulfilled, they are more likely to drop out.

Conclusion: creating optimal conditions for youth sport participation

By way of conclusion, we present some suggestions for optimal conditions that may enhance youth sport participation. First, practitioners need to create an environment in which youth feel competent. Such an environment is created when individuals receive praise from their parents, coaches and peers (Harter, 1992; Ullrich-French and Smith, 2006). Praise related to young people's individual improvement and effort, as opposed to their success in relation to others, is likely to enhance perceptions of competence more consistently (Papaioannou *et al.*, 2006). Young people also need to be reminded that their success is a result of their own actions (i.e. it was under their control) (Harter, 1978). As such, practitioners should create an environment in which young people are reminded of how they were successful and how they are able to be successful again. Finally, practitioners need to create an environment that allows young people to experience success (Harter, 1992). To create such an environment, practitioners could provide tasks that are challenging, without being too difficult, and also provide feedback regarding individual improvement.

In addition to creating an environment in which young people feel competent, young people also need to have the opportunity to develop friendships and relationships with their peers, coaches and other social agents. Developing a training and competitive environment in which young people are able to interact with their team mates, develop shared goals and values and experience a team-like atmosphere will help affiliation with peers (Weiss and Smith, 2002). Thus, practitioners may need to commit time to demonstrating the value of team work, providing an opportunity for young people to share team successes and challenges and create opportunities for young people to engage with their peers and other social agents (Knight *et al.*, 2011; Partridge *et al.*, 2008).

Finally, creating an enjoyable experience is paramount for young people to remain involved in sport. To create an enjoyable experience, practitioners are required to create an environment where young people feel supported in their participation through the development of friendships and various interactions, feel competent in their abilities and have the opportunities to feel the excitement and energy associated with the physical sensations of playing sport. Young people should be provided with the opportunity to just feel what it is like playing the sport, without always being constrained by the technical and tactical aspects of training or competition (Weiss and Ambrose, 2008; Weiss *et al.*, 2001). By creating a sporting environment that maximises the potential for young people to experience success, affiliation and enjoyment, there may be more chance of young people remaining in sport.

Compared to other leisure time activities, youth sport maintains a privileged status within many societies. As such, youth sport attracts media attention, research funding, policy-makers' time and an emotional investment from much of the general public. Given the range of benefits young people can gain from sport involvement, this privileged status appears positive. However, considerable numbers of young people are still either unable to participate, or choose not to participate in sport. Creating an environment that is focused upon the needs and requirements of young people will help to ensure that those children that have access to sport choose to participate, resulting in a potential lifetime of physical, psychological and social benefits.

References

Australian Bureau of Statistics (2009). *Sports and physical activity: a statistical overview, Australia.* Retrieved from www.abs.gov.au/AUSSTATS/abs@.nsf/DetailsPage/4156.02009?OpenDocument.

Bloom, B. (1985). *Developing talent in young people.* New York: Ballantine Books.

Brettschneider, W. and Naul, R. (2004). *Study on young people's lifestyles and sedentariness and the role of sport in the context of education and as a means of restoring the balance.* Retrieved from http://ec.europa.eu/sport/library/doc/c1/doc374_en.pdf.

Brustad, R. J., Vilhjalmsson, R. and Manuel Fonseca, A. (2008). Organized sport and physical activity promotion. In A. L. Smith and S. J. H. Biddle (Eds), *Youth physical activity and sedentary behaviour: challenges and solutions* (pp. 351–376). Champaign, IL: Human Kinetics.

Clark, W. (2008). *Kids' sport.* Component of Statistics Canada Catalogue no. 11–008-X Canadian Social Trends. Retrieved from www.statcan.gc.ca/pub/11008x/2008001/article/10573-eng.pdf.

Coakley, J. (2009). *Sport in society: issues and controversies* (10th edn). New York: McGraw-Hill.

Côté, J. (1999). The influence of the family in the development of talent in sport. *The Sport Psychologist, 13*, 395–417.

Côté, J. (2009). The road to continued sport participation and sport excellence. In T. Hung, R. Lidor and D. Hackfort (Eds), *International perspectives on sport and exercise psychology: psychology of sport excellence* (pp. 97–104). Morgantown: Fitness Information Technology.

Côté, J. and Hay, J. (2002). Children's involvement in sport: a developmental perspective. In J. M. Silva and D. E. Stevens (Eds), *Psychological foundations of sport* (pp. 484–502). Boston: Allyn and Bacon.

Côté, J., Baker, J. and Abernethy, B. (2007). Practice and play in the development of sport expertise. In R. Eklund and G. Tenenbaum (Eds), *Handbook of sport psychology* (3rd edn, pp. 184–202). Hoboken: Wiley.

English Football Association (2003). *Programme for excellence*. Retrieved from www.thefa.com/TheFA/RulesandRegulations/FARegulations/NewsAndFeatures/2003/Regs_ProgforExcellence.

Ewing, M. E., Gano-Overway, L. A., Branta, C. and Seefeldt, V. (2002). The role of sport in youth development. In M. Gatz, M. A. Messner and S. J. Ball-Rokeach (Eds), *Paradoxes of youth and sport* (pp. 31–48). Albany: New York Press.

Fraser-Thomas, J., Côté, J. and Deakin, J. (2005). Youth sport programmes: an avenue to foster positive youth development. *Physical Education and Sport Pedagogy, 10*, 19–40.

Gould, D. (1987). Understanding attrition in youth sport. In D. Gould and M. R. Weiss (Eds), *Advances in pediatric sport science: behavioural issues*, Vol. 2 (pp. 61–85). Champaign: Human Kinetics.

Gould, D., Feltz, D., Horn, T. and Weiss, M. (1982). Reasons for attrition in competitive youth swimming. *Journal of Sport Behaviour, 5*, 155–165.

Harter, S. (1978). Effectance motivation reconsidered. *Human Development, 21*, 34–64.

Harter, S. (1992). The relationship between perceived competence, affect, and motivational orientation within the classroom: processes and patterns of change. In A. K. Boggiano and T. S. Pittman (Eds), *Achievement and motivation: a social-developmental perspective* (pp. 77–115). Cambridge: Cambridge University Press.

Holt, N. L. and Knight, C. J. (in press). Sport participation. In B. B. Brown and M. Prinstein (Eds), *Encyclopedia of adolescence*. New York: Academic Press.

Japanese Statistics Bureau (2006). *2006 survey on time use and leisure activities*. Retrieved from www.stat.go.jp/english/data/shakai/2006/koudou-a/zenkoku/sports.htm.

Judge, L. W., Petersen, J. and Lydum, M. (2009). The best kept secret in sports: the 2010 Youth Olympic Games. *International Review for the Sociology of Sport, 44*, 173–191.

Klint, K. A. and Weiss, M. R. (1986). Dropping in and dropping out: participation motives of current and former youth gymnasts. *Canadian Journal of Applied Sports Sciences, 11*, 109–114.

Knight, C. J., Neely, K. C. and Holt, N. L. (2011). Parental behaviours in team sports: how do female athletes want parents to behave? *Journal of Applied Sport Psychology, 23*, 76–92.

Law, M., Côté, J. and Ericsson, K. A. (2007). Characteristics of expert development in rhythmic gymnastics: a retrospective study. *International Journal of Sport and Exercise Psychology, 5*, 82–103.

Longhurst, K. and Spink, K. S. (1987). Participation motivation of Australian children involved in organized sport. *Canadian Journal of Sport Science, 12*, 24–30.

McArdle, S. and Duda, J. L. (2002). Implications of the motivational climate in youth sports. In F. L. Smoll and R. E. Smith (Eds), *Children and youth in sport: a biopsychosocial perspective* (2nd edn, pp. 409–434). Dubuque: Kendall/Hunt.

National Sporting Goods Association (2009). *2009 youth participation in selected sports with comparisons to 2000.* Retrieved from www.nsga.org/files/public/2009YouthParticipationInSelectedSportsWithComparisons.pdf.

Olds, T., Dollman, J., Ridley, K., Boshoff, K., Hartshorne, S. and Kennaugh, S. (2004). *Children and sport* (Report for the Australian Sports Commission). Adelaide: University of South Australia.

Papaioannou, A., Bebetsos, E., Theodorakis, Y., Christodoulidis, T. and Kouli, O. (2006). Causal relationships of sport and exercise involvement with goal orientations, perceived competence and intrinsic motivation in physical education: a longitudinal study. *Journal of Sports Science, 24*, 367–382.

Partridge, J. A., Brustad, R. J. and Babkes Stellino, M. (2008). Social influence in sport. In T. S. Horn (Ed.), *Advances in sport psychology* (3rd edn, pp. 269–292). Champaign: Human Kinetics.

Pew Internet and American Life Project (2003). *America's online pursuits: the changing picture of who's online and what they do.* Principal author: Mary Madden. Retrieved 28 June 2007, from www.pewinternet.org/reports/pdfs/PIP_Online_Pursuits_Final.PDF.

Radtke, S. and Coalter, F. (2007). *Sports schools: an international review* (Report to the Scottish Institute of Foundation). Stirling: University of Stirling, Department of Sport Studies.

Ryba, T. and Kashope Wright, H. (2010). Sport psychology and the cultural turn: notes towards cultural praxis. In T. Ryba, R. J. Schinke and G. Tenenbaum (Eds), *The cultural turn in sport psychology* (pp. 3–28). Morgantown: Fitness Information Technology.

Sabo, D. and Veliz, P. (2008). *Go out and play: youth sports in America* (Report for the Women's Sports Foundation). Retrieved from www.womenssportsfoundation.org/~/media/Files/Research%20Reports/Go%20Out%20and%20Play%20report%209%2018%2008.pdf.

Seefeldt, V. D. and Ewing, M. E. (1996). *Youth sports in America: an overview.* Michigan State University (Originally published as Series 2, Number 11 of the PCPFS Research Digest). Retrieved from http://fitness.gov/youthsports.pdf.

Singapore Sports Council (2001). *National sports participation survey 2001.* Retrieved from http://research.nyc.sg/atoz.asp#Sports Participation.

Sport Canada (2009). Sport funding and accountability framework. Retrieved from www.pch.gc.ca/pgm/sc/pgm/cfrs/sfafelig09-eng.cfm.

Sport England (2003). *Young people and sport in England: trends in participation 1991–2002* (Research conducted for Sport England by MROI). Retrieved from www.sportengland.org/research/tracking_trends.aspx?sortBy=alpha&pageNum=3.

Sport and Recreation South Africa (2005). Participation patterns in sport and recreation activities in South Africa. Retrieved from www.kzndsr.gov.za/Portals/0/GIS/Participation%20patterns%20in%20sport%20and%20recreation%20activities%20in%20SA.pdf.

Sport and Recreation South Africa (2009). *A case for sport and recreation: an active and winning nation.* Retrieved from www.srsa.gov.za/MediaLib/Home/DocumentLibrary/CaseforSport_final-small.pdf.

Stamatakis, E. (2002). *Health survey for England 2002.* Retrieved from www.archive2.official-documents.co.uk/document/deps/doh/survey02/hcyp/hcyp01.htm.

Syed, M. (2010). *Bounce: how champions are made.* London: Fourth Estate.

Ullrich-French, S. and Smith, A. L. (2006). Social and motivational predictors of continued youth sport participation. *Psychology of Sport and Exercise, 10,* 87–95.

UNESCO (1978). *International charter for physical education and sport.* Retrieved from www.unesco.org/education/information/nfsunesco/pdf/SPORT_E.PDF.

Weiss, M. R. and Ambrose, A. J. (2008). Motivational orientations and sport behaviour. In T. S. Horn (Ed.), *Advances in sport psychology* (3rd edn, pp. 115–156). Champaign: Human Kinetics.

Weiss, M. R. and Smith, A. L. (2002). Friendship quality in youth sport: relationship to age, gender, and motivation variables. *Journal of Sport and Exercise Psychology, 24,* 420–437.

Weiss, M. R. and Williams, L. (2004). The why of youth sport involvement: a developmental perspective on motivational processes. In M. R. Weiss (Ed.), *Developmental sport and exercise psychology: a lifespan perspective* (pp. 223–268). Morgantown: Fitness Information Technology.

Weiss, M. R., Kimmel, L. A. and Smith, A. L. (2001). Determinants of sport commitment among junior tennis players: enjoyment as a mediating variables. *Pediatric Exercise Science, 13,* 131–144.

Weiss, M. R., Smith, A. L. and Stuntz, C. P. (2008). Moral development in sport and physical activity: theory, research, and intervention. In T. S. Horn (Ed.), *Advances in sport psychology* (3rd edn, pp. 187–210). Champaign: Human Kinetics.

Weiss, M. R., Smith, A. L. and Theeboom, M. (2007). 'That's what friends are for': children's and teenagers' perceptions of peer relationships in the sport domain. In D. Smith and M. Bar-Eli (Eds), *Essential readings in sport and exercise psychology* (pp. 439–454). Champaign: Human Kinetics.

Wold, B. and Kannas, L. (1993). Sport motivation among young adolescents in Finland, Norway and Sweden. *Scandinavian Journal of Medicine and Science in Sports, 3,* 283–291.

Woods, R. B. (2007). *Social issues in sport.* Champaign: Human Kinetics.

Wylleman, P. and Lavallee, D. (2004). A developmental perspective on transitions faced by athletes. In M. R. Weiss (Ed.), *Developmental sport and exercise psychology: a lifespan perspective* (pp. 503–524). Morgantown: Fitness Information Technology, Inc.

2 Physical activity during childhood and adolescence

Clare Hume and Jo Salmon

Introduction

In recent years, physical activity has received considerable attention, not just in the research literature, but also in the broader community, due to the known benefits of lifelong participation and concerns about the prevalence of this behaviour in the population. Even from infancy, it is recognised that physical activity is important for healthy growth and development; not just for physical health, but also for social and emotional wellbeing.

This chapter will draw on evidence from current research to explore issues related to physical activity among children (approximately 5–12 years) and adolescents (approximately 13–18 years; collectively labelled 'young people'). Specifically, this chapter will provide an understanding of the definitions of physical activity as they relate to young people; an overview of the characteristics of physical activity among these age groups; the health outcomes associated with physical activity in young people; the recommendations for young people's participation in physical activity; and the latest data on the prevalence of physical activity and interventions to promote physical activity in young people.

Characteristics of physical activity in young people

Physical activity in young people consists of a group of behaviours that, when performed, result in increases in energy expenditure above rest. These can be planned or unplanned behaviours. For example, exercise and sport are structured or planned activities, often for the purpose of improved or maintained physical fitness. Unplanned or incidental physical activity refers to behaviours where the primary goal is often not physical activity, but some other objective (e.g. riding a bike to the local convenience store or playing outdoors). Young people's physical activity is typically performed in four domains: leisure-time; home-based; school-based; and transport-related. Children's physical activity is substantially different from that of adolescents and from that of adults. One of the first studies to characterise physical activity patterns among children aged 6–10 years (Bailey *et al.*, 1995) found that:

1. children's physical activity is highly transitory in nature. That is, the type and intensity of children's activity changes rapidly and unexpectedly;
2. children spend most of their time engaged in physical activity that is low-intensity in nature, or requires low levels of energy to perform;
3. despite this, the tempo of children's physical activity is subject to rapid changes; and
4. children engage in short bursts of intense or vigorous physical activity that are interspersed with varying levels of low and moderate-intensity physical activity.

The types of physical activity in which children engage are also unique from those of adolescents and adults. Very young children spend much of their time in active play and games and less time in planned activities or active transport (e.g. walking or cycling) (Telford *et al.*, 2005). Children spend very little time in activities such as household chores; although this may vary culturally and between countries. The majority of children's physical activity is acquired as active play and leisure-based activities (e.g. walking their pet dog). As children reach early adolescence they spend more of their time in active transport (Hume *et al.*, 2009) and organised sports (Australian Bureau of Statistics, 2001) and less time in active play (Pellegrini and Smith, 1998). Although adolescents' physical activity more closely resembles that of adults (performed more frequently and for longer), their overall levels of physical activity decline through adolescence to young adulthood (Sallis *et al.*, 2000).

   These variations in how physical activity is accumulated from early childhood to late adolescence have meant that quantifying the type and amount of physical activity young people participate in, as well as the 'dose' of physical activity required for a health benefit, is challenging. There are four key dimensions to physical activity 'dose': duration or how long (e.g. the number of minutes or hours spent being physically active); frequency or how often (e.g. the number of days or sessions of physical activity); intensity (e.g. light, moderate, vigorous physical activity) which may be defined in terms of metabolic equivalent units of rest (Mets) where a brisk walk would result in three times the amount of energy expended (3 Mets) compared to rest; and type of physical activity (e.g. specific physical activity behaviours such as football, walking, riding a bicycle). Despite the challenges in quantifying physical activity dose, there is emerging evidence that young people's participation in physical activity benefits their short- and long-term health.

Physical activity and health among young people

While the literature examining the health benefits of physical activity for young people is less extensive than that for adults, emerging evidence suggests that physical activity plays a key role in preventing disease and promoting physical and psycho-social health throughout life. The prevalence of several chronic diseases such as cardiovascular disease (CVD), type 2 diabetes, obesity and osteoporosis place a substantial economic and social burden on modern society (Begg *et al.*, 2007). Diseases such as CVD and overweight and obesity have their origins in childhood (McGill *et al.*, 2000; Singh *et al.*, 2008) and this is of significant concern as risk factors for these conditions have been shown to track strongly from childhood into adulthood (Raitakari *et al.*, 2005).

Biddle *et al.* (2004) reviewed several studies examining associations of participation in physical activity during childhood with different measures of health status, both during youth and adulthood. That review suggests a likely beneficial effect of physical activity for prevention and treatment of overweight and obesity, although conflicting evidence regarding the immediate effect of physical activity on other health outcomes among children, particularly when measuring blood pressure and cholesterol, was reported. That review reported more consistent evidence of the influence of physical activity on bone health in childhood and adolescence, suggesting that physical activity is essential for the acquisition of peak bone mass in childhood, therefore potentially decreasing the likelihood of developing osteoporosis in adulthood. In addition to physical health, there is some support for the benefits of physical activity for a variety of psycho-social and psychological health outcomes among children (Biddle *et al.*, 2004). For example, physical activity has been found to be associated with reduced risk of depressive symptoms and anxiety, and improved self-esteem and self-concept in young people (Strong *et al.*, 2005).

There is some evidence to suggest that physical activity patterns in childhood may have influences on risk factors for disease in adolescence, as well as disease outcomes in later life, although considerable research remains to be performed in this area to confirm such suggestions. There is, however, strong evidence supporting the role of physical activity and positive health outcomes in adults. This has important implications for public health, as well as economic implications due to the significant economic costs associated with physical inactivity (Mathers *et al.*, 2001). Based on the likely positive relationship between physical activity and health, recommendations for how much and how often children and adolescents should be participating in physical activity have been proposed.

Physical activity recommendations for young people

The health benefits of physical activity have been widely recognised; however, the dose or amount and intensity of physical activity required to gain these benefits is currently unknown among youth. Despite this, guidelines on how much, how often and how intense physical activity should be, have been released from government bodies of several developed countries.

Recommendations from Canada suggest children and youth should achieve 90 minutes per day of moderate- to vigorous-intensity physical activity (MVPA) (Public Health Agency of Canada, 2002), while countries such as Australia (Australian Government Department of Health and Ageing, 2004), the United States (Strong *et al.*, 2005) and the United Kingdom (UK Department of Health, Physical Activity, Health Improvement and Prevention, 2004) all recommend young people perform at least 60 minutes per day of MVPA. Such guidelines are useful for monitoring population-level participation in physical activity; and the following section will describe recent data examining prevalence of physical activity across the youth population and how this has changed over time.

Prevalence of physical activity among young people

Estimates of the prevalence of physical activity in young people vary depending on how physical activity was assessed and what domains of physical activity were captured. In the United States, the 2007 Youth Risk Behaviour Surveillance Survey found that 26 per cent of girls and 44 per cent of boys in high school grades 9–12 reported any kind of physical activity for at least 60 minutes or more on five or more of the preceding seven days (Centers for Disease Control and Prevention, 2008). Approximately 25 per cent reported not participating in at least 60 minutes of physical activity on any of the previous seven days. Nationally in the United States, 56 per cent of adolescents (62 per cent boys, 50 per cent girls) played on at least one sports team in the 12 months preceding the survey. In contrast, three-quarters of 15–17-year-old Canadians reported participating in organised sport in 2007/2008, which was defined as 'physical activities that involve competition and rules, and develop specific skills' (Canadian Fitness and Lifestyle Research Institute, 2009). However, just 13 per cent of Canadian young people (5–19 years) met Canada's Physical Activity Guide of approximately 16,500 pedometer steps per day (Canadian Fitness and Lifestyle Research Institute, 2008).

A recent national survey of just under 4,500 children in Australia found that 40 per cent of children aged 9–13 years and 19 per cent of adolescents aged 14–16 years self-reported meeting physical activity recommendations (defined as spending 60 or more minutes in moderate- to vigorous-intensity physical activity on each of the four days assessed) (Commonwealth Scientific Industrial Research Organisation, Preventative Health National Research Flagship & University of South Australia, 2008). In the United Kingdom, it has been estimated that 70 per cent of boys and 60 per cent of girls are meeting national physical activity recommendations (UK Department of Health, Physical Activity, Health Improvement and Prevention, 2004). In contrast, the European Youth Heart Study used accelerometers to assess physical activity among more than 2,000 9- and 15-year-old youth and found approximately 98 per cent met the United Kingdom physical activity recommendations (Riddoch et al., 2004). However, there were significant cross-sectional declines among the older children with 89 per cent of 15-year-old boys and 62 per cent of girls meeting recommendations.

It is clear that making international comparisons of physical activity prevalence among young people is almost impossible due to the different measures used for assessing physical activity and also the different types or domains of physical activity that have been assessed (e.g. steps, organised sport, accumulated movement). These limitations in comparing levels of physical activity internationally were recognised in the adult physical activity research field some years ago and resulted in the development of the International Physical Activity Questionnaire (www.ipaq.ki.se) and more recently the Global Physical Activity Questionnaire (for use in developing countries) (www.who.int/chp/steps/GPAQ/en/index.html). Development of an international survey measure for assessing physical activity in young people that is relevant for most populations may be challenging; perhaps the use of objective instruments (such as pedometers or accelerometers) for population monitoring would overcome some of these challenges.

Irrespective of current physical activity prevalence rates in developed countries, there is consistent evidence that physical activity declines with age (Sallis *et al.*, 2000) and that young people can benefit from strategies to promote activity, no matter what age they are.

Physical activity interventions among young people

Over many years, several studies have trailed intervention strategies aiming to promote physical activity among young people, with mixed success (Salmon *et al.*, 2007). This may, in part, be due to the lack of use of behaviour change theories to guide such interventions, a limitation noted by Salmon *et al.* (2007). The importance of theory-based interventions has long been recognised (Glanz *et al.*, 2002) and, in recent years, interventions based on theories that consider the role of the broader physical and policy environments such as the Ecological Model, have been advocated (Sallis and Owen, 1999). One important aspect of the Ecological Model is the 'behaviour setting'. This model posits that behaviours such as physical activity occur in specific settings, and that the settings themselves are important environmental factors to consider (Sallis and Owen, 1999). Interventions aiming to promote physical activity among young people have been trialled in a variety of settings and some of the most recent, novel interventions will be described in this section.

Home- and family-based interventions

There is some evidence of effective intervention strategies targeting physical activity that are based in home and family settings. Strategies that typically incorporated the delivery of print materials to families and that provided group-based sessions which young people and their parent(s) were invited to attend, resulted in increases in physical activity in several studies (Beech *et al.*, 2003; Ransdell *et al.*, 2003; Robinson *et al.*, 2003; Story *et al.*, 2003); however, high attrition, small sample sizes and a lack of a control group for comparison in some studies mean the results should be interpreted with caution. One longer-term, well-designed study also shown to be effective in increasing physical activity used a diary method for young children over a three-year period (Saakslahti *et al.*, 2004). Using various modes of delivery, including annual meetings with parents, biannual delivery of print materials, an annual physical activity demonstration and a one-off radio programme for parents, this low-intensity intervention found that time spent in very active outdoor play increased significantly in intervention children compared to the control group. While there are some examples of effective home- and family-based interventions to promote physical activity in young people, many interventions have design limitations, use poor measures or have been conducted amongst ethnic minority groups or people experiencing socioeconomic disadvantage, and as such, the efficacy and generalisability of these interventions is difficult to determine (Salmon *et al.*, 2007). However, well designed studies in this setting do show promise for the promotion of physical activity in young people.

School-based interventions

Schools provide an ideal setting for the promotion of physical activity to young people (Salmon *et al.*, 2007; Timperio *et al.*, 2004). Many interventions aiming to promote physical activity in this setting have used a curriculum-based approach, although several studies have utilised an interdisciplinary approach, combining education sessions (e.g. promoting the benefits of increased physical activity, reducing time spent in sedentary pastimes) delivered via traditional teaching as well as multi-media methods, and delivery of physical activity or physical education sessions. In their review of intervention strategies, Salmon *et al.* (2007) found that the vast majority of curriculum-only interventions (nine of 11 studies) were not effective in increasing physical activity among children and adolescents. Studies that combined curriculum changes with physical activity or physical education sessions have also shown mixed results, with minimal increases in physical activity evident. One recent exception to this was the Switch-Play intervention by Salmon *et al.* (2008). Switch-Play was based on constructs from social cognitive theory and behavioural change theory, and was an 18-lesson group randomised controlled trial targeting physical activity, sedentary behaviour and weight gain prevention among 10–12-year-old Australian children. That four-arm trial examined the effects of a classroom-based programme targeting reduced sedentary behaviour (Group 1) with additional physical activity sessions that focused on improving fundamental motor skills (FMS) to increase physical activity (Group 2), and a combination of the two strategies (Group 3), compared to a group receiving 'usual care' (Group 4). Significant increases in boys' participation in objectively-measured vigorous-intensity physical activity were seen in the FMS group compared to controls (maintained at 12-months follow-up) (Salmon *et al.*, 2008), suggesting that interventions incorporating more than one strategy may be effective in promoting physical activity to children.

Another recent study that incorporated increased amounts of physical activity into a curriculum-based intervention was the 'Physical Activity Across the Curriculum' (PAAC) study, which aimed to increase physical activity and reduce gains in body mass index among 7–8-year-old children over a three-year period (Donnelly *et al.*, 2009). PAAC promoted the incorporation of 90 minutes per week of moderately to vigorously active academic lessons, and objective measures of physical activity among a sub-sample of participants showed significantly greater physical activity among children at intervention compared to control schools over the three years, suggesting that increasing physical activity using curriculum-based strategies may be effective among children.

Changing the physical environment within schools is another approach that has emerged in recent years. Incorporating ground markings in the school playground for games and activities (e.g. hopscotch, snakes and ladders) has been shown to be an effective strategy for increasing physical activity, as measured by heart rate telemetry during school in one study from the United Kingdom (Stratton and Leonard, 2002). Providing equipment for games and activity cards (showing examples of how to use the equipment) has also been found to be effective for promoting physical activity in Belgian children (Verstraete *et al.*, 2006). Although few studies have done so, a whole-of-school approach that combines curriculum-based strategies with physical activity or physical education sessions, and environmental changes has been advocated (Timperio *et al.*, 2004) as a likely method of achieving long-term changes in physical activity. Findings from two well known, large-scale interventions: Child and Adolescent Trial for Cardiovascular Health (CATCH) (Luepker *et al.*, 1996) and the Middle School Physical Activity and Nutrition study (M-SPAN) (Sallis *et al.*, 2003), support the use of curriculum-based strategies in conjunction with environmental and policy changes to achieve increases in physical activity among young people.

Neighbourhood- or community-based interventions

Although children spend much of their time at school, most of their leisure time is spent either at home or in their local community. Although limited by poor study designs, available data suggest this could be an important setting in which to base children's physical activity intervention programmes (Salmon *et al.*, 2007). One comprehensive study utilising multiple strategies (summer and after-school physical activity programmes, family newsletters, committees for improving the school environment, articles in the newspaper and physical activity at community events) was not shown to be effective (Pate *et al.*, 2003). However, two studies employing less comprehensive designs showed some increases in children's physical activity; a mass media campaign promoting the benefits of and self-efficacy for physical activity (Huhman *et al.*, 2007) and changes to the physical environment surrounding schools such as improving pedestrian crossings and footpaths (sidewalks) (Boarnet *et al.*, 2005). Although rigorous community-level studies using appropriate measurement tools are scarce, emerging evidence does suggest this may be a potentially effective setting for interventions aiming to increase children's physical activity. However, the challenge is being able to demonstrate effects.

In summary, the promotion of physical activity to young people is complex and studies to date have had limited success in achieving this goal. Future studies should be based on recognised behaviour-change theories, employ rigorous study designs with appropriate comparison groups, use valid and reliable measures of physical activity and increase the length of follow-up to allow conclusions about the long-term success of the intervention to be drawn.

Conclusions

This chapter aimed to provide an overview of the issues and opportunities related to physical activity in young people. The sporadic and unpredictable nature of children's physical activity means it is often a difficult behaviour to measure and change. Nonetheless, there is increasing evidence of the importance of physical activity for children's health both in the immediate and long-term, leading to the development of recommendations for the amount and intensity of physical activity needed for health. Several studies have examined the prevalence of physical activity among young people with a number of different measures used, and a variety of prevalence estimates reported. Intervention studies aiming to increase the prevalence of physical activity among children and adolescents have had equivocal results; however, several recent interventions have shown promise using a range of strategies in different settings.

Future research examining physical activity among young people should utilise rigorous study designs, use consistent measures of physical activity (e.g. objective measures) to provide higher levels of evidence for dose-response issues in relation to health outcomes, as well as better enabling the monitoring of compliance with physical activity recommendations, and improving comparisons within and between countries. The development and implementation of evidence-based interventions incorporating sound theoretical frameworks and that have suitable follow-up periods, is also recommended.

References

Australian Bureau of Statistics (2001). *Children's participation in cultural and leisure activities*. Canberra: Australian Bureau of Statistics.

Australian Government Department of Health and Ageing (2004). *Australia's physical activity recommendations for children and young people*. Canberra: Department of Health and Ageing.

Bailey, R. C., Olson, J., Pepper, S. L., Porszasz, J., Barstow, T. J. and Cooper, D. M. (1995). The level and tempo of children's physical activities: an observational study. *Medicine and Science in Sports and Exercise, 27*(7), 1033–1041.

Beech, B. M., Klesges, R. C., Kumanyika, S. K., Murray, D. M., Klesges, L., McClanahan, B., Slawson, D., Nunnally, C., Rochon, J., McLain-Allen, B. and Pree-Cary, J. (2003). Child- and parent-targeted interventions: the Memphis GEMS pilot study. *Ethnicity and Disease, 13*(Suppl. 1), S40–53.

Begg, S., Vos, T., Barker, B., Stevenson, C., Stanley, L. and Lopez, A. D. (2007). *The burden of disease and injury in Australia 2003. PHE 82*. Canberra: Australian Institute of Health and Welfare.

Biddle, S., Gorely, T. and Stensel, D. (2004). Health-enhancing physical activity and sedentary behaviour in children and adolescents. *Journal of Sports Sciences, 22*(8), 679–701.

Boarnet, M. G., Anderson, C. L., Day, K., McMillan, T. and Alfonzo, M. (2005). Evaluation of the California Safe Routes to School legislation: urban form changes and children's active transportation to school. *American Journal of Preventive Medicine, 28*(Suppl. 2), 134–140.

Canadian Fitness and Lifestyle Research Institute (2008). *Canadian physical activity levels among youth (CANPLAY), pedometer study bulletins, bulletin no.1.* Ontario: CFLRI, Healthy Living Unit, Public Health Agency of Canada, and the Interprovincial Sport and Recreation Council.

Canadian Fitness and Lifestyle Research Institute (CFLRI) (2009). *Sports participation in Canada, 2006/7 series, bulletin no.1.* Ontario: CFLRI, Canadian Heritage, and the Interprovincial Sport and Recreation Council.

Centers for Disease Control and Prevention (2008). Youth risk behaviour surveillance – United States, 2007. *Surveillance summaries, morbidity and mortality weekly report [MMWR], 57,* (SS-4).

Commonwealth Scientific Industrial Research Organisation, Preventative Health National Research Flagship, & University of South Australia (2008). *2007 Australian national children's nutrition and physical activity survey: main findings.* Canberra: Department of Health and Ageing.

Donnelly, J. E., Greene, J. L., Gibson, C. A., Smith, B. K., Washburn, R. A., Sullivan, D. K., DuBose, K., Mayo, M. S., Schmelzle, K. H., Ryan, J. J., Jacobsen, D. J. and Williams, S. L. (2009). Physical activity across the curriculum (PAAC): a randomized controlled trial to promote physical activity and diminish overweight and obesity in elementary school children. *Preventive Medicine, 49*(4), 336–341.

Glanz, K., Rimer, B. K. and Lewis, B. A. (2002). *Health behaviour and health education.* San Francisco: Jossey-Bass.

Huhman, M. E., Potter, L. D., Duke, J. C., Judkins, D. R., Heitzler, C. D. and Wong, F. L. (2007). Evaluation of a national physical activity intervention for children: VERB campaign, 2002–2004. *American Journal of Preventive Medicine, 32*(1), 38–43.

Hume, C., Timperio, A., Salmon, J., Carver, A., Giles-Corti, B. and Crawford, D. (2009). Walking and cycling to school: predictors of increases among children and adolescents. *American Journal of Preventive Medicine, 36*(3), 195–200.

Luepker, R. V., Perry, C. L., McKinlay, S. M., Nader, P. R., Parcel, G. S., Stone, E. J., *et al.* (1996). Outcomes of a field trial to improve children's dietary patterns and physical activity. The Child and Adolescent Trial for Cardiovascular Health. CATCH collaborative group. *Journal of the American Medical Association, 275*(10), 768–776.

McGill, H. C., Jr., McMahan, C. A., Herderick, E. E., Malcom, G. T., Tracy, R. E. and Strong, J. P. (2000). Origin of atherosclerosis in childhood and adolescence. *American Journal of Clinical Nutrition, 72*(Suppl. 5), 1307S–1315S.

Mathers, C. D., Vos, E. T., Stevenson, C. E. and Begg, S. J. (2001). The burden of disease and injury in Australia. *Bulletin of the World Health Organisation, 79*(11), 1076–1084.

Pate, R. R., Saunders, R. P., Ward, D. S., Felton, G., Trost, S. G. and Dowda, M. (2003). Evaluation of a community-based intervention to promote physical activity in youth: lessons from Active Winners. *American Journal of Health Promotion, 17*(3), 171–182.

Pellegrini, A. D. and Smith, P. K. (1998). Physical activity play: the nature and function of a neglected aspect of playing. *Child Development, 69*(3), 577–598.

Public Health Agency of Canada (2002). *Canada's Physical Activity Guide for Youth.* Ottawa: Public Health Agency of Canada.

Raitakari, O. T., Juonala, M. and Viikari, J. S. (2005). Obesity in childhood and vascular changes in adulthood: insights into the Cardiovascular Risk in Young Finns Study. *International Journal of Obesity, 29*(Suppl. 2), S101–104.

Ransdell, L. B., Taylor, A., Oakland, D., Schmidt, J., Moyer-Mileur, L. and Shultz, B. (2003). Daughters and mothers exercising together: effects of home- and community-based programmes. *Medicine and Science in Sports and Exercise, 35*(2), 286–296.

Riddoch, C. J., Andersen, L. B., Wedderkopp, N., Harro, M., Klasson-Heggebo, L., Sardinha, L. B., Cooper, A. and Ekelund, U. (2004). Physical activity levels and patterns of 9- and 15-yr-old European children. *Medicine and Science in Sports and Exercise*, *36*(1), 86–92.

Robinson, T. N., Killen, J. D., Kraemer, H. C., Wilson, D. M., Matheson, D. M., Haskell, W. L., Pruitt, L. A., Powell, T. M., Owens, A. S., Thompson, N. S., Flint-Moore, N. M., Davis, G. J., Emig, K. A., Brown, R. T., Rochon, J., Green, S. and Varady, A. (2003). Dance and reducing television viewing to prevent weight gain in African-American girls: the Stanford GEMS pilot study. *Ethnicity and Disease*, *13*(Suppl. 1), S65–77.

Saakslahti, A., Numminen, P., Salo, P., Tuominen, J., Helenius, H., and Valimaki, I. (2004). Effects of a three-year intervention on children's physical activity from age 4 to 7. *Pediatric Exercise Science*, *16*, 167–180.

Sallis, J. F. and Owen, N. (1999). *Physical activity and behavioural medicine*. Thousand Oaks: Sage Publications.

Sallis, J. F., Prochaska, J. J. and Taylor, W. C. (2000). A review of correlates of physical activity of children and adolescents. *Medicine and Science in Sports and Exercise*, *32*(5), 963–975.

Sallis, J. F., McKenzie, T. L., Conway, T. L., Elder, J. P., Prochaska, J. J., Brown, M., Zive, M. M., Marshall, S. J. and Alcaraz, J. E. (2003). Environmental interventions for eating and physical activity: a randomized controlled trial in middle schools. *American Journal of Preventive Medicine*, *24*(3), 209–217.

Salmon, J., Ball, K., Hume, C., Booth, M. and Crawford, D. (2008). Outcomes of a group-randomized trial to prevent excess weight gain, reduce screen behaviours and promote physical activity in 10-year-old children: switch-play. *International Journal of Obesity*, *32*(4), 601–612.

Salmon, J., Booth, M. L., Phongsavan, P., Murphy, N. and Timperio, A. (2007). Promoting physical activity participation among children and adolescents. *Epidemiologic Reviews*, *29*, 144–159.

Singh, A. S., Mulder, C., Twisk, J. W., van Mechelen, W. and Chinapaw, M. J. (2008). Tracking of childhood overweight into adulthood: a systematic review of the literature. *Obesity Reviews*, *9*(5), 474–488.

Story, M., Sherwood, N. E., Himes, J. H., Davis, M., Jacobs, D. R., Jr., Cartwright, Y., Smyth, M. and Rochon, J. (2003). An after-school obesity prevention programme for African-American girls: the Minnesota GEMS pilot study. *Ethnicity and Disease*, *13*(Suppl. 1), S54–64.

Stratton, G. and Leonard, J. (2002). The effects of playground markings on the energy expenditure of 5–7-year-old school children. *Pediatric Exercise Science*, *14*, 170–180.

Strong, W. B., Malina, R. M., Blimkie, C. J. R., Daniels, S. R., Dishman, R. K., Gutin, B., Hergenroeder, A. C., Must, A., Nixon, P. A., Pivarnik, J. M., Rowland, T., Trost, S. and Trudeau, F. (2005). Evidence based physical activity for school-age youth. *Journal of Pediatrics*, *146*, 732–737.

Telford, A., Salmon, J., Timperio, A. and Crawford, D. (2005). Examining physical activity among 5- to 6- and 10- to 12-year-old children: the Children's Leisure Activities Study. *Pediatric Exercise Science*, *17*, 266–280.

Timperio, A., Salmon, J. and Ball, K. (2004). Evidence-based strategies to promote physical activity among children, adolescents and young adults: review and update. *Journal of Science and Medicine in Sport*, *7*(Suppl. 1), 20–29.

UK Department of Health, Physical Activity, Health Improvement and Prevention (2004). *At least 5 a week*. London: Department of Health.

Verstraete, S. J., Cardon, G. M., De Clercq, D. L. and De Bourdeaudhuij, I. M. (2006). Increasing children's physical activity levels during recess periods in elementary schools: the effects of providing game equipment. *European Journal of Public Health*, *16*(4), 415–419.

Part II

Transitions in sport and physical activity participation

3 Tracking physical activity, energy balance and health from childhood to adulthood

Paul A. Ford

Introduction

There is considerable interest in physical activity from practitioners, policy-makers and the public, because of the impact low activity levels may have upon health. The relationship is of significant current international interest due to the association with rising obesity levels; both during childhood and adulthood, spanning both genders, and different ethnicities and socio-economic status. The World Health Organization (2009) reports that globally there are more than 1 billion overweight adults, with at least 300 million of them classified as obese.

Similarly, approximately 17.6 million children under the age of five, worldwide, are estimated to be overweight. The occurrence of obese children aged six to eleven years old has more than doubled since the 1960s. Flodmark *et al.* (2006) observe that in most scenarios, it is more difficult to treat obesity once it has occurred, therefore literature related to the impact that physical activity may have upon these figures is of great interest. The objective of this chapter is to demonstrate the relationship between physical activity and health, and to show how these variables may change throughout the transition from childhood to adulthood.

Theoretical orientation

The underlying assumption for this chapter is that there is a negative relationship between physical activity and health (Figure 3.1). Simply stated, the more active an individual is (x axis) the lower the risk of a negative health condition (y axis). Furthermore, the more active a lifestyle an individual leads, the lower the risk of developing a negative health condition and ill-health throughout life. Within Figure 3.2, the lower line represents an individual who leads an active life, whereas the upper line represents an individual who leads an inactive lifestyle for a prolonged period of time.

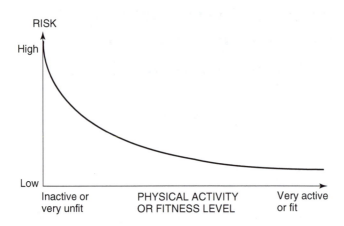

Figure 3.1 Relationship between physical activity and health risk factors.

Source: Adapted from Chief Medical Officer, 2004.

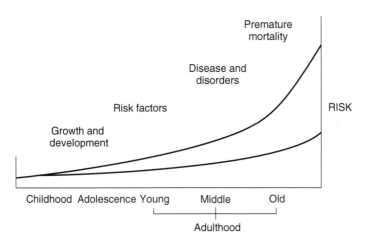

Figure 3.2 Impact of low and high physical activity adherence upon health risk factors throughout life.

Source: Adapted from Chief Medical Officer, 2004.

Review of literature

What is energy balance?

Energy is consumed in the form of food as it is required for cellular, metabolic and mechanical work, known as energy expenditure (EE). EE within the body for basic physiological functions is known as resting EE. There is an increase in EE when food is consumed, known as the thermic effect of a meal. This is because energy is expended to digest, metabolise and store ingested macronutrients. The actual amount of energy required for this process depends on the complexity of the food composition, but it is approximately 10 per cent of the caloric content of the meal (Goran and Treuth, 2001). Another source of EE is that used for mechanical work during physical activity, which is the most variable component of EE, with the duration, type and intensity of activity each affecting the metabolic rate. The combination of these variables forms an individual's total EE (Goran and Treuth, 2001). If an individual consumes more energy than s/he can expend, it is classi-fied as a 'positive' energy balance, whereas the reverse is known as a 'negative' energy balance. If a positive energy balance occurs, the excess energy is likely to be stored as excess body fat: this is because it is the preferred means of storing energy, due to limited storage capacity for carbohydrates and fat storage occurring at a lower metabolic cost than for carbohydrates (Goran and Treuth, 2001).

Excess body fat and negative health conditions

Obesity is the definition given to the storage of excess accumulation of body fat (Flodmark *et al.*, 2006). The obesity classification in adults is most commonly defined by a body mass index (BMI) greater than 30 kg.m^{-2}. However, diagnosis and definition of obesity in children is more problematic, because the degree and severity of body fatness depends upon growth and maturation, as well as on gen-der (Kiess *et al.*, 2006). Currently, the supported notion of a BMI greater than the 95th percentile of a reference population in children is the classification of obesity (Higgins *et al.*, 2001). Cole *et al.* (2000) have produced international reference values for children aged 2–18 years old, based on six-month intervals, which have been adopted by the International Obesity Task Force. The authors have adopted the >95th percentile for gender-specific obesity classifications from their study of six countries, each comprising over 10,000 participants. Individuals between the 85th and 95th percentiles are classed as overweight, as an indication of emerging body fatness. However, these guidelines are based on data from only six countries, which means that these classification curves could be geographically and ethni-cally biased. There is also growing belief that using BMI is not necessarily the correct procedure (e.g. Higgins *et al.*, 2001), due to the limitations of the assess-ment technique, and suggestions that a more direct measure of body composition may be of better validity.

Notwithstanding identification issues, many review articles have highlighted that the development of obesity is commonly associated with many comorbid cardiovascular disease (CVD) medical conditions, such as type II diabetes mel-litus, atherosclerosis, endothelial dysfunction, hypertension and hyperlipidemia (Ebbeling *et al.*, 2002). Furthermore, there are psycho-social consequences of obesity, with individuals developing negative self-image, low self-esteem and being stereotyped as 'lazy' and unhealthy (Must and Strauss, 1999). Additionally, the development of breathing disorders is associated with obesity (Reilly *et al.*, 2003), although there is no causality, meaning that it is not appropriate to infer direct cause and effect. It should be noted, however, that these correlates of obesity have not been well researched directly in children, as most of these conditions do not manifest until adulthood (Rowland, 2001).

Nevertheless, to avoid the development of such conditions, it is important to address the obesity situation early; reviewers have repeatedly highlighted that childhood obesity is repeatedly tracked through to adulthood (Rowland, 2001). For example, 26–41 per cent of children who are obese at pre-school age and 42–63 per cent of obese school-aged children become obese adults (Chief Medical Officer, 2004). Raitakari *et al.* (2005) suggest that it is this continuation of obesity into adulthood that leads to the development of CVD risk factors in adulthood, rather than CVD development during childhood. On the other hand, Williams *et al.* (1992) suggest that excess adiposity during childhood is associated with early development of atherosclerotic lesions, and therefore CVD risk. Supporting this, Tracy *et al.* (1995) identified fatty streaks in coronary arteries during paediatric autopsies, which were associated with negative blood pressure and lipid profiles, and obesity status. Must and Strauss (1999) record that adults, who were obese children, have a greater risk of morbidity, independent of their adult weight.

What is the relationship between physical activity and health?

Having established this link between excess body fat and negative health conditions, it still remains difficult to identify the underlying cause(s): the contributors to a positive energy balance, within both childhood and adulthood, are very complex. There are many interrelated multi-disciplinary factors, including cultural, behavioural and biological (genetic and hormonal) variables that affect both energy intake and expenditure (Sallis, 2000). The potential variables for an individual's total EE, affecting both energy balance and the storage of excess body fat are highlighted in Figure 3.3.

Though physical activity is the main source of flexibility among an individual's total EE, to date, most interventions designed to reduce excess body fat have largely focused on using both controlled diets and exercise interventions. This is due to the complexity surrounding excess body fat accumulation in terms of it being multi-dimensional, as previously described. Goran *et al.* (1999) suggest that even 1–2 hours of physical activity alone may be insufficient to bring energy balance when calorific intake is high.

However, the continuing rise of obesity and the number of studies with a poor success rate using controlled diets to reduce excess body fat, have encouraged more recent studies to address long-term intervention strategies that increase EE in relation to changing body composition (Bond-Brill *et al.*, 2002): and cross-sectional studies and literature reviews are focusing on the development of CVD risk factors and other negative variables (Wannamethee and Shaper, 2001; Froberg and Andersen, 2005). Despite this, reviewers such as Twisk (2001) conclude that results of previous research are too inconclusive to make substantial health statements, especially for children and young people. Several reviews and cross-sectional studies have highlighted only weak to moderate associations between

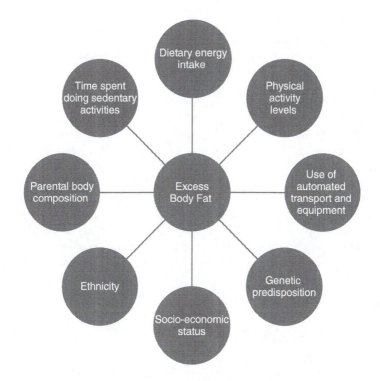

Figure 3.3 Variables associated with excess body fat accumulation.

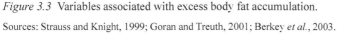

Sources: Strauss and Knight, 1999; Goran and Treuth, 2001; Berkey *et al.*, 2003.

these physical and psychological health associations and activity levels in child-hood (Katzmarzyk *et al.*, 1998; Ribeiro *et al.*, 2004). Limitations of previous research within this area include small sample sizes, crude and inconsistent assess-ment of activity levels, uncontrolled maturational variances, insufficient knowl-edge of risk factors clustering during youth and debate whether activity levels are a product of fitness and health, or vice versa (Katzmarzyk *et al.*, 1998; Twisk, 2001; Biddle *et al.*, 2004; Ribeiro *et al.*, 2004).

Many epidemiological studies and reviews have related the use of physical activ-ity programmes alone with a decreased risk of developing excess accumulation of body fat in adults (Yu *et al.*, 2003; Must and Tybor, 2005) and children (Rowland, 2001; Abbott and Davies, 2004). In terms of longitudinal assessment, Guo *et al.* (1999) noted that increasing physical activity levels resulted in decreased total body fatness during growth, and an increase in fat-free mass, which would in turn help to increase resting EE and maintain future energy balance (Stieger and Cunliffe, 2006). Moreover, and as previously mentioned, for the apparent inverse relationship between physical activity and fatness, the consensus is that the size of reduction in excess body fat accumulation is dependent upon the intensity and duration (known as the amount) of the activity (Goran and Treuth, 2001). In summary, Biddle *et al.* (2004) suggest that 1–3 per cent body fat reductions can be observed in effective activity intervention studies.

Nevertheless, much of the supporting research is cross-sectional based and therefore there is limited definitive cause and effect (Goran *et al.*, 1999; Biddle *et al.*, 2004). Although positive findings have been mentioned, longitudinal studies by Johnson *et al.* (2000) and Ekelund *et al.* (2002) have failed to show a firm link between low EE and body fatness, which is perhaps an indication of the complexity of the factors that are involved in body fat accumulation. Twisk (2001) suggests that the varying methods of the activity and adiposity assessment influence the pattern of the results. Similarly, Goran *et al.* (1999) note that physical activity alone, and subsequent increased EE, may be insufficient to avert weight gain and body fat accumulation due to the individual child's state of growth and maturation. Flodmark *et al.* (2006) conclude that the varying outcome variables, investigation and follow-up periods mean that many results cannot be processed within a meta-analysis, which further contributes to lack of definitive consensus and agreement. In addition, although authors have discussed 'dose-response' relationships between the amount of activity and adipose tissue reductions (Bond-Brill *et al.*, 2002), they are unable to draw firm conclusions as there is insufficient evidence to establish the size of the dose-response relationship (Wilmore, 2001), particularly in children. To add to these challenges, in adults there is a notion that there are 'responders' and 'non-responders' to the same exercise intervention, based on genetic predispositions (Bouchard *et al.*, 1994).

Even so, it would be inappropriate to conclude that lack of definitive data means that the importance of physical activity and active lifestyles should not be promoted consistently through childhood and adulthood. The accumulated current knowledge, expert opinion, much of the theory and common sense provide support for a drive for activity recommendations and lifelong encouragement of positive lifestyles to help address reduced participation rates in adulthood (Twisk, 2001).

Physical activity level recommendations

Several physical activity recommendations and guidelines have been formulated for both adults and children, and are promoted on the basis of speculated health benefits. In 1995, the Center for Disease Control and Prevention, in collaboration with the American College of Sports Medicine (ACSM), after reviewing literature within the area, introduced a radical change in how the dose of exercise and activity was viewed, in terms of what was necessary for health promotion and disease prevention (Pate *et al.*, 1995). The radical view was that adults should accumulate 30 minutes of moderate-intensity activity as a minimum on preferably every day of the week, to reduce the chances of negative health conditions. More recently published documents from the United Kingdom (UK) government further support this recommendation, highlighting that adults should be achieving 60 minutes of moderate-intensity activity to optimise health (Chief Medical Officer, 2004; Department of Health, 2004). However, as previously discussed, the amount and quality of literature and evidence relating to adults' physical activity levels, dose-response, and health consequences is far superior to that available for children, where the evidence base is considerably weaker (Cavill *et al.*, 2001).

In terms of appropriate guidelines for children, the Children's Lifetime Physical Activity Model (C-LPAM) was formed by Corbin *et al.* (1994), which was an adaptation of the adult Lifetime Physical Activity Model (LPAM). The C-LPAM states both a minimum standard recommendation and an optimal functioning recommendation, focusing on development of basic motor skills; learning and enjoying lifelong activity experiences; increasing aerobic fitness, flexibility, muscle strength and endurance; controlling body fatness and bone mineral density; and decreasing the development of disease risk factors. The C-LPAM significantly highlights that accumulation is the best way for children to meet activity guidelines, as this suits their natural sporadic, non-sustained activity patterns (Corbin *et al.*, 1994). The minimum standard guidelines for the C-LPAM are 3–4 kcal. kg^{-1}.day^{-1}, at moderate intensity levels (e.g. walking) on most days of the week, for around 30–60mins, accumulated in bouts >10min. The optimal standard recommendation is activity of 6–8 kcal.kg^{-1}.day^{-1}, which is >60mins of activity, that can be accumulated on most days of the week. In conclusion, the authors identify that these guidelines are not definitive, but are a good beginning for separating expectations between children and adults. Corbin and Pangrazi (1999) reinforced these recommendations, stating that children should accumulate intermittent bouts of activity in minimum periods of 10–15 minutes. Cavill *et al.* (2001) lend their support to these recommendations, but note that they may be refined when future research is performed. Based on this discussion, in the UK, the 'Choosing Health' document (Department of Health, 2004) has highlighted these activity guidelines and prescriptions for children.

More recently, Andersen *et al.* (2006) proposed more challenging physical activity recommendations for children, using several health markers in their large sample cross-sectional study of 9- and 15-year old participants. They conclude that perhaps 90 minutes of moderate activity each day are required to prevent CVD development during childhood. However, as frequently mentioned, these recommendations are limited, since causality is absent in the cross-sectional design. Hence, any form of recommendation based on health consequences remains contentious, due to the debate over the manifestations during childhood, and through into adulthood. Tudor-Locke and Bassett (2004) have tried to put a more practical generalised figure on these guidelines, in terms of the number of steps required each day in adults and children. But there is limited scientific supporting evidence for such guidelines, and it may still be insufficient for some children due to their individual circumstances, state of maturation and initial training status (Blair *et al.*, 2004).

How do physical activity levels change throughout life?

Because of the association between low physical activity levels and negative health conditions, particularly in adulthood, it is of significant interest to identify how childhood physical activity levels relate to adulthood. It has been shown in numerous studies that there is a reduction in physical activity levels as individuals get older, from childhood to adolescence, and adolescence to adulthood. It also seems that this decrease is more significant amongst females than males (Riddoch *et al.*, 2004), although this is debated (Sleap and Warburton, 1997). Such reductions are associated with variables including the conservation of EE to support maturational development processes during puberty, as well as a reduced accessibility to structured physical activity opportunities and lower social desirability to participate (Biddle *et al.*, 2004). Moreover, Biddle *et al.* (2004) associate the common adolescent decline in physical activity levels with changes in perceptions of participation, in terms of perceived competence, self-consciousness of body shape and general motivation to participate in more peer-acceptable ventures. Anderssen *et al.* (2006) have highlighted that it is the activities of peers that have greater impact upon adolescent physical activity adoption than their parents' physical activity status, which may have been more important during earlier childhood. It seems that as individuals progress along their physical development pathway, their psychological and behavioural perspectives change, with concurrent impact upon their physical activity levels (Biddle *et al.*, 2004).

However, if it can be shown that increased physical activity levels in childhood lead to more active lifestyles throughout life, it would support the rationale to make sure that delivery of sport, exercise and physical activity at a young age is appropriate and conducive to maintaining adherence. Malina (1996), Twisk *et al.* (2000), Trudeau *et al.* (2004) and Trudeau and Shephard (2005) identified a low to moderate relationship between activity statuses in childhood compared to adulthood, using cross-sectional methods. But it was evident that inactive lifestyles in childhood were more directly associated with inactive lifestyles in adulthood. This suggests that it may be sensible to try to address inactivity during childhood as it increases the likelihood of an inactive adult.

Yet only a few investigations have directly measured the impact of physical activity intervention upon adult adherence. Twisk (2001) does highlight that there is no evident threshold for physical activity in childhood that influences adult participation in sport and exercise and that more evidence is required. Trudeau *et al.* (1998, 1999) addressed the effects of school physical education delivery effects, in terms of five hours of 'quality' provision for the intervention group, versus two hours of normal provision for the control group, on adult participation rates. It was identified more than 20 years after the intervention that 42.1 per cent compared to 25.9 per cent of the intervention and control group respectively, completed three hours of moderate-high intensity exercise per week. This indicated a possible positive effect of childhood physical activity experiences on long-term adult participation. However, the difference was observed only amongst females. Within a similar investigation, Telama *et al.* (2006) found that participation in organised youth sport increased the probability of high activity in adulthood in males more than females. These studies highlight the need to take into account the context of the interventions, given the long-established leisure research, which acknowledges its interaction with gender differences in participation in sport and physical education.

A review by Martens (1996) highlights the importance of fun in facilitating life-long physical activity adoption from childhood. Similarly, an individual's parental and peer support has been identified as an important source of encouragement, involvement and facilitation to affect adherence of a long-term physically active lifestyle, especially for younger children (Gustafson and Rhodes, 2006). Likewise, interventions and messages to demonstrate the benefits of physical activity upon health have been shown to be important in maintaining participation in sport and exercise (Heitzler *et al.*, 2006). In addition, conducive environmental factors, such as safe and enjoyable spaces, and increased socio-economic status of the individual may have an impact upon increasing adherence to an active lifestyle (Franks *et al.*, 2005).

Limits to existing knowledge and future directions

A significant issue for the tracking of physical activity levels throughout life is the accurate assessment of physical activity, which can be challenging, since there is a wide use of different measurement tools between studies, leading to ambiguous results. More standardised approaches should allow for clearer understanding of the relationship between physical activity and health throughout life, directly related to contributing factors of change during this time course. Although there is some evidence, as presented above, there is no definitive conclusion that activity levels track from childhood into adulthood, mainly because of the research problems of effective assessment procedures and the long-term nature of such studies (Trudeau *et al.*, 2004).[1] Twisk (2001) recommends that to maximise adult participation in sport and physical activity, total populations should be considered as the target populations, rather than just children and adolescents, in order to help reduce the associated affects of negative health outcomes. There is evident need to align multi-disciplinary practitioners to address inactive lifestyles throughout life, since sport, exercise and physical activity adherence is clearly multifaceted, with the impact of the different variables consistently changing as individuals get older.

Note

1. Editors' note: it is also desirable that researchers working in this area become aware of the long-established leisure research on sport and active leisure participation, which strongly supports the relationships between activity levels and life cycle stage, gender and socio-economic status which are reported in this chapter.

References

Abbott, R. A. and Davies, P. S. W. (2004). Habitual physical activity and physical activity intensity: their relation to body composition in 5.0-10.5-y-old children. *European Journal of Clinical Nutrition*, 58, 285–291.

Andersen, L. B., Harro, M., Sardinha, L. B., Froberg, K., Ekelund, U., Brage, S. and Anderssen, S. A. (2006). Physical activity and clustered cardiovascular risk in children:

42   *P. A. Ford*

a cross-sectional study (The European Youth Heart Study). *The Lancet, 368*(9532), 299–304.

Anderssen, N., Wold, B. and Torsheim, T. (2006). Are parental health habits transmitted to their children? An eight year longitudinal study of physical activity in adolescents and their parents. *Journal of Adolescence, 29*, 513–524.

Berkey, C., Rockett, H., Gillman, M. and Colditz, G. (2003). One-year changes in activity and in inactivity among 10- to 15-year old boys and girls: relationship to change in body mass index. *Pediatrics, 111*, 836–843.

Biddle, S. J. H., Gorely, T. and Stensel, D. J. (2004). Health-enhancing physical activity and sedentary behaviour in children and adolescents. *Journal of Sports Sciences, 22*, 679–701.

Blair, S. N., LaMonte, M. J. and Nichaman, M. Z. (2004). The evolution of physical activity recommendations: how much is enough? *American Journal of Clinical Nutrition, 79*, S913–920.

Bond-Brill, J., Perry, A. C., Parker, L., Robinson, A. and Burnett, K. (2002). Dose-response effect of walking exercise on weight loss. How much is enough? *International Journal of Obesity, 26*, 1484–1493.

Bouchard, C. A., Tremblay, J.-P., Despres, J. P., Thériault, G., Nadeau, A., Lupien, P. J., Moorjani, S., Prud'homme, D. and Fournier, G. (1994). The response to exercise with constant energy intake in identical twins. *Obesity Research, 2*, 400–410.

Cavill, N., Biddle, S. and Sallis, J. F. (2001). Health enhancing physical activity for young people: statement of the United Kingdom expert consensus conference. *Pediatric Exercise Science, 13*, 12–25.

Chief Medical Officer. (2004). *At least five a week*. Department of Health Publication, UK.

Cole, T. J., Bellizzi, M. C., Flegal, K. M. and Dietz, W. H. (2000). Establishing a standard definition for child overweight and obesity worldwide: international survey. *British Medical Journal, 320*, 1240–1245.

Corbin, C. B. and Pangrazi, R. P. (1999). Physical activity for children: in pursuit of appropriate guidelines. *European Journal of Physical Education, 4*, 136–138.

Corbin, C. B., Pangrazi, R. P. and Welk, G. J. (1994). Toward an understanding of appropriate physical activity levels for youth. *PCPFS Research Digest, 1*(98), 1–7.

Department of Health (2004). *Choosing health – making healthy choices easier* (White Paper). Department of Health Publication, UK.

Ebbeling, C. B., Pawlak, D. B. and Ludwig, D. S. (2002). Childhood obesity: public-health crisis, common sense cure. *The Lancet, 360*, 473–482.

Ekelund, U., Åman, J., Yngve, A., Renman, C., Westerterp, K. and Sjöström, M. (2002). Physical activity but not energy expenditure is reduced in obese adolescents: a case-control study. *American Journal of Clinical Nutrition, 76*, 935–941.

Flodmark, C.-E., Marcus, C. and Britton, M. (2006). Interventions to prevent obesity in children and adolescents: a systematic literature review. *International Journal of Obesity, 30*, 579–589.

Franks, P. W., Ravussin, E., Hanson, R. L., Harper, I. T., Allison, D. B., Knowler, W. C., Tataranni, P. A. and Salbe, A. D. (2005). Habitual physical activity in children: the role of genes and the environment. *American Journal of Clinical Nutrition, 82*, 901–908.

Froberg, K. and Andersen, L. B. (2005). Mini review: physical activity and fitness and its relations to cardiovascular disease risk factors in children. *International Journal of Obesity, 29*, S34–39.

Goran, M. I. and Treuth, M. S. (2001). Energy expenditure, physical activity, and obesity in children. *Pediatric Clinic of North America, 48*(4), 931–953.

Goran, M. I., Reynolds, F. D. and Lindquist, C. H. (1999). Role of physical activity in the prevention of obesity in children. *International Journal of Obesity*, *23*(S3), S198–233.

Guo, S. S., Zeller, C., Chumlea, W. C. and Siervogel, R. M. (1999). Aging, body composition, and lifestyle: the Fels longitudinal study. *American Journal of Clinical Nutrition*, *70*, 405–411.

Gustafson, S. L. and Rhodes, R. E. (2006). Parental correlates of physical activity in children and early adolescents. *Sports Medicine*, *36*(1), 79–97.

Heitzler, C. D., Martin, S. L., Duke, J. and Huhman, M. (2006). Correlates of physical activity in a national sample of children aged 9–13 years. *Preventive Medicine*, *42*, 254–260.

Higgins, P. B., Gower, B. A., Hunter, G. R. and Goran, M. I. (2001). Defining health-related obesity in prepubertal children. *Obesity Research*, *9*, 233–240.

Johnson, M. S., Figueroa-Colon, R., Herd, S. L., Fields, D. A., Min Sun, M. S., Hunter, G. R. and Goran, M. I. (2000). Aerobic fitness, not energy expenditure, influences subsequent increase in adiposity in black and white children. *Pediatrics*, *106*(4), e50.

Katzmarzyk, P. T., Malina, R. M., Song, T. M. K. and Bouchard, C. (1998). Physical activity and health-related fitness in youth: a multivariate analysis. *Medicine and Science in Sports and Exercise*, *30*(5), 709–714.

Kiess, W., Blüher, S., Kapellen, T., Garten, A., Klammt, J., Kratzsch, J. and Körner, A. (2006). Physiology of obesity in childhood and adolescence. *Current Paediatrics*, *16*, 123–131.

Malina, R. M. (1996). Tracking of physical activity and physical fitness across the lifespan. *Research Quarterly in Exercise and Sport*, *67*(3), 48–57.

Martens, R. (1996). Turning kids on to physical activity for a lifetime. *Quest*, *48*, 303–310.

Must, A. and Strauss, R. S. (1999). Risks and consequences of childhood and adolescent obesity. *International Journal of Obesity and Related Metabolic Disorders*, *23*, S2–11.

Must, A. and Tybor, D. J. (2005). Physical activity and sedentary behaviour: a review of longitudinal studies of weight and adiposity in youth. *International Journal of Obesity*, *29*, S84–96.

Pate, R. R., Pratt, M., Blair, S. N., Haskell, W. L., Macera, C. A., Bouchard, C., Buchner, D., Ettinger, W., Heath, G. W., King, A. C., Kriska, A., Leon, A. S., Marcus, B. H., Morris, J., Paffenbarger, Jr., R. S., Patrick, K., Pollock, M. L., Rippe, J. M., Sallis, J. and Wilmore, J. H. (1995). Physical activity and public health. A recommendation from the Centers for Disease Control and Prevention and the American College of Sports Medicine. *Journal of the American Medical Association*, *273*, 402–407.

Raitakari, O. T., Juonala, M. and Viikari, J. S. A. (2005). Obesity in childhood and vascular changes in adulthood: insights into the cardiovascular risk in Young Finns study. *International Journal of Obesity*, *29*, S101–104.

Reilly, J. J. Methven, E., McDowell, Z. C., Hacking, B., Alexander, D., Stewart, L. and Kelnar, C. J. H. (2003). Health consequences of obesity: systematic review. *Archives of Disease in Childhood*, *88*, 748–752.

Ribeiro, J. C., Guerra, S., Oliveira, J., Teixeira-Pinto, A., Twisk, J. W. R., Duarte, J. A. and Mota, J. (2004). Physical activity and biological risk factors clustering in pediatric population. *Preventive Medicine*, *39*, 596–601.

Riddoch, C. J., Andersen, L. B., Wedderkopp, N., Harro, M., Klasson-Heggebo, L., Sardinha, L. B., Cooper, A. R. and Ekelund, U. (2004). Physical activity levels and patterns of 9- and 15-yr-old European children. *Medicine and Science in Sports and Exercise*, *36*(1), 86–92.

Rowland, T. W. (2001). The role of physical activity and fitness in children in the prevention of adult cardiovascular disease. *Progress in Pediatric Cardiology*, *12*, 199–203.

44   *P. A. Ford*

Sallis, J. F. (2000). Overcoming inactivity in young people. *The Physician and Sportsmedicine, 28*(10), 31–33.

Sleap, M. and Warburton, P. (1997). Physical activity levels of 5-11-year-old children in England: cumulative evidence from three direct observation studies. *International Journal of Sports Medicine, 17*(4), 248–253.

Stiegler, P. and Cunliffe, A. (2006). The role of diet and exercise for the maintenance of fat-free mass and resting metabolic rate during weight loss. *Sports Medicine, 36*(3), 239–262.

Strauss, R. and Knight, J. (1999). Influence of the home environment on the development of obesity in children. *Pediatrics, 103*, e85.

Telama, R., Yang, X., Hirvensalo, M. and Raitakari, O. (2006). Participation in organized youth sport as a predictor of adult physical activity: a 21-year longitudinal study. *Pediatric Exercise Science, 17*, 76–88.

Tracy, R. E., Newman, W. P., Wattigney, W. A., Scrinivalan, S. R., Strong, J. P. and Berenson, G. S. (1995). Histological features of atherosclerosis and hypertension from autopsies of young individuals in a defined geographic population: the Bogalusa Heart Study. *Atherosclerosis, 116*, 163–179.

Trudeau, F. and Shephard, R. J. (2005). Contribution of school programmes to physical activity levels and attitudes in children and adults. *Sports Medicine, 35*(2), 89–105.

Trudeau, F., Laurencelle, L. and Shephard, R. J. (2004). Tracking of physical activity from childhood to adulthood. *Medicine and Science in Sports and Exercise, 36*(11), 1937–1943.

Trudeau, F., Laurencelle, L., Tremblay, J., Rajic, M. and Shephard, R. J. (1998). Follow-up of the Trois-Rivières Growth and Development longitudinal study. *Pediatric Exercise Science, 10*, 368–377.

Trudeau, F., Laurencelle, L., Tremblay, J., Rajic, M. and Shephard, R. J. (1999). Daily primary school physical education: effects on physical activity during adult life. *Medicine and Science in Sport and Exercise, 31*, 111–117.

Tudor-Locke, C. and Bassett, D. R. (2004). How many steps/day are enough? Preliminary pedometer indices for public health. *Sports Medicine, 34*(1), 1–8.

Twisk, J. W. R. (2001). Physical activity guidelines for children and adolescents. *Sports Medicine, 31*(8), 617–627.

Twisk, J. W. R., Kemper, H. C. G. and van Mechelen, W. (2000). Tracking of activity and fitness and the relationship with cardiovascular disease risk factors. *Medicine and Science in Sport and Exercise, 32*, 1455–1461.

Wannamethee, S. G. and Shaper, A.G. (2001). Physical activity in the prevention of cardiovascular disease. *Sports Medicine, 31*(2), 101–114.

Williams, D. P., Going, S. B., Lohman, T. G., Harsha, D. W., Srinivasan, S. R., Webber, L. S. and Berenson, G. S. (1992). Body fatness and risk for elevated blood pressure, total cholesterol, and serum lipoprotein ratios in children and adolescents. *American Journal of Public Health, 82*(3), 358–363.

Wilmore, J. H. (2001). Dose-response: variation with age, sex, and health status. *Medicine and Science in Sports and Exercise, 33*(6), S622–634.

World Health Organization. www.who.int/dietphysicalactivity/publications/facts/obesity/en, accessed 16.07.09.

Yu, S., Yarnell, J. W. G., Sweetman, P. M. and Murray, L. (2003). What level of physical activity protects against premature cardiovascular death? The Caerphilly study. *Heart, 89*, 502–506.

4 Rethinking participant development in sport and physical activity

Dave Collins, Richard Bailey,
Martin Toms, Gemma Pearce,
Áine MacNamara and Paul A. Ford

Policy context for sport and physical activity

Engagement in sport is widely perceived to be so worthwhile that governments around the world invest large sums of public money in its promotion. The United Kingdom (UK), in particular, has demonstrated great faith in the potential of sport both in its own right and for the achievement of wider social goals. For example, school sport alone has received more than £1 billion since 2003 (Green, 2006). In parallel, the sport policy community in the UK has changed in a short period of time from a relatively unknown arena to a significant focus. The announcement of London as the host of the 2012 Olympic Games has merely added impetus to this process.

As sport has become increasingly politicised, there has been a significant shift in both policy rhetoric and funding from an emphasis on mass participation physical activity towards elite sport (Green, 2006). It is relatively clear why governments would seek to promote participation in sport at a grassroots level: it has been claimed to contribute to a variety of personal and social outcomes, such as health, education, social inclusion and neighbourhood renewal (Coalter, 2007). The rationale for investment in elite sport is less clear. Nevertheless, successive policy documents have spoken of the importance of elite sport in increasingly confident terms, culminating in the publication of *Playing to Win: A New Era for Sport* (DCMS, 2008) which placed performance and excellence at its very core. Reflecting this perception, funding for elite sport in Britain has risen exponentially since 1997 and is set to continue up to and beyond the 2012 Olympics (DCMS, 2008, p. 4).

Despite this increased investment, however, there seem to be problems with the underlying reasoning about allocation. At a superficial level, there seems to be an assumption that the development of mass participation is synergistic with elite sport. For example, the justification for investment in high performance sport in *Game Plan* is based on the expectation that elite sport produces a number of virtuous outcomes, including economic benefits, grassroots participation, a 'feel good factor' and a positive 'national "image" abroad' (DCMS/Strategy Unit, 2002, p. 117). However, even government policy documents make it clear that each of these claims are, at best, inconclusive (e.g. DCMS/Strategy Unit, 2002).

In practice, the allocation of resources has always been finite, and development of elite sport has usually occurred at the expense of mass participation (Girginov and Collins, 2004). This is not inevitable, but there is a tendency because 'the scale of provision, the span of time needed and other favourable contextual policies to provoke major lifestyle and participation changes are huge, challenging and beyond the sport policy community, which is usually marginal' (Collins, 2008, p. 78). This situation is exacerbated by the prestige associated with elite sporting events, against which grassroots participation seems unable to compete. Therefore, there has been a general international movement away from unified and collaborative provision towards separate policy delivery.

The consequence of this contextual discussion is that the objectives of sport for all and elite sport are presented as structurally distinct and incompatible. Almost all structures, systems and initiatives are built on this twin track approach, where competitive sport and (non-competitive) physical activity are seen as separate concerns. We argue in this chapter that this split is more about structural simplification and organisational power than rational pursuit of goals. Whilst it may be necessary to establish separate agencies for provision to different audiences, we suggest that it is a categorical error to generalise this to all elements of the sport system. This is not merely an academic concern, as the underlying principles of sports development express themselves in the practical organisation of structures. Our primary concern is with participant development, by which we mean the trajectory of engagement of those participating in sport and physical activity throughout the lifespan. In this context, the twin track approach has largely been taken for granted by policy-makers and deliverers, albeit using different metaphors to capture the point. For example, most models of sports development are premised on a broad foundation of recreational participants who feed into progressively higher and more selective levels, as players move up a 'pyramid' of performance (Kirk *et al.*, 2005); other popular metaphors that presume the same basic process are 'foundation stones' and 'trickle down' (Kirk and Gorely, 2000). Houlihan (2000) has suggested that versions of this viewpoint characterise many UK sports development policy statements, and Kirk *et al.* (2005, p. 2) argue that its influence can be seen in numerous international sports participation models, and that 'the assumptions underpinning the . . . model continue to have a powerful residual influence on thinking about junior sport participation and sport development in sport policy'.

In the discussion that follows, we offer a framework for reconceptualising participant development in sport and physical activity (the addition of physical activity will become clear as our argument develops). This framework stands in contrast to the twin track and 'pyramid' models that have dominated policy discourse, and presents a rationale for a more unified and coherent approach to sport development for all participants. Rather than a comprehensive theory, we are fundamentally concerned with stimulating debate. However, we are also eager to offer a counter to certain practices that may be incompatible with the development of a rational and fair framework of sport for all people.

An alternative structure for the process: the participant continuum

Our first revision lies in how the development process is structured, and its aims and objectives across the lifespan. Participant development in sport and physical activity is dynamic and non-linear, and there are multiple pathways that individuals may take as they progress in their activity (Abbott *et al.*, 2005). This non-linearity, coupled with the importance of 'key events and transitions' in the developmental pathway (Ollis *et al.*, 2006), makes it essential that support systems offer flexibility, individual optimisation and 'return routes' as features of any formal 'pathway to excellence'. As we will suggest in this chapter, however, it is equally important that similar characteristics, constraints and requirements also appear to apply to the development of participation in all contexts. As such, and notably for this developmental perspective, we suggest that the twin track approach to participant development may be philosophically and practically flawed. In short, the existence of distinct organisations, methodologies and initiatives for the promotion of sport performance and exercise participation may well be more hindrance than help, at least when the rather esoteric needs of the elite are removed from the picture.

Defining excellence

We start our account for this approach in the performance-excellence world of competitive sport. Traditionally, excellence in sport has been conceptualised in terms of outcome measures in the form of medals, records and victories (Penney, 2000). More recently however, and reflecting growing interest in lifelong participation in sport and physical activity, there has been a call to expand this definition to include excellence in terms of personal participation and improvement (Miller and Kerr, 2002). As such, we suggest that excellence can be usefully considered in terms of a continuum across three different 'worlds'.[1] The first two worlds lie mainly in competitive sport, from club competitor to world-class performer. These are as follows:

- Elite Referenced Excellence (ERE): excellence in the form of high-level sporting performance where achievement is measured against others with the ultimate goal of winning at the highest level possible, or;
- Personal Referenced Excellence (PRE): excellence in the form of participation and personal performance, where achievement is more personally referenced by, say, completing a marathon or improving one's personal best time.

The first category is clearly concerned with performance excellence in high-level sport such as national and international competition. Conversely, the second advocates excellence as the achievement of developmentally appropriate challenges across the length of one's lifespan as well as the acquisition of those personal qualities that contribute to lifelong health and well-being (Cimons, 1999). As such, accomplishments such as completing a marathon, improving a personal best, playing for a local club team, regular mountaineering and hill walking, or even (enthusiastically) digging the garden can be considered as the pursuit of 'excellence' when, from the performer's perspective, these activities are measured in terms of personal achievement (Weiss and Chaumenton, 1992).

To be truly adequate, however, one other sporting world must be explicitly considered.[2] In this review, this third perspective is defined as follows:

• Participation for Personal Well-being (PPW): taking part in physical activity to satisfy needs other than personal progression.

Typical motivations for PPW might include the improvement of one's social life (e.g. making and keeping friends), the enhancement of one's social identity (by being a member of a high status group or club), personal renewal (through activity which is fulfilling) and the maintenance of aspects of self-concept (staying in good shape). However, our suggestion relates not just to the existence of these three worlds but also the necessity for effective and smooth transition between them.

The need for a continuum between these worlds

A key driver for the approach espoused by this chapter is the contention that the three worlds described above are interrelated, at least in developmental terms (cf. Jess and Collins, 2003). These ideas are critically considered in subsequent sections. For the moment, however, the need for enabling a degree of fluidity between the three should be apparent, such as in meeting the aim of 'lifelong physical activity'.

This Three Worlds Continuum is presented schematically in Figure 4.1.

The hypothesis is that, built on a common fundamental skills base, all individuals should be empowered to progress back and forth between the three types

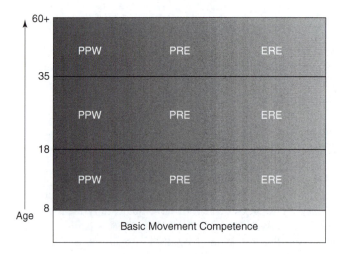

Figure 4.1 The Three Worlds Continuum.

of activity contexts. On this basis, young elite performers can subsequently stay involved at a participation level whilst late developers or returners can attempt to move into the ERE and PRE worlds at any age, practicalities notwithstanding. In short, at any age/stage and in progression from one to the next, easy movement between the three worlds is important. We examine the commonality of causation in a subsequent section. Suffice to say at this point, age boundaries to the different stages are somewhat arbitrary. In fact, age transitions are dependent on a combination of factors, including physiological and societal concerns, with high inter-individual variation.

Both the categories and the continuum are based on historical and pragmatic imperatives. Major but somewhat distinct stakeholders are apparent for each of the categories (e.g. UK Sport/British Olympic Association for ERE, Home Country Sports Councils and National Governing Bodies for sport for PRE, and Health Organisations/Local Health Trusts for PPW). Of course, as with the categories themselves, some overlap is usually apparent. For the needs of a central government, however, fluid movement across the continuum is essential, since each aspect is crucial at some point of the lifespan.

Conceptual barriers to participant development

Further evidence of the need for a new approach comes from a critical consideration of some of the parameters implicit within other participant development approaches. We consider first the largely physiological precepts which underpin the widely influential Long-Term Athlete Development model (LTAD) (Balyi and Hamilton, 1996, 2003).

Critical periods – training opportunities which MUST be exploited

The LTAD model proposes the existence of critical periods, in which some unique, special and otherwise unobtainable advantage is obtained from effective exploitation of the period so described. Thus, for example, the identification of a critical period for strength gains between the ages of 10 and 12 years suggests this focus is imperative and that, if not realised within this age phase, these gains will never be fully achieved. There are obvious and strong implications to the use of the 'critical' label, together with significant consequences for important constructs in elite sport, such as early specialisation.

Of course, it is plausible that there may be critical periods when developmental response is greater in relation to a controlled training stimulus, and this may enhance ERE chances, *especially at that age*. However, there is a lack of supporting population-specific evidence. In this regard, Suslov (2002) identifies the complexity in quantifying physical activity and training in young participants, as well as controlling this during an investigation. He further credits this complexity for the lack of agreement in the literature as to the objective influence of the optimal training loads during critical periods and whether they may maximise final athletic capacity. Moreover, Suslov highlights that coaches should be aware of the importance of training to advance all fitness components throughout childhood and adolescence during non-critical periods as well as those identified as critical, principally because of individualised development rates of anatomical, neurological, muscular and metabolic parameters. Most interestingly for the present purpose, Saltin (2005) questions the implicit theorising behind specialised training of young people with direct reference to critical periods, asking if coaches are trying to enhance development to increase performance at the same age with the consequent danger that current success may be at the expense of higher level success later.

In short, the evidence on which many implications of the LTAD model are based, such as the necessity of early selection/specialisation to exploit these 'once in a lifetime' opportunities, is not apparent. For example, the 'strength critical window' in relation to testosterone increases in males during maturation is certainly a plausible trainability opportunity: however, whether it will affect end-athletic performance seems unclear. Of course, this is not to say that key physiological processes and changes, such as the transition through Peak Height Velocity and its accompanying challenges to coordination and performance (Malina and Bouchard, 1991), are not important influences. It is simply that these changes are not monotonic in their influence, but rather differential based on mediation by psychological and social factors.

In a somewhat similar vein, the concept of early specialisation has also been promoted by some as a means of allowing an individual to obtain a higher performance capacity, due to opportunities for deliberate practice for a longer period (Ericsson *et al.*, 1993). Certainly, Balyi and Hamilton (2003) have addressed the positive aspects of such concepts with direct reference to sports such as gymnastics: the maturational changes in flexibility tend to favour athletes achieving optimal performance during late adolescence; and consequently, expert skill acquisition must be obtained as early as possible. However, such early/intensive specialisation is also related to outcomes such as over-training and burnout (Bompa, 1995; Balyi and Hamilton, 2003), and could have a significant influence on subsequent progress (or lack thereof) between the Three Worlds. Interestingly, more recent research demonstrates the achievement of excellence with less than the mythical 10,000 hours of deliberate practice, with such achievements often promoted by social, psychological and other environmental factors (Baker *et al.*, 2003).

Perhaps reflecting these ideological challenges, the long-term periodised concepts of the LTAD model account for negative consequences of specialisation by incorporating generalised sport/exercise training during maturational progression with more advanced specialisation occurring during adolescent maturation. Nevertheless, Rutenfranz and Singer (1980) have suggested that even generic physical activity increase between the ages of 15–17 in boys is associated with sports performance improvement. Crucially, it seems that specific training may be unnecessary as generic improvement in athletic capabilities can provide an effective starting point for *later* specialisation but *better* eventual achievement. The downsides of early specialisation for lifelong sport and physical activity or self-image issues for example, suggest that its necessity requires more advanced investigation. Other challenges come from the characteristics of effective talent development environments, which appear to significantly mediate the impact of practice regimes with physically precocious young performers (Martindale *et al.*, 2005). In summary, evidence for the necessity of early selection/specialisation is not forthcoming, unlike the proposal that psychosocial factors co-act with physical and practice regimes to enhance efficacy or, if started early, to precipitate dropout.

Developmental stages, critical moments, critical episodes or 'deliberate experience'?

Other key drivers postulated to the development outcome relate to progression through a prescribed and generic series of stages and/or the differential impact imposed by incidents with high personal significance. Typical of these later experiences may be major wins or losses, selection/de-selection from a squad or embarrassing moments. Referred to by Côté and Hay (2002) as 'critical incidents', these examples characterise the short and distinct experiences which are likely to be impactful. Such incidents, together with the generic and linear stages of progression through a developmental pathway, are the underpinning principles of Côté's Developmental Model of Sport Participation (DMSP; Côté, 1999). The DMSP extended Bloom's (1985) earlier work with talented individuals through qualitative interviews with elite Canadian and Australian gymnasts, basketball players, netball players, hockey players, rowers and tennis players. Progression from the early 'sampling' phase can take one of three forms: children can become involved more seriously in one or two sports in the specialising phase; they can chose to stay involved in sport as a recreational activity; or they can drop out of sport. Likewise, at the 'specialising' phase, players have three options available to them: recreation; drop out; or progress to the 'investment phase', when they aspire to a high level of performance in one sport. Those players who have reached the investment years can subsequently progress to either recreational sport, or simply drop out.

Two important qualifiers need to be embraced within these potentially competing constructs (LTAD and DMSP). First, it needs to be stressed that critical incidents can be chronic as well as acute (for example, the experience of poor coaching, long-term parental pressure or coping unsuccessfully with overly severe training loads). As such, the incidents (or what might be more correctly termed critical *episodes*) will inevitably interact with the more prescriptively driven developmental stages. As a result, we contend that the pathway can be neither generic nor linear, especially when the individuals' responses to these critical episodes, whether they act as spur or terminator for example, is taken into consideration. Second, the extent to which the participants' metacognitive skills, that might simply be called their attitude, lead them to interpret and exploit experiences as positive or negative. Ollis *et al.* (2006) refer to this as 'deliberate experience'; where long and careful consideration of a hard experience can often result in positive development.

The main implication from all these ideas is the central role played by an individual's metacognitive skills. In short, thinking positively may be crucial for optimising development. As crucial mediators, these characteristics are arguably more important precursors of positive development than the experiences themselves. As Aldous Huxley (1932) observed, 'Experience is not what happens to a man; it is what a man does with what happens to him'. Metacognitive skills appear to be the mechanism through which experience is internalised and exploited (cf. Dweck, 2006).

Social advantage and psycho-behavioural/metacognitive skill

Participant development is impacted by a wide variety of psychosocial factors, including the possession of one or more advantage-conferring environmental parameters. For example, many writers suggest that a range of environmental factors (e.g. family, schooling, geographical location, date of birth and place of birth) can influence the likelihood of children being identified as talented in the first place (e.g. Perleth *et al.*, 2000; Côté *et al.*, 2007). One such factor, now acknowledged by many (e.g. Helsen *et al.*, 1998), involves individuals' birth dates with regard to the age grouping system in any particular activity – their 'relative age'. Young athletes 'lucky' enough to be born in the first half of the selection year are significantly more likely to be identified as talented because they are relatively older and more physically mature than their peers (Helsen *et al.*, 1998). Conversely, and reflecting other aspects of serendipitous experience, highly able children who are relatively younger, have never been exposed to certain activities, do not have access to appropriate facilities or do not have the social or familial support to engage their ability, are much more likely to remain undetected (Côté, 1999; Martindale *et al.*, 2005). For these reasons, many researchers in talent identification increasingly disregard the effectiveness of early identification processes in sport and instead place the emphasis on the development of the multi-dimensional factors that underpin the capacity young athletes need to realise their potential (Abbott and Collins, 2004). This line of research seeks to neutralise (or at least minimise) the role of luck (Bailey, 2007) by systematically developing all the components of talent so that individuals have both the ability and capacity for choice to engage in sport and physical activity targeted at either PRE or ERE, or, typically at earlier ages, both (Abbott and Collins, 2004; Martindale *et al.*, 2005). Notably and, to our minds unfortunately, this trend often lies contrary to the techniques and initiatives pursued by central governments.

Greater focus on these metacognitive factors, the internal characteristics which help participants to make the most of their chances, represents a move towards a truly inclusive talent development model (Dweck, 2006). Abbott and her colleagues point to the importance of considering, identifying and developing those factors (which they term psycho-behavioural characteristics) which over the course of time may facilitate development (Abbott *et al.*, 2007). They offer the example of a lack of mental focus (Gould *et al.*, 2002) as a factor that might hinder the development of a young, but otherwise talented athlete. In fact, Abbott *et al.* (2002) question whether, in the absence of key characteristics such as a positive work ethic, an individual can be considered talented at all. Certainly, the subsequent development and deployment of a positive work ethic can result in unexpected and non-linear changes in development and performance (Abbott *et al.*, 2002), reflecting the dynamic conception of talent. Simonton (1999) offers further support for this and proposes that talent is not a static entity but emerges over time, both endogenously and in reaction to environmental factors. Simonton's model of talent development also accounts for the multiple factors that influence talent and suggests that these factors (e.g. innate ability, environmental factors, motivation and learning strategies) interact in a multiplicative manner. So, even if a young athlete has the physical attributes to succeed in sport, the potential to develop is also dependent on other determinants of success such as commitment, motivation and the availability of developmental opportunities (Abbott and Collins, 2004; Baker and Horton, 2004). The availability of additional, socially mediated factors such as parental resource, social support and familial influence also play a significant part.

From our Three Worlds perspective, this understanding of talent as multiplicative and dynamic highlights the limitations of uni-dimensional talent identification models since these are based on linear and additive factors. In contrast, Simonton (2001) suggests that genetic traits do not manifest themselves at birth but instead develop according to epigenetic trajectories. Within this dynamic perspective, talent may manifest itself early or late in the performer's career and is constantly transforming throughout the maturational process. This perspective suggests that the traits constituting talent emerge with variable growth curves and with diverse fits and starts (Simonton, 1999). Recognising the importance of environmental factors (Ericsson *et al.*, 1993), talent development is amenable to acceleration or retardation according to environmental incentives and stimulation. In other words, even if epigenetic trajectories are under genetic control, the exploitation of these is not.

Social factors, metacognitive skills and participation

Hopefully, this brief review of an expanding literature base offers a strong case for the role of psycho-behavioural characteristics in facilitating (or perhaps causing) effective progression towards both ERE and PRE. Possession and effective deployment of these skills smoothes the pathway to excellence and allows the developing performer to make the most of his/her social advantages. But does such an advantageous process also exist for young people developing towards a more participatory orientation?

Certainly, if the Three Worlds idea is accepted, enhancement towards any part of the spectrum will facilitate the others, as long as the young person's perceptions are not jaded by low perceived competence or overuse/burnout (Butcher *et al.*, 2002). However, it is also worth considering the other factors which lead young people to desist from physical activity and, conversely and more interestingly, the factors which seem to help them sustain engagement (Allender *et al.*, 2006). Similar constructs do appear important for both PRE and PPW, and this is not surprising given the balance of physiological, social and psychological factors that have already emerged in ERE/PRE. Physical competence, both actual and perceived, has already been stressed (Boyd *et al.*, 2002; Horn and Harris, 2002), whilst concerns with societal norms, social physique anxiety (Sabiston *et al.*, 2007) and other social pressures appear to play a large part, especially for young women (Whitehead and Biddle, 2008). Most important to the current context, however, is the way in which these various characteristics are mediated by personal perceptions and characteristics, such as locus of causality (Chatzisarantis *et al.*, 2003), low self-consciousness (Cox *et al.*, 2006) and self-determination (e.g. Chatzisarantis and Hagger, 2009).

In short, it seems that there are compelling reasons to pursue an integrated model across the Three Worlds *and* there is an emerging argument to examine the impact of developing metacognitive strategies within an integrated framework as an educational route to facilitating movement across the continuum. This being so, it is worth asking which approaches, developed against which structural models, offer the best way to tackle this challenge.

Moving forward

Traditional models have tended to portray participant development as a relatively simple affair, in which participants' entry and engagement in sport and physical activity is almost exclusively determined by their interests and in which their success is the result of their ability and effort. Clearly, such factors are of vital importance, but so too are a host of mediating elements, such as developmental maturation, the provision of skills within an effective developmental environment, socialisation and ultimately luck. Crucially, and reflecting suggestions made in the preceding two sections, we do not believe that participant development can be adequately understood through uni-disciplinary approaches. On the contrary, we suggest that any complex system benefits from the enhanced vision provided by multiple lenses. The main message is that whilst the different factors impacting on engagement can be profitably analysed as discrete elements that offer value, they should not be used solely and in isolation as the basis of policies and recommendations. This warning is especially noteworthy in light of the fact that the two most influential models of development (LTAD and DMSP) are explicitly based on relatively narrow disciplinary perspectives (physiology and developmental psychology, respectively[3]).

The applied aim for any model in this context is to explain, predict and enable the modification of human behaviour. Unfortunately, the ability of models like LTAD and DMSP to account for the patterns of participation in different national contexts is equivocal. For example, Côté's description of young people's socialisation into sport (Côté and Hay, 2002) has received support from MacPhail *et al.*'s (2003) study of an athletics club in England. Notably, these examinations come from a uni-disciplinary approach. However, both Côté's model and Balyi's (2001,

2002) much more detailed and prescriptive phased account, have been thrown into doubt by Toms' (2005) study of young cricketers' socialisation into their sport. In keeping with our inter-disciplinary proposals, and the evidence presented in this review, Toms found involvement in their sports club was contingent on positive, socially mediated episodes, psychological support and motivation, as well as physical ability, and that the actual, real world experiences of these young people did not follow a linear trajectory (see Figure 4.2). Similar findings of non-linearity and a complex interaction of influences are increasingly common in investigations of related topics (e.g. Ollis *et al.*, 2006).

None of this discussion is intended to argue against the need for models of participant development. On the contrary, our belief is that models like LTAD and DMSP have proved to be extremely valuable in promoting a developmental, evidence-based perspective in sport. There are weaknesses in terms of their content, but even more so in their scope and application. Models are intended to represent meaningful conjectures about the varied factors that impact on a particular phenomenon or situation, their possible inter-relationships or causal sequence. Their value lies in the extent to which they can be critically evaluated to investigate their coherence, their evidential basis or their internal consistency. Time and testing may see some models develop or contribute to an emerging theory. Others will wither and die. That is the nature of science (Popper, 1934). The point is that it is the testing of models, not their creation, that is of greatest value. This suggests that policy-makers and practitioners ought to view all models with caution: they are provisional, and permanently so.

Figure 4.2 A thematic conceptual model of the development of experiences of U13 young cricketers.

Source: Toms, 2005.

A biopsychosocial approach

As an alternative to simple, uni-disciplinary models of participant development, we suggest the adoption and application of a biopsychosocial approach. To date, biopsychosocial approaches are relatively new to the sport and exercise sciences. In the present context, a biopsychosocial perspective undermines simple equations of participant development with biological maturation, psychological development or social factors. Consider an exemplar of the explicative benefits which accrue from this more complex but, we contend, more powerful approach. We wonder whether some of the well-known stage models of youth sport and physical activity, in which young players are claimed to progress through discrete developmental phases related directly to their maturational readiness, are mediated by rather mundane social factors like transitions within schooling systems and different access to specialist teaching and facilities. In a similar fashion, the widely acknowledged and often considered dropout from physical activity by young women is difficult to explain by a uni-disciplinary approach. It is neither due to hormonal change, nor peer pressure nor social expectation, but rather to a subtle and probably individual-specific interplay between these, and other factors drawn from all three biopsychosocial domains. Extending this argument to its logical application, a fitness indexed activity programme, a self-concept boosting initiative, or a 'group vote for content' physical education programme are unlikely to generate a significant impact *in isolation*. Notably, all three have been tried in recent years. Rather, effective models and effective interventions are almost of necessity required to address all three components and their interaction. In short, the biopsychosocial approach offers an effective basis for modelling and manipulating this crucial but complex facet of human behaviour.

Three-dimensional modelling of participant development

The holistic nature of development described above obviously co-acts with the Three Worlds Continuum across the lifespan. This co-action, important if research and intervention are to effectively address lifelong physical activity participation, is more effectively represented by a three-dimensional, rather than a two-dimensional model. Consider, then, Figure 4.3 in which the

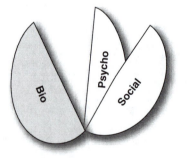

Figure 4.3 The biopsychosocial (BPS) sphere.

three segments of a sphere represent the elements of the bio-psycho-social complex.

The virtue of an image like this is that it allows us to include a third dimension that is integral to participant development: namely the different pathways of development through time. Accordingly, consider the addition of a z-axis for age, as presented in Figure 4.4, and the variety of approaches that can be taken across the lifespan. At an early age (the bottom of the sphere), the number of options available to an individual is small and the emphasis predominantly bio-psycho, even though all three elements must be addressed. As a consequence, but a theoretically and empirically examinable one, guidelines are going to be more prescriptive and investigations comparatively simple.

As the participant ages and develops (moving towards and through the 'equator'), the number of permutations becomes greater, as reflected by the larger area within which a particular dynamic (combination of biological, psychological and social factors) can be envisaged. In short, there are a large number of options, relating to the characteristics of the participant and his/her environment,

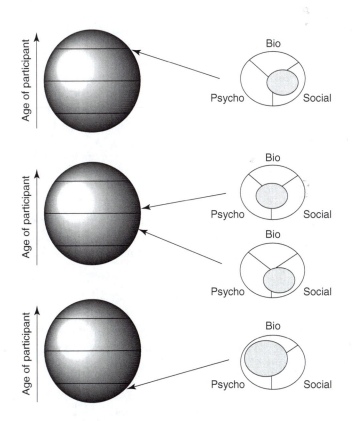

Figure 4.4 Different participant ages/stages and applications of the biopsychosocial sphere.

together with the objective of the process (for example, ERE, PRE or PPW). We present two exemplars from the many possible permutations. The upper option shows a predominantly psycho-social focus, ideal perhaps for promoting activity uptake and adherence through the late teens and early twenties. The lower option depicts a largely psychological focus; best perhaps for an aspiring elite player about to make the key transition to university. As the participant reaches old age, the number of permutations decrease towards an almost exclusively PPW orientation, with a comparatively small number of different options at the pole. In keeping with research findings, investigation/intervention programmes at this late stage might focus on predominantly social issues, with biological and psychological well-being seen as associated but fringe benefits.

The main objective of all this artwork, supported by the emergent arguments developed within the chapter, is to depict diagrammatically the following criteria of an effective model of participant development.

- Investigations *and* interventions focused on this important but complex aspect of human behaviour *must* be inter-disciplinary. In each case, however, the focus will be driven by an empirically/theoretically justified balance between the biopsychosocial domains.
- The balance between domains will change, based on the objective (ERE, PRE or PPW), together with environmental and personal characteristics, as the participant moves through the Three Worlds Continuum.
- Mapping the domain balance for an individual as s/he progresses through ages and stages will enable an evaluation of preparedness for new challenges. In a similar vein, dropout or non-participation may be better understood by means of a series of intra-individual development maps, enabling a search for causative trends.
- Consequently, investigations/interventions and the funding models and policies which underpin them must be driven by a clear awareness and explicit consideration of inter-disciplinary issues.

The Venn diagrams may offer a convenient way to qualitatively summarise the thrust of many different programmes, and it is possible to envisage a quantitative and empirical equivalent, which could be employed in the meta-analysis of approaches and their relative impact.

Final thought

On the basis of the complex, multifaceted trajectory towards an effective and genuinely lifelong pathway to sport and physical activity presented in this chapter, the role of optimising educational processes is demonstrably crucial. Development of the various precursors of effective sport and physical activity, actual and perceived movement competence, metacognitive skills and the optimum biopsychosocial balance must be nurtured and deployed effectively within the primary and secondary school system. The exploitation of the captive audience, coupled with the genuinely educational processes we espouse, can provide the structure and skill set upon which initiatives across the lifespan can be designed to meet the needs of particular groups. There is evidence to suggest that this approach can cater for the full range of physical activity whilst even making a contribution to wider aspects of cognitive and social development. In fact, empirical data from a pilot study based on these ideas offers further support (Abbott *et al.*, 2007). We commend this as a way forward, as well as a way to more effectively reconceptualise sport-related social policy.

Notes

1 Our use of the terms 'worlds' to describe our framework explicitly reflects Karl Popper's cosmology in which three worlds are ontologically distinct, but necessarily and continually interacting (Popper, 1972).
2 One other potentially orthogonal categorisation is apparent, namely personal development, in which involvement is focused on 'character building'. Involvement in martial arts, for example, is often typified by this focus. For the present purposes, however, we assume this to be subsumed within the PPW motive.
3 We are not suggesting, of course, that either of these models set out to provide a comprehensive account of participant development. However, we do maintain that this is the way they have been interpreted by some initiative funders and national sports groups.

References

Abbott, A. and Collins, D. (2004). Eliminating the Dichotomy Between Theory and Practice in Talent Identification and Development: Considering the Role of Psychology. *Journal of Sports Sciences*, *22*, 395–408.

Abbott, A., Button, C., Pepping, G.-J. and Collins, D. (2005). Unnatural Selection: Talent Identification and Development in Sport. *Nonlinear Dynamics, Psychology and Life Sciences*, *9*, 61–88.

Abbott, A., Collins, D., Martindale, R. and Sowerby, K. (2002). *Talent Identification and Development: An Academic Review*. Edinburgh: sportscotland.

Abbott, A., Collins, D., Sowerby, K. and Martindale, R. (2007). *Developing the Potential of Young People in Sport*. Edinburgh: sportscotland.

Allender, S., Cowburn, G. and Foster, C. (2006). Understanding Participation in Sport and Physical Activity among Children and Adults: A Review of Qualitative Studies. *Health Education Research*, *21*, 826–835.

Bailey, R. P. (2007). Talent Development and the Luck Problem. *Sport, Ethics and Philosophy*, *1*, 367–376.

Baker, J. and Horton, S. (2004). A Review of Primary and Secondary Influences on Sport Expertise. *High Ability Studies*, *15*, 211–228.

Baker, J., Côté, J. and Abernethy, B. (2003). Sport-Specific Practice and the Development of Expert Decision Making in Team Ball Sports. *Journal of Applied Sport Psychology*, *15*, 12–25.

Balyi, I. (2001). *Sport System Building and Long-Term Athlete Development in British Columbia*. Victoria, BC: SportsMed BC.

Balyi, I. (2002). Long-Term Athlete Development: The System and Solutions. *Faster, Higher, Stronger*, *14*(January), 6–9.

Balyi, I. and Hamilton, A. (1996). Planning for Training and Performance: The Training to Win Phase. *BC Coach*, 9–26.

Balyi, I. and Hamilton, A. (2003). Long-Term Athlete Development Update: Trainability in Childhood and Adolescence. *Faster, Higher, Stronger, 20*, 6–8.

Bloom, B. S. (Ed.). (1985). *Developing Talent in Young People*. New York: Ballantine Books.

Bompa, T. (1995). *From Childhood to Champion Athlete*. West Sedona, AZ: Veritas Publishing.

Boyd, M. P., Weinmann, C. and Yin, Z. (2002). The Relationship of Physical Self-Perceptions and Goal Orientations to Intrinsic Motivation for Exercise. *Journal of Sport Behaviour, 25*, 1–18.

Butcher, J., Lindner, K. J. and Johns, D. P. (2002). Withdrawal from Competitive Youth Sport. *Journal of Sport Behaviour, 25*, 145–163.

Chatzisarantis, N. and Hagger, M. (2009). Effects of an Intervention Based on Self-Determination Theory on Self-Reported Leisure-Time Physical Activity Participation. *Psychology and Health, 24*, 29–48.

Chatzisarantis, N., Hagger, M., Biddle, S., Smith, B. and Wang, J. (2003). A Meta-Analysis of Perceived Locus of Causality in Exercise, Sport, and Physical Education Contexts. *Journal of Sport and Exercise Psychology, 25*, 284–306.

Cimons, M. (1999). Youth Movement: Children and Teens Vulnerable to Sports Injury. *Runners' World, 34*, 42.

Coalter, F. (2007). *A Wider Social Role for Sport*. London: Routledge.

Collins, M. (2008). Public Policies on Sports Development: Can Mass and Elite Sport Hold Together? In V. Girginov (Ed.), *Management of Sports Development*. Oxford: Butterworth-Heinemann.

Côté, J. (1999). The Influence of the Family in the Development of Talent in Sport. *The Sport Psychologist, 13*, 395–417.

Côté, J. and Hay, J. (2002). Children's Involvement in Sport: A Developmental Perspective. In J. Silva and D. Stevens (Eds), *Psychological Foundations of Sport* (pp. 484–502). Boston: Allyn and Bacon.

Côté, J., Baker, J. and Abernethy B. (2007). Practice to Play in the Development of Sport Expertise. In R. Eklund and G. Tenenbaum (Eds), *Handbook of Sport Psychology* (pp. 184–202). Hoboken: Wiley.

Cox, L., Coleman, L. and Roker, D. (2006). *Understanding Participation in Sport: What Determines Sports Participation among 15-19 Year Old Women?* London: Sport England.

DCMS (2008). *Playing to Win*. London: DCMS.

DCMS/Strategy Unit (2002). *Game Plan: A Strategy for Delivering Government's Sport and Physical Activity Objectives*. London: Cabinet Office.

Dweck, C. (2006). *Mindset*. New York: Random House.

Ericsson, K., Krampe, R. and Tesch-Römer, C. (1993). The Role of Deliberate Practice in the Acquisition of Expert Performance. *Psychological Review, 100*, 363–406.

Girginov, V. and Collins, M. (Eds) (2004). Sport in Eastern Europe. *International Journal of the History of Sport, 21*(5), Special issue.

Gould, D., Dieffenbach, K. and Moffett, A. (2002). Psychological Characteristics and their Development in Olympic Champions. *Journal of Applied Sport Psychology, 14*, 172–204.

Green, M. (2006). From 'Sport for All' to Not About 'Sport' at All? *European Sport Management Quarterly, 6*, 217–238.

Helsen, W., Starkes, J. and Van Winckel, J. (1998). The Influence of Relative Age on Success and Dropout in Male Soccer Players. *American Journal of Human Biology*, *10*, 791–798.

Horn, T. and Harris, A. (2002). Perceived Competence in Young Athletes. In F. Smoll and R. Smith (Eds), *Children and Youth in Sport: A Bio-psycho-social Perspective* (pp. 435–464). Dubuque: Kendall-Hunt.

Houlihan, B. (2000). Sporting Excellence, Schools and Sports Development. *European Physical Education Review*, *6*, 171–193.

Huxley, A. (1932). *Texts and Pretexts*. London: Chatto and Windus.

Jess, M. and Collins, D. (2003). Primary Physical Education in Scotland. *European Journal of Physical Education*, *8*, 103–118.

Kirk, D. and Gorely, T. (2000). Challenging Thinking about the Relationship Between School Physical Education and Sport Performance. *European Physical Education Review*, *6*, 119–134.

Kirk, D., Brettschneider, W.-D. and Auld, C. (2005). *Junior Sport Models Representing Best Practice Nationally and Internationally*. Canberra: Australian Sports Commission.

MacPhail, A., Gorely, T. and Kirk, D. (2003). Young People's Socialisation into Sport: A Case Study of an Athletics Club. *Sport, Education and Society*, *8*, 251–267.

Malina, R. and Bouchard, C. (1991). *Growth, Maturation, and Physical Activity*. Champaign: Human Kinetics.

Martindale, R., Collins, D. and Daubney, J. (2005). Talent Development: A Guide for Practice and Research Within Sport. *Quest*, 57, 353–375.

Miller, P. and Kerr, G. (2002). The Athletic, Academic and Social Experiences of Intercollegiate Student-Athletes. *Journal of Sport Behaviour*, *25*, 346–367.

Ollis, S., MacPherson, A. and Collins, D. (2006). Expertise and Talent Development in Rugby Refereeing: An Ethnographic Enquiry. *Journal of Sports Sciences*, *24*, 309–322.

Penney, D. (2000). Physical Education, Sporting Excellence and Educational Excellence. *European Physical Education Review*, *6*, 135–150.

Perleth, C., Schatz, T. and Mönks, F. (2000). Early Identification of High Ability. In K. Heller, F. Mönks, R. Sternberg and R. Subotnik (Eds), *International Handbook of Giftedness and Talent* (pp. 297–316). Oxford: Elsevier.

Popper, K. R. (1934). *Logik der Forschung*. Tübingen: Mohr.

Popper, K. R. (1972). *Objective Knowledge: An Evolutionary Approach*. Oxford: Oxford University Press.

Rutenfranz, J. and Singer, R. (1980). The Influence of Sport Activity on the Development of Physical Performance Capacities of 15–17-Year-Old Boys. In K. Berg and K. Eriksson (Eds), *Children and Exercise IX* (pp. 99–108). Baltimore: University Park Press.

Sabiston, C., Sedgwick, W., Crocker, P., Kowalski, K. and Stevens, D. (2007). Social Physique Anxiety in Adolescents. *Journal of Adolescent Research*, *22*, 78–101.

Saltin, B. (2005). The Search for and Fostering of the Young Talent. Paper presented at the opening of ASPIRE Academy, Doha, Qatar, November.

Simonton, D. (1999). Talent and its Development: An Emergenic and Epigenetic Model. *Psychological Review*, *106*, 435–457.

Simonton, D. (2001). Talent Development as a Multidimensional, Multiplicative, and Dynamic Process. *Current Directions in Psychological Science*, *10*, 39–43.

Suslov, F. (2002). About the Sensitive Age Periods in the Development of Physical Capacities. *Modern Athlete and Coach*, *40*, 31–33.

Toms, M. (2005). The Developmental Socialisation of Young People in Club Sport. Unpublished PhD Thesis, Loughborough University.

Weiss, M. and Chaumenton, N. (1992). Motivational Orientations in Sport. In T. Horn (Ed.), *Advances in Sport Psychology* (pp. 61–99). Champaign: Human Kinetics.

Whitehead, S. and Biddle, S. (2008). Adolescent Girls' Perceptions of Physical Activity. *European Physical Education Review, 14*, 243–262.

5 Transitions in competitive sports

Paul Wylleman, Paul De Knop and Anke Reints

Introduction

While at first glance the athletic career seems to be continuous in nature, that is a global 'start-to-finish' period, autobiographical reports reveal that (former) elite athletes actually outline their sport participation in terms of specific events which did – or sometimes did not – occur during their career. For example, five-time Olympic gold medal winner Steve Redgrave reviewed his rowing career in terms of events such as a disappointing experience during his first Junior World Championships, his first Olympic medal, ending the collaboration with a rowing partner, establishing a new rowing partnership, his anticipated but unrealised athletic retirement after his fourth gold medal, the turbulent periods in his marriage, or his 'date with destiny' when going for his fifth gold medal at the 2000 Olympic Games (Redgrave and Townsend, 2001). In another example, legendary tennis player Pete Sampras (2008) linked his career to events and periods such as starting out in tennis, a period of wavering commitment, the winning moments at Wimbledon, and setting a new record of winning 14 Grand Slam titles. Interestingly, former elite athletes review the development of their athletic career not only in terms of performance-related events per se but refer also to events or periods that have shaped their personal development. This emphasis is, for example, underlined by Sampras who explicitly introduces his autobiography with the statement that he also wanted to acknowledge those events (e.g. his first coach spending time in jail, his mentor stricken by cancer and dying at an early age, a career-threatening injury) which 'aren't the things that come to most people's minds at the mention of my name' (i.e. 14 Grand Slam titles) but of which he wanted to 'reveal what they meant and how they affected me'.

During the past decades, sport psychologists have shown a clear interest not only in the development of the (elite) athletic career – which can span 15 to 25 years (Sosniak, 2006; Wylleman *et al.*, 1993) – in general, but also in the occurrence of these career-related events or 'career transitions' in particular (Wylleman *et al.*, 2004a; Wylleman *et al.*, 2004b). This interest has resulted in research-driven publications and special journal issues (e.g., Wylleman *et al.*, 2004a), as well as in the propagation of specific guidelines (FEPSAC, 2003a, 2003b) by the European Federation of Sport Psychology (FEPSAC) aimed at assisting (former) elite athletes in coping with these career transitions, which have been reported to be one of the most commonly encountered issues for applied sport psychologists (Murphy, 1995).

This chapter will address the development of the athletic career and the occurrence and influence of career transitions from a lifespan perspective. First, a brief overview of sport psychology research into the concept of career transitions will be given. Second, using Wylleman and Lavallee's (2004) lifespan model, a description of the athletic career development and occurrence of career transitions will be provided. This lifespan model will also be used to illustrate the developmental challenges faced by athletes with regard to four career transitions, followed by a brief overview of its use in providing career support services to talented, elite and former elite athletes. Finally, recommendations and perspectives for future research on career transitions will be formulated.

A sport psychology perspective on career transitions faced by elite athletes

An initial perspective used by sport psychologists to study career transitions was focused upon one single event, namely the termination of further participation in competitive sports amongst elite and young talented athletes. Empirical studies conducted as early as the 1960s–1970s (e.g. Haerle, 1975; Mihovilovic, 1968) revealed that former athletes experienced a wide range of psychological, interpersonal, social and financial problems initiated by a range of negative or even traumatic experiences (e.g. alcohol and substance abuse, acute depression, eating disorders, identity confusion, decreased self-confidence, attempted suicide) related to not only the athletic retirement itself, but also to a problematic post-athletic career (e.g. Blinde and Stratta, 1992; Sinclair and Orlick, 1993). With regard to the event of discontinuing participation in competitive sports among young talented athletes, research conducted during the 1980s showed that young athletes' experience of dropout shared similarities with those of the retiring adult athlete. The often definite, unexpected, unprepared and off-time withdrawal from active involvement in competitive sport made them, to a large extent, prone to problems of adjustment, similar to those experienced by retiring adult athletes (e.g. Weiss and Chaumeton, 1992; Wylleman *et al.*, 1994).

A second and subsequent perspective was based upon empirical findings that made relative the traumatic character of career termination (Alfermann, 2000; Wylleman *et al.*, 1993). More particularly, the perspective of studying one single event (i.e. the career termination) was abandoned in favour of conceptual frameworks acknowledging the transitional process underlying this career transition (Coakley, 1983; McPherson, 1980). In particular, the Model of Human Adaptation to Transition by Schlossberg and colleagues (Charner and Schlossberg, 1986; Schlossberg, 1981, 1984) was employed to operationalise the process of career transitions faced by athletes (e.g. Baillie and Danish, 1992; Parker, 1994; Sinclair and Orlick, 1994; Swain, 1991). In the first instance, the model defined a career transition as 'an event or non-event which results in a change in assumptions about oneself and the world and thus requires a corresponding change in one's behaviour and relationships' (Schlossberg, 1981, p. 5). Second, it provided a description of three major sets of factors interacting during the transitional process of retirement, namely the characteristics of the athlete experiencing the transition (e.g. psychosocial competence, gender, age, previous experience with a transition of a similar nature), the perception of the particular transition (e.g. role change, affect, occurrence of stress), and the characteristics of the pre- and post-transition environments (e.g. the evaluation of internal support systems, institutional support). In the wake of this approach, other conceptual models were proposed based on actual (former) elite athlete-related research or applied work with retired elite athletes (Wylleman *et al.*, 1999). For example, Taylor and Ogilvie's (1998) domain-specific model viewed the career transition process amongst elite athletes in terms of the causal factors initiating the transitional process, the developmental factors related to transition adaptation, the coping resources affecting the responses to career transitions, the quality of adjustment to career transition, and the possible treatment issues for distressful reactions to career transition. The athletic career transition model of Stambulova (1997, 2003) focused on the athlete's ability to cope effectively with the transitional process by taking into account the dynamic balance between transition resources and barriers. Stambulova (2000) showed that athletes' ineffectiveness to cope with transitions is related to, amongst others, a low awareness of transition demands, a lack of resources, or an inability to analyse the transitional situation, which may lead athletes to perceive a need for psychological support. Both models enabled the (further) concrete and sport-specific development of sport psychological career interventions.

Building upon the conceptual frameworks of transitions, and taking into account the empirical data underlining the importance of the pre- and post-transition periods and environments, sport psychologists' perspective broadened during the late 1990s from the career ending transition to include other transitions elite athletes face during their actual athletic career. As sport psychologists focused more on a succession of 'normative' (i.e. predictable and anticipated) transitions, a link was made with research on talent development such as that of Bloom (1985a) and colleagues who revealed that it took talented individuals across different talent fields (music and art, mathematics and science, swimming and tennis) not only ten to 15 years to attain a mature and complex talent as international-level performers, but that their development occurred in three consecutive normative, that is predictable and anticipated, stages. Described as 'signposts along a long and continuous learning process' (Bloom, 1985b, p. 537) these normative stages included the 'early years' (i.e. the beginning instruction of young athletes with teaching and learning leading them to make relatively rapid progress in a few years), the 'middle years' (i.e. talented athletes almost fully committed to their sport, increasingly putting aside other interests and working with precision and accuracy in all aspects of their sporting endeavours towards the highest goals in sport) and the 'later years' (i.e. almost all of the elite athletes' time is dedicated to perfecting their talent to the highest level, with participation in international contests as evidence of progress and achievement in sport). Strongly linked to Bloom's (1985a) research, Salmela

(1994) described three normative career transitions based upon the athletes' level of athletic development, namely, the stage from initiation to development, the stage from development to perfection, and the stage from perfection to career termination. The analytical athletic career model of Stambulova (1994) empirically identified five normative stages among Russian athletes, each describing the demands put to athletes and their coping resources. These stages include the preparatory stage, the stage of the start into specialisation, the stage of intensive training in the chosen sport, the culmination stage and the final stage followed by the career end. From the perspective of talent development and on the basis of qualitative research with families of young rowers, Côté (1999) presented the Developmental Model of Sport Participation which identifies four stages, namely, the stage of the sampling years, the stage of the specialising years, the stage of the investment years and the stage of the recreational years. Finally, two other stage-like conceptualisations were also presented which focused not upon the process of career development but rather on that of career retirement and the post-athletic career. Based upon research among retired elite female gymnasts, Kerr and Dacyshyn (2000) formulated the phases of 'Retirement' (the actual withdrawal from sport), 'Nowhere Land' (period of uncertainty and disorientation) and of 'New Beginnings' (the start in a new setting). Using prospective qualitative data, Torregrosa *et al.* (2004) proposed Spanish Olympic athletes' perceptions of how they presumed their process of disengaging from elite sports would take place in the future in three stages, namely the initiation/training stage, the maturity performance stage and the anticipation of retirement stage.

As research confirmed that talented and elite athletes were confronted with normative stages and transitions during, as well as after, their athletic career, it was argued that a better understanding of the other developmental transitions (e.g. psychological, psychosocial) they face was also required in order to more fully understand how athletes are able to cope with these transitions (Wylleman *et al.*, 1999). This need for a 'whole career/whole person approach' (Alfermann and Stambulova, 2007) found its reflection in Wylleman and Lavallee's (2004) lifespan model on career transitions.

A lifespan perspective on the career development of elite athletes

Based upon research on transitions and on experience with the provision of applied sport psychological support to, amongst others, student-athletes, elite athletes and former Olympians, Wylleman and Lavallee (2004) formulated a lifespan model in which a developmental or 'whole career' approach (i.e. from young to former-elite athlete) is combined with a holistic or 'whole person' approach (i.e. development in different domains) perspective (see Figure 5.1).

This lifespan model reflects the concurrent, interactive and reciprocal nature of the development of athletes in four domains (i.e. athletic, psychological, psychosocial, academic and vocational) as delineated by domain-specific normative transitions. The first layer represents transitions in the athletic development, including the initiation stage (i.e. 6–7-year-olds are introduced to organised

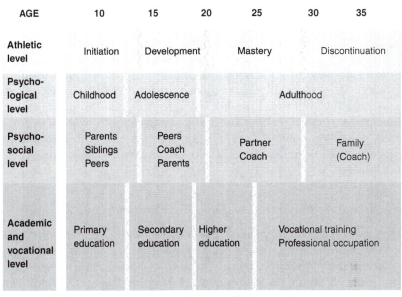

AGE	10	15	20	25	30	35
Athletic level	Initiation	Development		Mastery		Discontinuation
Psycho-logical level	Childhood	Adolescence			Adulthood	
Psycho-social level	Parents Siblings Peers	Peers Coach Parents		Partner Coach		Family (Coach)
Academic and vocational level	Primary education	Secondary education	Higher education		Vocational training Professional occupation	

Note: A dotted line indicates the approximate age at which the transition occurs.

Figure 5.1 A developmental perspective on transitions faced by athletes at athletic, individual, psychosocial and academic-vocational levels.

Source: reproduced from Wylleman and Lavallee (2004, p. 516) with permission.

competitive sports), the development stage (i.e. 12–13-year-old athletes are recognised as being talented, bringing with it an intensive level of training and competition), the mastery stage (i.e. from about 18 to 19 years of age, with participation at the highest competitive level), and the discontinuation stage (i.e. elite athletes' transition out of competitive sports). While normative in nature, the specific ages at which these transitions occur may vary depending upon the type of sport, the athletes' characteristics (e.g. early versus late maturation), or gender. The second layer reflects the major transitions and stages in athletes' psychological development, including childhood, adolescence and (young) adulthood. The third layer is indicative of transitions in athletes' psychosocial development and denotes those individuals who are perceived by athletes as being (most) significant during that particular transition or stage (e.g. parents, coach, peers, lifetime partner). The final layer represents stages and transitions at academic (primary education/elementary school, secondary education/high school, higher education) and vocational level (may also start after secondary education, involving full- or part-time occupation in the field of professional sports).

This lifespan model, which has been used in research on transition experiences of, amongst others, rookie ice-hockey players (Bruner *et al.*, 2008), adolescent event riders (Pummell *et al.*, 2008), Olympic swimmers (Reints and Wylleman,

2009a), floret fencers (Germeau, 2009), retired elite judokas (Reints *et al.*, 2008), and in research on the provision of athletic and post-athletic career support services (Reints and Wylleman, 2009b), illustrates that athletes will face normative transitions in different domains of development throughout as well as after their athletic career. As a transition creates 'a developmental conflict between "what the athlete is" and "what he or she wants or ought to be"' (Alfermann and Stambulova, 2007, p. 717), athletes will need to be able to cope effectively with each transition separately, as well as with the effects of their interaction, in order to progress developmentally in all domains. Four transitional challenges will be considered in the next paragraphs, followed by a brief overview of how this lifespan model has been integrated into the provision of career support services to talented, elite and retired athletes.

A transitional challenge during the initiation stage of athletic development

During the initiation stage, young talented athletes face, at a psychological level, the transitional challenge of (motivational and cognitive) readiness for structured competitive sport. From a motivational point of view, young athletes' participation in competitive sport can be linked to, amongst others, internally driven motivators (e.g. interest in the sport, friendship relations). As intrinsic motivation provides for a stronger and more long lasting impetus, it is essential that young talented athletes are embedded into an environment emphasising this type of motivation. It is important to acknowledge that the development of this motivational readiness may be enhanced (or challenged) by the strong (but generally well-meant) involvement of young athletes' parents (Wylleman *et al.*, 2006). From a cognitive point of view, readiness refers to young athletes' capacity for abstract reasoning, as well as for an understanding of roles, responsibilities and relational characteristics relevant to the setting of athletic competition. As a child's role-taking abilities are not fully developed until 8–10 years of age (van der Meulen and Menkehorst, 1992), young athletes may experience considerable frustration with a lack of (full) understanding of their own roles and those of the adults involved in the context of competitive sports and thus could lose interest for continued sport participation because they do not have the cognitive capacities to handle the demands placed on them. Moreover, as children do not effectively distinguish between the various contributors to achievement outcomes until around 10–12 years of age (Fry and Duda, 1997), young athletes may not be able to accurately estimate their own ability or understand the cause/s of performance outcomes. It thus becomes important that youth sport coaches are aware of the fact and take into account that young athletes in the transition stage need to be supported in such a way that their motivational and cognitive readiness is developed and sustained.

A transitional challenge during the development stage of athletic development

At the end of the development stage, 16- to 18-year-old talented athletes face the transition from junior level into senior level or (semi-)professional sports and then into more high-level (national or international) competitions. While having been at the top end as junior elite athletes, first-year senior athletes will generally be at the lower end in terms of athletic prowess and/or achievement. In fact, one in two novice senior athletes will experience this transition as difficult (e.g. financial problems, illnesses, injuries, self-doubts) and will possibly experience a career-high injury-rate (Australian Sports Commission, 2003). Many first-year seniors may also move away from home (e.g. into a professional football academy, own private accommodation). It should not be surprising that, on average, only one junior elite athlete in three actually makes a successful transition into the senior elite ranks (Australian Sports Commission, 2003; Bussmann and Alfermann, 1994). Successfully completing the junior–senior transition takes novice senior athletes on average 2.1 years (Australian Sports Commission, 2003), and involves having not only a coach providing supportive and transition-related assistance to first- and second-year seniors, but also a supportive family and financial support (Robertson-Wilson and Côté, 2002; Rea, 2003).

A transitional challenge during the mastery stage of athletic development

During the mastery stage, elite athletes will encounter transitions at academic and vocational levels. In view of the value attributed by parents and by society at large to an academic formation and degree, and taking into account the risks (e.g. career-ending injury) and disadvantages (e.g. unfulfilled academic potential, lack of financial security and stability) of elite sport, many athletes will continue their academic development into higher education. Reints *et al.* (2008) showed that amongst 15 Flemish retired elite judokas, two in three continued their academic career into higher education, with 60 per cent of them graduating successfully from university. As student-athletes, they will need to be more personally involved in developing their academic career, be able to cope with the relatively high degree of freedom to (not) attend academic activities, have more systematic planning to study, be committed enough to direct time to academic activities, and cope with the changing social environment (De Knop *et al.*, 1999). Significantly, the academic success rate of elite student-athletes graduating from university (71 per cent) was found to be higher than the average amongst other 'regular' students (De Knop *et al.*, 1999). A survey (Reints and Wylleman, 2009a) examining the career development experiences of 44 former and 64 active Flemish athletes revealed, amongst others, that four active elite athletes in ten (55 per cent female) and six retired athletes in ten (36 per cent female) had obtained a diploma in higher education.

Elite athletes transiting out of an academic career will strongly be influenced by the choices made when entering higher education (e.g. selection of a specific subject of study or a major) as well as by the status of their sport career. Some elite athletes may choose to further their academic endeavours as the status of student-athlete provides them with the opportunity of not having to develop a vocation (other than that of being an elite athlete), of being able to enjoy the support provided to student-athletes (e.g. financial, logistic, coaching), and of bridging one or more years in preparation of a major competition (e.g. Olympic Games).

A transitional challenge during the discontinuation stage of athletic development

The discontinuation of the athletic career may involve 5 to 7 per cent of elite athletes who retire annually, on average, at the age of 34 years (North and Lavallee, 2004). Depending upon type of sport, the age of making this transition may vary (Wylleman *et al.*, 1993). For example, North and Lavallee (2004) found that elite athletes from gymnastics, diving, swimming, ice skating and judo planned to retire in the 24–30 year age category, with those from sailing, golf, equestrian and shooting planning their retirement well after the age of 40. Transitional challenges faced by retiring/retired elite athletes include, amongst others, adjusting to a new life and lifestyle following the sport career in which they are suddenly 'like everyone else', missing the sport atmosphere and the competition, dealing with bodily changes and changes in subjective well-being, or adapting to a new social status and vocational responsibilities (e.g. Cecić Erpič *et al.*, 2004; Stephan *et al.*, 2007). Reints *et al.* (2008) found that seven out of 15 former elite judokas reported to have experienced problems in adapting to their post-athletic career life, such as increased responsibilities, changed financial situation, lack of goal-oriented work and working with fixed hours. Particular to the vocational challenges faced by former elite athletes is the phenomenon of 'occupational delay' (Naul, 1994): as few will have had the opportunity to actively employ the knowledge and skills gained in higher education (e.g. via summer jobs, vocational or in-service training), retired elite athletes may lack the relevant professional skills, experience and relational networks necessary for vocational success and therefore may need to return to higher (post-graduate) education or to basic vocational training in order to gain up-to-date or new professional knowledge and skills. Once entering the job market, they may find themselves 'at the bottom of the ladder', being confronted not only with lower wages (in comparison to their non-athletic peers) than could be expected on the basis of their age (and athletic achievements), but also with younger co-workers or colleagues who may have seniority over them. Former elite athletes will need motivational readiness and interpersonal skills to integrate into such a professional setting. Several former elite athletes may in fact (e.g. due to lack of financial stability) turn to their family-of-origin for support, or even 'return home' to live with their parents and may then also experience interpersonal (or intergenerational) problems. Taking into account these challenges, it should not be surprising that vocational training is an important part of career support services for athletes in view of their post-athletic career (Reints and Wylleman, 2009b).

A lifespan approach to the provision of career support services

While it has assisted career support service providers and sport psychologists in gaining a better overview and understanding of the multi-level transitional demands put on athletes and the resources available to them, this lifespan model has also enabled them to provide more specific means and support to cope effectively with these transitions (Stambulova, 2000). As such, it has assisted in creating a holistic view of elite athletes and their social environments during their athletic and post-athletic career (Alfermann and Stambulova, 2007). It has therefore also been proposed to the Athletes' Commission of the International Olympic Committee (Wylleman and Waser, 2007) as well as to the International Athletes' Forum (Wylleman and Parker, 2004) as a conceptual framework for support services to (former) elite athletes and Olympians. The lifespan model has also been used in the further development and provision of athlete career services in Scotland, France and Flanders (Bouchetal Pellegri *et al.*, 2006; Van Aken *et al.*, 2008; Wylleman and Debois, 2007; Wylleman and Taelman, 2007). Using this lifespan model, the Flemish career support services for elite athletes of Topsport Vlaanderen (Wylleman and Taelman, 2007; Wylleman, 2008) developed a proactive and educational approach aimed at teaching young talented athletes, from the athletic development stage onward, those lifestyle skills required at the time of the onset of a particular transitional challenge and career stage for them to cope efficiently and effectively with that particular challenge or stage. Services were delineated in function to three major transitions and career stages, namely (primary, secondary, higher) education (from age nine onwards), the athletic career (from age 14–16 onwards) and the post-athletic career (from 26–28 years of age onwards). They focused on empowering athletes by assisting them to acquire lifestyle skills specific to their stage of development, including time management skills (from age ten onwards), transition skills (from 14 years of age), media skills (for 16-year-olds), relationship skills (from age 18 onwards), financial management skills (22 years of age onwards), as well as networking skills (from the age of 26 years onwards). This approach provides for the reported long-term career development needs of younger talented athletes coming through the elite athlete system (North and Lavallee, 2004). The model was also used to develop and provide a developmentally structured mental skills approach in which the teaching, training and use of mental (e.g. concentration, self-control) and lifestyle skills are delineated in parallel with the age-related mental capabilities and resources of 12–18-year-old elite athletes in different sports (e.g. athletics, cycling, tennis, swimming, volleyball) (Wylleman, 2006).

Recommendations and conclusions

As transitions can be described as turning points 'at which talent may be derailed or may flourish' (Dweck, 2009) a strong need remains to broaden the existing knowledge on the transitional challenges faced by athletes. In the first instance, as existing transitional models are generally based upon normative transitions, researchers should look into the occurrence of non-normative transitions. These idiosyncratic transitions, which are generally unpredicted, unanticipated and involuntary in nature, do not occur in a set plan or schedule but are the result of important events that take place in an individual's life and to which it responds (Schlossberg, 1984). For elite athletes, these transitions may include a sudden change of personal coach, an athletic injury, or a non-event such as an unanticipated de-selection for a major championship after years of preparation. The unpredictable and/or involuntary nature of these types of transition will require researchers to develop further existing models such as Stambulova's (1997, 2003) athletic career transition model, as well as to consider new conceptual models which include the mechanisms required by athletes to cope successfully with this type of transition. In the second instance, existing transitional models should be made more specific. For example, while transiting from national to international level is a normative transition present in all sports the ages at which this transition occurs may be very sport-specific (e.g. female gymnastics versus male rowers). It is therefore important to look more closely into the diversity with which career transition models attend to sport-, gender- or cultural-specific characteristics (e.g. Seiler *et al.*, 1998). In a similar vein, while Wylleman and Lavallee's (2004) lifespan model has been instrumental in developing and propagating a 'whole career/whole person approach' (Alfermann and Stambulova, 2007) by including a developmental perspective on the occurrence of transitions in four domains of development (i.e. athletic, psychological, psychosocial, academic and vocational), a need exists to investigate further whether other domains should be included in which talented, elite and/or former elite athletes are confronted with (normative) transitions. For example, athletes' financial status may change during their athletic career and become a challenge as they enter or leave elite status (Reints and Wylleman, 2009a).

From an applied perspective, sport psychology and career support services focused on preparing for and coping with transitional challenges need to be evaluated based on their effectiveness, user-friendliness and applicability across the range of athletes. Furthermore, a clear need exists for the development of a specific methodology to evaluate athletes' perceptions of the transitions occurring throughout their sports career, and of the way in which they are able to cope with these transitions. For example, the Athletes' Retirement Decision Inventory (ARDI) (Fernandez *et al.*, 2006) is an example of a conceptually valuable instrument with which athletes' perceptions of the reasons for the transition into the discontinuing stage can be assessed. Finally, taking into account the relevance of the holistic or 'whole person' approach, the inclusion of other experts who are significant to athletes' successful coping with transitional challenges such as experts in the fields of sports medicine, sports physiotherapy, financial management, human resource and personnel management, should be considered for inclusion in career support services. It is this type of interdisciplinary cooperation which will become more and more relevant as elite athletes are increasingly supported by a multidisciplinary team of service providers in order to ensure that they progress developmentally throughout their athletic career (Wylleman and Kahan, 2004).

In conclusion, continued research on, as well as the provision of high quality career transition and career management support based on a lifespan perspective, will be required in order to maximise talented and elite athletes' opportunities to progress optimally throughout, as well as after, their athletic career.

References

Alfermann, D. (2000). Causes and consequences of sport career termination. In D. Lavallee and P. Wylleman (Eds), *Career transitions in sport: International perspectives* (pp. 45–58). Morgantown: Fitness Information Technology.

Alfermann, D. and Stambulova, N. (2007). Career transitions and career termination. In G. Tenenbaum and R. C. Eklund (Eds.), *Handbook of sport psychology* (3rd edn, pp. 712–733). New York: Wiley.

Australian Sports Commission (2003). *How do elite athletes develop? A look through the 'rear-view mirror'. A preliminary report from the National Athlete Development Survey (NADS)*. Canberra: Australian Sports Commission.

Baillie, P. H. F. and Danish, S. J. (1992). Understanding the career transition of athletes. *The Sport Psychologist, 6*, 77–98.

Blinde, E. and Stratta, T. (1992). The 'sport career death' of college athletes: involuntary and unanticipated sports exits. *Journal of Sport Behaviour, 15*, 3–20.

Bloom, B. S. (Ed.). (1985a). *Developing talent in young people*. New York: Ballantine.

Bloom, B. S. (1985b). Generalisations about talent development. In B. S. Bloom (Ed.), *Developing talent in young people* (pp. 507–549). New York: Ballantine.

Bouchetal Pellegri, F., Leseur, V. and Debois, N. (2006). *Carrière sportive. Projet de vie*. Paris: INSEP-Publications.

Bruner, M. W., Munroe-Chandler, K. J. and Spink, K. S. (2008). Entry into elite sport: a preliminary investigation into the transition experiences of rookie athletes. *Journal of Applied Sport Psychology, 20*, 236–252.

Bussmann, G. and Alfermann, D. (1994). Drop-out and the female athlete: a study with track-and-field athletes. In D. Hackforth (Ed.), *Psycho-social issues and interventions in elite sport* (pp. 89–128). Frankfurt: Lang.

Cecić Erpič, S., Wylleman, P. and Zupančič, M. (2004). Characteristics of the sports career termination and adaptation to post career transitions in perspective. *Psychology of Sport and Exercise, 1*, 45–60.

Charner, I. and Schlossberg, N. K. (1986). Variations by theme: the life transitions of clerical workers. *The Vocational Guidance Quarterly*, 212–224.

Coakley, J. J. (1983). Leaving competitive sport: retirement or rebirth? *Quest, 35*, 1–11.

Côté, J. (1999). The influence of the family in the development of talent in sport. *The Sport Psychologist, 13*, 395–417.

De Knop, P., Wylleman, P., Van Hoecke, J. and Bollaert, L. (1999). Sports management – a European approach to the management of the combination of academics and elite-level sport. In S. Bailey (Ed.), *Perspectives – the interdisciplinary series of physical education and sport science. Vol. 1. School sport and competition* (pp. 49–62). Oxford: Meyer & Meyer Sport.

Dweck, C. S. (2009). Foreword. In F. D. Horowitz, R. F. Subotnik and D. J. Matthews (Eds), *The development of giftedness and talent across the life span* (pp. xi–xiv). Washington, DC: American Psychological Association.

FEPSAC (2003a). FEPSAC position statement #5 'sports career termination'. In E. Apitzsch and G. Schilling (Eds), *Sport psychology in Europe. FEPSAC – an organisational platform and a scientific meeting point* (pp. 96–97). Biel: European Federation of Sport Psychology.

FEPSAC (2003b). FEPSAC position statement #3 'sports career transitions'. In E. Apitzsch and G. Schilling (Eds), *Sport psychology in Europe. FEPSAC – an organisational platform and a scientific meeting point* (pp. 101–102). Biel: European Federation of Sport Psychology.

Fernandez, A., Stephan, Y. and Fouquereau, E. (2006). Assessing reasons for sports career termination: development of the Athletes' Retirement Decision Inventory (ARDI). *Psychology of Sport and Exercise*, 7, 407–421.

Fry, M. D. and Duda, J. L. (1997). A developmental examination of children's understanding of effort and ability in the physical and academic domains. *Research Quarterly for Exercise and Sport*, 68, 331–344.

Germeau Y. (2009). *Carrièretransities bij elite atleten: Kwalitatief onderzoek naar de invloed van de Olympische Spelen en carrièrebeëindiging op de carrièreontwikkeling van elitezwemmers en elite floretschermers* [Career transitions among elite athletes: a qualitative study into the influence of the Olympic Games and the career discontinuation on the career development of elite swimmers and elite floret fencers]. Unpublished master dissertation. Vrije Universiteit Brussel.

Haerle, R. K. (1975). Career patterns and career contingencies of professional baseball players: an occupational analysis. In D. W. Ball and J. W. Loy (Eds), *Sport and social order* (pp. 461–519). Reading, MA: Addison-Wesley.

Kerr, G. and Dacyshyn, A. (2000). The retirement experiences of elite, female gymnasts. *Journal of Applied Sport Psychology*, 12, 115–133.

McPherson, B. D. (1980). Retirement from professional sport: the process and problems of occupational and psychological adjustment. *Sociological Symposium*, 30, 126–143.

Mihovilovic, M. (1968). The status of former sportsmen. *International Review of Sport Sociology*, 3, 73–93.

Murphy, S. (1995). Transitions in competitive sport: maximising individual potential. In S. Murphy (Ed.), *Sport psychology interventions* (pp. 334–346). Champaign: Human Kinetics.

Naul, R. (1994). The elite athlete career: sport pedagogy must counsel social and professional problems in life development. In D. Hackfort (Ed.), *Psycho-social issues and interventions in elite sport* (pp. 237–258). Frankfurt: Lang.

North, J. and Lavallee, D. (2004). An investigation of potential users of career transition services in the United Kingdom. *Psychology of Sport and Exercise*, 5, 77–84.

Parker, K. B. (1994). 'Has-beens' and 'wanna-bes': transition experiences of former major college football players. *The Sport Psychologist*, 8, 287–304.

Pummell, B., Harwood, C. and Lavallee, D. (2008). Jumping to the next level: a qualitative examination of within-career transition in adolescent event riders. *Psychology of Sport and Exercise*, 9, 427–447.

Rea, T. (2003). *An examination of the normative transitions experienced by professional football players in academy setting*. Unpublished master dissertation. Loughborough University.

Redgrave, S. and Townsend, N. (2001). *A golden age*. London: BBC Books.

Reints, A. and Wylleman, P. (2009a). *Career development and transitions of elite athletes*. Paper presented at the Symposium: Managing elite sports: a multidisciplinary perspective on the management of elite sports in Flanders. Barcelona, Spain: Centre d'Alt Rendiment (C.A.R.) Sant Cugat, 16 November.

Reints, A. and Wylleman, P. (2009b). *Athletic and post-athletic career support services: evaluation of supply and user satisfaction using a mixed-method study*. Paper presented at the 12th World Congress of Sport Psychology. Marrakesh, Morocco: ISSP, 17–21 June.

Reints, A., Wylleman, P. and Dom, L. (2008). *Kwalitatief onderzoek naar relatie tussen beroepsgerichte na-carrièreplanning en huidige beroepssituatie van Vlaamse ex-topjudoka's* [Qualitative research into the relationship between profession-oriented past-career planning and current professional situation of Flemish former elite judokas]. During the Congres VSPN 'Van wetenschap naar praktijk'. Amsterdam, the Netherlands: Vereniging Sportpsychologie Nederland – VUAmsterdam.

Robertson-Wilson, J. and Côté, J. (2002). *The role of parents in children's hockey participation*. Report for the Canadian Hockey Association. p. 46.

Salmela, J. H. (1994). Phases and transitions across sports career. In D. Hackfort (Ed.), *Psycho-social issues and interventions in elite sport* (pp. 11–28). Frankfurt: Lang.

Sampras, P. (2008). *A champion's mind: lessons from a life in tennis*. New York: Crown Publishers.

Schlossberg, N. K. (1981). A model for analyzing human adaptation. *The Counseling Psychologist, 9*, 2–18.

Schlossberg, N. K. (1984). *Counseling adults in transition: linking practice with theory*. New York: Springer.

Seiler, R., Anders, G. and Irlinger, P. (Eds). (1998). *Das leben nach dem spitzensport. La via apre's le sport de haut niveau* [Life after elite level sport]. Paris: INSEP.

Sinclair, D. A. and Orlick, T. (1993). Positive transitions from high-performance sport. *The Sport Psychologist, 7*, 138–150.

Sinclair, D. A. and Orlick, T. (1994). The effects of transition on high performance sport. In D. Hackfort (Ed.), *Psycho-social issues and interventions in elite sports* (pp. 29–55). Frankfurt: Lang.

Sosniak, A. (2006). Retrospective interviews in the study of expertise and expert performance. In K. A. Ericsson, N. Charness, P. J. Feltovich and R. R. Hoffman (Eds), *The Cambridge handbook of expertise and expert performance* (pp. 287–302). New York: Cambridge University Press.

Stambulova, N. (1994). Developmental sports career investigations in Russia: a post-Perestroika analysis. *The Sports Psychologist, 8*, 221–237.

Stambulova, N. (1997). Sociological sports career transitions. In J. Bangsbo, B. Saltin, H. Bonde, Y. Hellsten, B. Ibsen, M. Kjfr and G. Sjxgaard (Eds), *Proceedings of the second annual congress of the European College of Sport Science* (pp. 88–89). Copenhagen: ECSS.

Stambulova, N. (2000). Athlete's crises: a developmental perspective. *International Journal of Sport Psychology, 31*, 584–601.

Stambulova, N. (2003). Symptoms of a crisis-transition: a grounded theory study. In N. Hassmen (Ed.), *SIPF yearbook 2003* (pp. 97–109). Örebro: Örebro University Press.

Stephan, Y., Torregrosa, M. and Sanchez, X. (2007). The body matters: psychophysical impact of retiring from elite sport. *Psychology of Sport and Exercise, 8*, 73–83.

Swain, D. A. (1991). Withdrawal from sport and Schlossberg's model of transitions. *Sociology of Sport Journal, 8*, 152–160.

Taylor, J. and Ogilvie, B. C. (1998). Career transition among elite athletes: is there life after sports? In J. M. Williams (Ed.), *Applied sport psychology: personal growth to peak performance* (pp. 429–444). Mountain View: Mayfield.

Torregrosa, M., Boixadós, M., Valiente, L. and Cruz, J. (2004). Elite athletes' image of retirement: the way to relocation in sport. *Psychology of Sport and Exercise, 5*, 35–43.

Van Aken, I., Wylleman, P., Taelman, K., De Knop, P. and Clonen, J. (2008). Het recht van een getalenteerd kind om al dan niet sportkampioen te worden [The right of the young talented athlete to (not) become a champion]. *Tijdschrift Jeugd- en Kinderrechten, 2*, 101–109.

van der Meulen, M. and Menkehorst, H. (1992). Intensieve sportbeoefening in ontwikkelingspsychologisch perspectief [Intensive sports participation in developmental psychological perspective]. In M. van der Meulen, H. A. B. M. Menkehorst and F. C. Bakker (Eds), *Jeugdig sporttalent: Psychologische aspecten van intensieve sportbeoefening* [Talented young athletes: psychological aspects of intensive sport participation] (pp. 93–114). Amsterdam: Vereniging Sportpsychologie Nederland.

Weiss, M. and Chaumeton, N. (1992). Motivational orientations in sport. In T. S. Horn (Ed.), *Advances in sport psychology* (pp. 61–99). Champaign: Human Kinetics.

Wylleman, P. (2006). *A developmental approach to mental skills training of talented young tennis players*. During the 11th Annual Conference of the European College of Sport Sciences. Lausanne: ECSS, 5–8 July.

Wylleman, P. (2008). *From talented to elite to retired athlete: a holistic perspective on career development and transitions*. During the Personal Lifestyle Conference 2008 'The Contribution of Performance Lifestyle to Athlete Legacy'. London: UKSport, 14 May.

Wylleman, P. and Debois, N. (2007). *Lifestyle and career management*. During the FAST Professional workshop. Halkidiki, Greece: Forum for Applied Sport psychologists in Topsport, 4 September.

Wylleman, P. and Kahan, N. (2004). *The cooperation between an elite archer, the coach, team manager, physiotherapist and sport psychologist: a case-study*. During the 9th Annual Conference of the European College of Sport Sciences. Clermont-Ferrand, France: ECSS, 3–6 July.

Wylleman, P. and Lavallee, D. (2004). A developmental perspective on transitions faced by athletes. In M. Weiss (Ed.), *Developmental sport and exercise psychology: a lifespan perspective* (pp. 507–527). Morgantown: FIT.

Wylleman, P. and Parker, R. (2004). *Lifestyle management for elite athletes: a European perspective*. In Book of abstracts of the 12th European Congress on Sport Management (p. 263).

Wylleman, P. and Taelman, K. (2007). *Carrièrebegeleiding en de combinatie van studie en topsport* [Career management and the combination of study and elite sport]. During the 10th ENAS Conference 'Securing the Future of University Sport'. Ghent: European Network of Academic Sport Services – Universiteit Gent, 9 November.

Wylleman, P. and Waser, J. (2007). *Services to athletes*. During the IOC Athletes' Commission meeting. Lausanne: IOC, 6 February.

Wylleman, P., Alfermann, D. and Lavallee, D. (2004a). Career transitions in perspective. *Psychology of Sport and Exercise*, 5, 7–20.

Wylleman, P., Lavallee, D. and Alfermann, D. (Eds). (1999). *FEPSAC Monograph Series. Career transitions in competitive sports*. Lund: European Federation of Sport Psychology FEPSAC.

Wylleman, P., Lavallee, D. and Theeboom, M. (2004b). Successful athletic careers. In C. Spielberger (Ed.), *Encyclopedia of applied psychology* (pp. 511–518). San Diego: Elsevier Ltd.

Wylleman, P., De Knop, P., Theeboom, M. and De Greef, A. (1994). Research into the (non-)participation of youth in organised sports in Flanders. In W. Duquet, P. De Knop and L. Bollaert (Eds.), *Youth, leisure and physical activity* (pp. 145–160). Brussel: VUB.

Wylleman, P., De Knop, P., Verdet, M.-C. and Cecić Erpič, S. (2006). Parenting and career transitions of elite athletes. In S. Jowett and D. Lavallee (Eds), *Social psychology of sport* (pp. 233–247). Champaign: Human Kinetics.

Wylleman, P., De Knop, P., Menkehorst, H., Theeboom, M. and Annerel, J. (1993). Career termination and social integration among elite athletes. In S. Serpa, J. Alves, V. Ferreira and A. Paula-Brito (Eds), *Proceedings of the VIII World Congress of Sport Psychology* (pp. 902–906). Lisbon: International Society of Sport Psychology.

Part III

Sport and physical activity during adulthood among various populations

6 The transtheoretical model and physical activity adherence

Elizabeth A. Fallon

The World Health Organization defines health as 'a state of complete physical, mental and social well-being, and not merely the absence of disease' (World Health Organization, 2006). Substantial evidence demonstrates that regular physical activity is an essential component of physical and psychological health (Physical Activity Guidelines Advisory Committee, 2008). Despite the obvious importance of physical activity, however, 60 per cent of the world's population does not accumulate enough physical activity to attain the health benefits (World Health Organization, 2002). To achieve maximum individual and public health impact, however, recommended levels of physical activity must be attained early in life and maintained across the entire lifespan.

At the foundation of our ability to successfully address the physical inactivity epidemic is the development and empirical testing of health behaviour theories and models. These theories/models are essential for: (1) systematically explaining and predicting behaviour and behaviour change; and (2) providing frameworks for the development, implementation and evaluation of physical activity interventions. Thus, the purpose of this chapter is to discuss the transtheoretical model for the initiation of physical activity as well as the model's potential for explaining long-term adherence to physical activity.

Transtheoretical model

The transtheoretical model of behaviour change proposes that individuals move through six stages of readiness to change over time, with periods of progression and relapse (Prochaska and Velicer, 1997). These six stages are:

- Precontemplation – no intention to begin physical activity within the next six months.
- Contemplation – intention to begin physical activity within the next six months.
- Preparation – Intention to begin physical activity within the next month or irregular or insufficient physical activity (not meeting recommended levels).
- Action – meeting physical activity recommendations within the past six months.

- Maintenance – meeting physical activity recommendations for more than six consecutive months.
- Termination – meeting physical activity recommendations for more than five years and having 0 per cent temptation to not exercise and 100 per cent self-efficacy to meet physical activity recommendations.

The transtheoretical model also proposes that movement through these stages is a result of changes in four primary cognitive and behavioural constructs. *Self-efficacy* is the situation-specific confidence to overcome a high-risk circumstance without relapse to sedentary habits (Bandura, 1977; Prochaska and Velicer, 1997). As self-efficacy for physical activity increases, forward progression through the stages is more likely. *Temptation* is the intensity of urges to not engage in physical activity in the midst of a difficult situation. Thus, a decrease in temptation is needed for forward progression through the stages of change. *Decisional balance* is the weighing of the pros and the cons of engaging in physical activity. As the pros of physical activity outweigh the cons, forward movement through the stages is expected. Finally, the *processes of change* are five cognitive and five behavioural processes used to progress through the stages of change (see Table 6.1 for

Table 6.1 Experiential and behavioural processes of change

Experiential (Cognitive) Processes of Change	
Consciousness Raising	Seeking and gaining new information, awareness, understanding and feedback about physical activity or sedentary lifestyle.
Dramatic Relief	Changes in affect related to changes in physical activity or sedentary lifestyle.
Self-reevaluation	Emotional and cognitive appraisal of self-image regarding physical activity or sedentary behaviour.
Environmental Reevaluation	Cognitive and affective assessment of how physical activity or sedentary lifestyle affects the physical and social environment.
Social Liberation	Awareness, availability, and acceptance of alternative, physically active lifestyles in society.
Behavioural Processes of Change	
Counterconditioning	The substitution of physical activity for sedentary behaviours.
Reinforcement Management	Changing the contingencies that control or maintain the sedentary lifestyle.
Stimulus Control	Removing cues for sedentary behaviour and adding cues for physically active behaviour.
Helping Relationships	Identification and use of open, trusting, accepting, and supportive relationships for physical activity.
Self-liberation	The choice and commitment to change and remain physically active; includes the belief that change is possible and sustainable.

Source: Prochaska and Velicer (1997) and Burkholder and Nigg (2002).

definitions of each process of change). For physical activity, the more an individual uses these processes of change, the more likely they will progress through the stages of change.

To date, most research has focused on the model's ability to initiate physical activity by moving individuals through the earlier stages of change (i.e. precontemplation, contemplation, preparation and action stages). As such, we know very little about the model as it applies to maintenance of physical activity over the long term (i.e. maintenance and termination stages). Yet, as stated earlier, it is long-term adherence to physical activity that is needed for maximal health outcomes. Therefore, it is prudent to move behavioural research forward by investigating theoretical frameworks pertaining to long-term adherence and testing physical activity interventions based on these frameworks.

Initiation vs. adherence

Several interventions based on the transtheoretical model have proven successful for the initiation of physical activity (Hutchison *et al.*, 2009). Unfortunately, too few interventions have been able to document adherence beyond six months after the intervention concludes (Adams and White, 2003, 2005; Hutchison *et al.*, 2009). This lack of long-term effectiveness may be due to several factors. First, many interventions do not fully employ all of the transtheoretical model constructs (Hutchison *et al.*, 2009). Thus, changing only one or two of the primary constructs in the model may lead to a brief period of initiation of physical activity, but may not be sufficient for long-term adherence. Second, many interventions are too brief, lasting three months or less, or lack sufficient intensity to effectively change long-term behaviour (Hutchison *et al.*, 2009). Sedentary behaviour, which has been learned over several years, often requires a great amount of trial and error before finding the strategies that will ultimately lead to a physically active lifestyle. Thus, interventions that are too short, or lack a sufficient amount of provider contact are less likely to result in long-term adherence. Third, interventions may not be delivered the way they are intended to be delivered (Adams and White, 2003). Often referred to as a lack of intervention fidelity, failing to deliver an intervention the way it was intended can reduce its effectiveness both for initiation as well as long-term adherence.

In addition to these factors, low rates of long-term adherence may be due to an underlying (and unfounded) assumption that the psychosocial, behavioural and environmental factors responsible for physical activity initiation are the same factors necessary for long-term adherence. This assumption is evidenced by a lack of models/theories developed to explain, predict and provide intervention frameworks for long-term adherence to physical activity. The transtheoretical model is one of the few health behaviour change models that explicitly differentiates between initiation and maintenance of behaviour by including the maintenance and termination stages of change. The inclusion of these stages provides researchers with a valuable starting point for the empirical study of theory as it applies to long-term (>six months) physical activity adherence. Thus, the purpose of the remainder of this chapter is three-fold: (1) to summarise research examining the transtheoretical model as it applies to long-term adherence (action/maintenance/termination stages); (2) to identify the limitations of this research; and (3) to propose future directions for research and application of the transtheoretical model for long-term adherence to physical activity.

Validity of the termination stage for physical activity

The transtheoretical model was originally developed for smoking cessation and applying this model to the initiation and maintenance of physical activity brings about conceptual differences in the model's application. One question that arises is whether the termination stage is a valid stage of change for an ongoing positive health behaviour, such as physical activity. Historically, many researchers have assumed that the termination stage is not a valid stage of change for physical activity and omitted the termination stage from literature reviews (Adams and White, 2003, 2005; Bridle et al., 2005; Marcus and Simkin, 1994; Reed, 1999). The following studies, however, have directly tested the validity of this stage of change for physical activity.

Seminal research examining the validity of the termination stage for physical activity was equivocal, with one study providing empirical evidence for the existence of the termination stage (Cardinal, 1999) and another study refuting the existence of the termination stage (Courneya and Bobick, 2000). When reading these studies closely, it becomes evident that both studies failed to fully and exclusively study the original definition of termination as described by Prochaska and Velicer (1997), which is meeting physical activity recommendations for more than five years and having 0 per cent temptation to not exercise and 100 per cent self-efficacy to meet physical activity recommendations. Thus, following the development of the temptation to not exercise scale (Hausenblas et al., 2001), Fallon and Hausenblas (2001) conducted a third study to test the validity of the termination stage. Specifically, gym members' self-reported stage of change, physical activity, self-efficacy and temptation was assessed. As the transtheoretical model would suggest, those in the maintenance stage reported less self-efficacy and less temptation to not exercise. It is important to note, however, that only one participant in the study met Prochaska's original definition of the termination stage by reporting 0 per cent temptation and 100 per cent self-efficacy. These findings suggest there are statistically significant differences between individuals in the maintenance and termination stages, but do not fully support Prochaska's original definition of termination.

The results of Fallon and Hausenblas (2001) may be interpreted in different ways. Some may overlook the differences found between individuals in the maintenance and termination stages and conclude that the termination stage is not valid for physical activity because so few people met Prochaska's original definition of termination. Others may place greater importance on the differences between the maintenance and termination groups and view the lack of individuals reporting 0 per cent temptation and 100 per cent self-efficacy as a reflection of the conceptual difference that emerges when applying a model originally created for the cessation of a negative behaviour to the initiation and long-term adherence to a positive behaviour. A third interpretation of the Fallon and Hausenblas (2001) study is that 0 per cent temptation and 100 per cent self-efficacy for physical activity are possible, but it takes longer than five years to reach this definition of termination.

Thus, the next step was to empirically examine the validity of the five-year time requirement originally proposed for the termination stage. Using a self-report survey, total number of years of physical activity, current physical activity levels and all five constructs of the transtheoretical model (i.e. stage of change, self-efficacy, temptation, decisional balance and processes of change) were assessed (Fallon and Hausenblas, 2004). Participants were grouped into the following stages: maintenance (exercising more than six months, but less than five years), 5–10 year termination (exercising between five and ten years), and >ten-year termination (exercising longer than ten years). Similar to the previous study (Fallon and Hausenblas, 2001), those in the maintenance stage reported less self-efficacy, less use of processes of change and greater temptation to not exercise compared to those in the termination stages. But no differences in constructs emerged when comparing the two termination stages (5–10 year and >ten-year termination stages). This study provides additional evidence of significant psychosocial differences between individuals in maintenance and termination stages. Additionally, because there was no evidence that adhering to exercise for more than ten years results in significant changes in the transtheoretical model constructs, it appears that there is validity to the termination stage's five-year time frame.

In summary, these studies show there are differences among individuals who have been exercising for less than six months (action), those exercising more than six months but less than five years (maintenance) and those exercising more than five years (termination). For practitioners, this may mean expanding the time frame of existing physical activity interventions (typically three to six months), such that contact with participants is maintained as long as five years. What behavioural science has not been able to provide conclusive evidence for is: (1) how frequently practitioners need to have contact with participants during the maintenance phase; and (2) what specific content should be included in these maintenance interventions. Typically, the most successful transtheoretically-based interventions for initiation of physical activity provide weekly contact with an interventionist for three to six months. There is no empirical evidence, however, of how often to meet with individuals attempting to maintain their physical activity. With regard to the content of these interventions, however, research has provided a small amount of evidence, which is discussed below.

Movement through action, maintenance and termination stages

If we momentarily assume that the termination stage is a valid stage for physical activity behaviour, the next topic of interest is how the transtheoretical model constructs (i.e. self-efficacy, decisional balance, processes of change and temptation) operate to effect movement through the later stages of change (action, maintenance and termination).

Marshall and Biddle (2001) conducted a meta-analytic review of research examining the core constructs of the transtheoretical model. Results showed that self-efficacy was the only construct associated with the action and maintenance stages of change, suggesting that increases in self-efficacy during the action stage are necessary for successful movement into maintenance.

Although the Marshall and Biddle (2001) review was comprehensive (71 published studies), it is important to note several limitations of the study. First, temptation to not exercise was not included in their review due to a lack of physical activity research incorporating this construct prior to 2001. Second, 54 of 71 studies were based on cross-sectional data, six were longitudinal, ten were quasi-experimental and one was a randomised control trial. Cross-sectional studies are prone to overestimating the relationship between constructs and behaviour (Weinstein, 2007). Thus, a review based on such a large proportion of cross-sectional studies may also overestimate the relationship between constructs and physical activity.

Third, in addition to the large proportion of cross-sectional studies included in the review, it is also important to note the limited number of studies examining construct relationships for action and maintenance stages. Specifically, self-efficacy had the most independent samples (16 studies), followed by decisional balance (13 studies) and processes of change (five studies). Therefore, with so few studies examining construct associations between action and maintenance, and fewer still using longitudinal data sets and randomised control trials, our understanding of how the transtheoretical constructs operate to move individuals from action to maintenance is limited.

Our current understanding of stage transitions is further clouded by the likely presence of moderating and/or mediating factors that impact the ability of the transtheoretical constructs to influence stage transition (Marshall and Biddle, 2001). For example, an abundance of research shows that men are more physically active than women and higher socioeconomic status groups are more active than low socioeconomic status groups. Thus, it is possible that members of these subgroups use transtheoretical model constructs differently. If this is the case, it would change how practitioners develop transtheoretically-based interventions for physical activity.

The presence of moderating variables for construct associations among action, maintenance and termination stages of change was confirmed by Fallon et al. (2005). Using a self-report survey assessing all of the transtheoretical model constructs, results indicated that sex moderated the transtheoretical model constructs. Specifically, compared to men, women reported lower barriers efficacy, greater pros for physical activity and greater use of behavioural and experiential processes of change. To examine stage associations, the remaining analyses were conducted separately for men and women. Results suggested that:

- To move from action to maintenance, men should decrease their affect temptation to not exercise and women should increase in environmental re-evaluation and social liberation.

- To move from maintenance to termination, men need to increase their barriers efficacy and environmental re-evaluation and decrease their affect temptation to not exercise, while women should increase their barriers efficacy.

The strength of this study is the inclusion of all of the transtheoretical model constructs and the separation of analyses by sex, giving researchers and practitioners empirical confirmation that men and women may require different interventions to promote long-term maintenance of physical activity. The major limitation of this study, however, is its reliance on cross-sectional data.

A more recent study used a 12-month longitudinal design to examine the influence of processes of change on stage movement (Lowther *et al.*, 2007). Of the 734 stage transitions occurring throughout the study, 56 transitioned from action to maintenance. Results indicate that decreasing the use of environmental evaluation and self-reevaluation while increasing the use of helping relationships, social liberation, counter-conditioning and self-liberation increase the odds of progressing from action to maintenance. Although the longitudinal design of this study provides stronger evidence for construct transitions than cross-sectional designs, failing to include all of the transtheoretical model constructs in the study may lead to the overestimation of the importance of the processes of change. Additionally, the low number of stage transitions from action to maintenance may not provide adequate power.

In summary, we have few studies providing an empirical basis for the intervention content necessary to move individuals from action to maintenance and from maintenance to termination. Preliminary evidence suggests that the only construct consistently associated with moving an individual through the later stages of change is self-efficacy, such that continued increases in self-efficacy are associated with later stages of change. This is not to say that other transtheoretically-based constructs are unable to produce forward stage progression; rather we have insufficient evidence at this time to provide practitioners with any firm conclusions for which constructs are best to develop their intervention materials.

Implications for future research

While there have been recent advances in the validation of the termination stage for physical activity and understanding stage transitions among action, maintenance and termination, the following limitations need to be addressed by future research before we will be successful in understanding and influencing long-term physical activity adherence. First, most samples are convenience samples and represent middle to high socioeconomic status, well-educated and primarily Caucasian populations. Thus, replication of studies using more diverse and randomly selected samples is advised. Second, the majority of studies use cross-sectional designs, which have been criticised for their likelihood for bias when examining the relationship among psychosocial constructs and behaviour (Weinstein, 2007). Thus, prospective studies controlling for past physical activity behaviour and randomised control intervention trials are needed to advance this area of research (Rothman,

2000; Weinstein, 2007). Third, many studies have relied on self-reported measures of leisure-time physical activity, which can be subject to self-presentation biases, inaccurate recall and do not assess other types of physical activity important for health (e.g. transportation activity, household activities and occupational activity). Therefore, future investigations of the transtheoretical model's application to physical activity adherence should measure multiple types of physical activity and incorporate accelerometry or other objective methods of physical activity measurement. Fourth, similar to the lack of studies examining transportation/household/ occupational activity, only a few studies (Cardinal and Kosma, 2004; Shirazi *et al.*, 2007) have examined the utility of the transtheoretical model for adherence to resistance training activities. Thus, researchers should examine the extent to which the transtheoretical model may operate differently for aerobic and anaerobic exercise behaviour. Fifth, too few studies have simultaneously examined all of the transtheoretical constructs, with extremely limited attention given to the temptation construct. As research examining the transtheoretical model and physical activity adherence moves forward, it is imperative to include all of the constructs to truly understand how the model works as a whole. Otherwise, we may be under-/ over-estimating the usefulness of a particular construct within the model. Finally, researchers should investigate the extent to which identifying and documenting moderating and mediating variables may improve our ability to understand and predict stage movement and long-term physical activity adherence.

Implications for practitioners

While research examining the utility of the transtheoretical model for long-term adherence to physical activity is ongoing, the following recommendations can be made for practitioners offering physical activity interventions. First, interventions lasting at least three months will substantially increase the likelihood of effecting long-term physical activity adherence (Hutchison *et al.*, 2009). Second, interventions providing participants with several provider contacts and mediums by which to receive advice (e.g. face-to-face contact, theory-based newsletters, group sessions, and/or encouraging phone calls) will be more effective in the long-term (Hutchison *et al.*, 2009). Third, the most successful transtheoretically-based interventions to date have included all of the constructs in some capacity (Hutchison *et al.*, 2009). But if time and resources are limited, an intervention's chances of effecting long-term adherence are optimised by focusing on increases in self-efficacy (Fallon and Hausenblas, 2004; Fallon *et al.*, 2005). Finally, as research identifies and documents moderating variables (such as sex) it may be beneficial for practitioners to carefully modify existing evidence-based interventions to better accommodate and target specific subgroups within the larger population.

Conclusion

Regular physical activity participation has the potential to make a significant public health impact for prevention and treatment of chronic diseases. Unfortunately, too few people currently meet physical activity guidelines, and fewer still are able to meet guidelines across the lifespan. While we have made significant gains in recent years to understand initiation of physical activity behaviour through theoretically-based interventions, we know very little about long-term (>six months) physical activity behaviour change. This chapter has outlined recent developments in our understanding of the transtheoretical model as it applies to long-term adherence, but much more opportunity for empirical investigation remains.

References

Adams, J. and White, M. (2003). Are activity promotion interventions based on the transtheoretical model effective? A critical review. *British Journal of Sports Medicine, 37,* 106–114.

Adams, J. and White, M. (2005). Why don't stage-based activity promotion interventions work? *Health Education Research, 20,* 237–243.

Bandura, A. (1977). Self-efficacy: toward a unifying theory of behavioural change. *Psycholgical Review, 84,* 191–215.

Bridle, C., Riemsma, R. P., Patternden, J., Sowden, A. J., Mather, L., Watt, I. S. and Walker, A. (2005). Systematic review of the effectiveness of health behaviour interventions based on the transtheoretical model. *Psychology and Health, 20,* 283–301.

Burkholder, G. J. and Nigg, C. (2002). Overview of the transtheoretical model. In P. M. Burbank and D. Riebe (Eds), *Promoting exercise and behaviour change in older adults: interventions with the transtheoretical model* (pp. 57–84). New York: Springer Publishing Company, Inc.

Cardinal, B. J. (1999). Extended stage of model of physical activity behaviour. *Journal of Human Movement Studies, 37,* 37–54.

Cardinal, B. J. and Kosma, M. (2004). Self-efficacy and the stages and processes of change associated with adopting and maintaining muscular fitness-promoting behaviours. *Research Quarterly for Exercise and Sport, 75,* 186–196.

Courneya, K. S. and Bobick, T. M. (2000). No evidence for a termination stage in exercise behaviour change. *Avante, 6,* 75–85.

Fallon, E. A. and Hausenblas, H. A. (2001). Transtheoretical model of behaviour change: does the termination stage exist for exercise? *Journal of Human Movement Studies, 40,* 465–479.

Fallon, E. A. and Hausenblas, H. A. (2004). Transtheoretical model of behaviour change: does it take five years to reach termination? *American Journal of Health Studies, 19,* 35–44.

Fallon, E. A., Hausenblas, H. A. and Nigg, C. R. (2005). The transtheoretical model and exercise adherence: examining construct associations in later stages of change. *Psychology of Sport and Exercise, 4,* 420–433.

Hausenblas, H. A., Nigg, C., Dannecker, E. A., Downs, D. S., Gardner, R. E., Fallon, E. A., Focht, B. C. and Loving, M. G. (2001). A missing piece of the transtheoretical model applied to exercise: development and validation of the temptation to not exercise scale. *Psychology and Health, 16,* 381–390.

Hutchison, A. J., Breckon, J. D. and Johnston, L. H. (2009). Physical activity behaviour change interventions based on the transtheoretical model: a systematic review. *Health Education & Behaviour, 36*(5), 829–845.

Lowther, M., Mutrie, N. and Scott, E. M. (2007). Identifying key processes of exercise behaviour change associated with movement through the stages of exercise behaviour change. *Journal of Health Psychology, 12*, 261–272.

Marcus, B. H. and Simkin, L. R. (1994). The transtheoretical model: applications to exercise behaviour. *Medicine and Science in Sports and Exercise, 26*, 1400–1404.

Marshall, S. J. and Biddle, S. J. (2001). The transtheoretical model of behaviour change: a meta-analysis of applications to physical activity and exercise. *Annals of Behavioural Medicine, 23*, 229–246.

Physical Activity Guidelines Advisory Committee (2008). *Physical Activity Guidelines Advisory Committee Report.* Washington, DC: U.S. Department of Health and Human Services.

Prochaska, J. O. and Velicer, W. F. (1997). The transtheoretical model of health behaviour change. *American Journal of Health Promotion, 12*, 38–48.

Reed, G. R. (1999). Adherence to exercise and the transtheoretical model of behaviour change. In S. J. Bull (Ed.), *Adherence issues in sport and exercise* (pp. 19–46). New York: John Wiley & Sons.

Rothman, A. J. (2000). Toward a theory-based analysis of behavioural maintenance. *Health Psychology, 19*(1 Suppl), 64–69.

Shirazi, K. K., Wallace, L. M., Niknami, S., Hidarnia, A., Torkaman, G., Gilchrist, M. and Faghihzadeh, S. (2007). A home-based, transtheoretical change model designed strength training intervention to increase exercise to prevent osteoporosis in Iranian women aged 40–65 years: a randomized controlled trial. *Health Education Research, 22*, 305–317.

Weinstein, N. D. (2007). Misleading tests of health behaviour theories. *Annals of Behavioural Medicine, 33*, 1–10.

World Health Organization (2002). *The world health report 2002 – reducing risks, promoting healthy life.* Geneva, Switzerland.

World Health Organization (2006). Constitution of the World Health Organization. Retrieved 18 December 2009, from www.who.int/governance/eb/who_constitution_en.pdf.

7 Physical exercise as a social marker among middle-aged people in Sweden

Lars-Magnus Engström

Introduction

In modern society we have systematically and successfully made our daily lives less physically active. Technological development has made it possible to avoid physical effort and an increasing proportion of men and women are physically inactive during their leisure time (Haskell *et al.*, 2007). We use computers, time-saving apparatus and various household appliances to an ever greater extent. Centrally located lifts and escalators often appear to be the most apparent and comfortable way of getting from one floor to another. Using the car for short distances also seems to be an obvious alternative. In short, our daily tasks have become much less physically demanding.

A sedentary lifestyle is not without its problems, however. The human body needs to move in order to function optimally and there is scientific consensus about the importance of physical activity for health. Several common illnesses are associated with physical inactivity, such as cardiovascular diseases, adult onset (Type II) diabetes, high blood pressure, obesity, osteoporosis, joint and back problems and cancer of the colon (Andersen *et al.*, 2006; Carnethon *et al.*, 2003; Haskell *et al.*, 2007; Pedersen and Saltin, 2006).

Interestingly, the situation has developed into something of a paradox. The more knowledge we acquire about physical inactivity being a threat to health, the less active we seem to become in our daily lives. A number of physical cultures have developed as a result, to which people relate in different ways, and which to varying degrees have become incorporated into people's lifestyles. In other words, physical exercise should be seen in cultural context, and cannot simply be understood from a biological point of view, even though to a great extent physical exercise, or its lack, has biological and medical consequences.

To whom is this socio-culturally produced physical exercise meaningful? The object of this chapter is to highlight how exercise in middle age, e.g. deliberately chosen physical training, is related to current social position and to previous cultural capital and experiences of sport during adolescence.

The answers to these questions are of vital importance in understanding how lifelong engagement in sport and physical activity develops. Since physical activity is fundamental for both a healthy life and for quality of life, identifying central and governing factors for an active lifestyle is important – and will create good opportunities to design interventions that increase people's physical activity. The results of this study, drawn on empirical data from about 2,000 men and women followed from 15 to 53 years of age, give us unique opportunities to highlight this area and increase our understanding of how exercise habits develop.

Theoretical starting points and earlier research

My analysis of the exercise habits of middle-aged men and women is based on Pierre Bourdieu's theoretical frame of reference and conceptual framework (Engström, 2008). Adopting Bourdieu's perspective allows us to highlight different principles or logics within the field of sport that give an activity meaning (Bourdieu, 1990). In this culture, both the role of the individual and whether individuals attempt to enter the arena at all are dependent on how the individual's habitus relates to the sports culture in question. Bourdieu (1984, p. 170) describes habitus:

> The habitus is necessity internalised and converted into a disposition that generates meaningful practices and meaning-given perceptions; it is a general, transposable disposition which carries out a systematic, universal application – beyond the limits of what has been directly learnt – of the necessity inherent in the learning conditions.

For example, an individual who participates in keep-fit activities must find participation meaningful, or at least acceptable, and perceive physical training as essential. Habitus, the underlying generative principle for differences in taste and unconscious strategies, has to be in harmony with the present contribution in society. However, if it is to be meaningful, habitus has to be related to some of Bourdieu's key concepts. People's different status, power and influence are dependent on the assets – economic, cultural or social – they possess and can display. According to Bourdieu, the habitus of different classes more or less harmonises with what is on offer in the field of sport. Several studies have pointed out that it is middle class and the upper middle class individuals, with their proportionately high economic and/or cultural capital, who are especially attracted to the exercise activities on offer (Bourdieu, 1978; Cole et al., 2006; Mäkinen et al., 2009; Scheerder et al., 2002; Scheerder et al., 2005, Shilling, 1993; Stempel, 2005; Wilson, 2002). This research, along with my own (Engström, 2008), supports Bourdieu's thesis that the taste for sport can be read socially. The possibility of choice is both limited to and ruled by the cultural and social context within which an individual has been brought up and now occupies. People's preferences and taste for various practices in the field of sport can thus clearly be seen as cultural expressions.

Many longitudinal studies have found a low to moderate association between sports activities during adolescence and exercise habits in adulthood (Scheerder et al., 2006; Seefeldt et al., 2002; Tammelin, 2005; Telama et al., 2005). However, such studies have seldom involved detailed multivariate analyses that take into account the confounding effects of social background factors, or the variety of sporting experiences associated with later exercise habits. An exception is Scheerder *et al.* (2006), who showed that highly diverse sports patterns during late adolescence were linked to active participation in sport as an adult. Females with non-competitive engagement appear to be more likely to continue involvement in sports activities in later life. Level of education was also positively related to active involvement in sports for adults.

Against this background, the following questions can be formulated:

1. Can a combination of two indicators of social position, indicating cultural as well as economic capital, give a stronger relationship between social position and exercise habits than using the indicators separately?
2. Since exercise in middle age is characterised by a logic in which physical training is central, does a habitus imprinted during childhood and youth and in harmony with this logic have a greater significance than a logic based on competition and ranking?
3. Are those who secured high cultural capital during childhood and adolescence, and thereby increased their opportunity to reach a high social position later in life, more likely to devote their time to physical exercise than those with a lower cultural capital?

Research design

The individuals included in this follow-up study were first contacted in 1968, when they were 15 years of age. I contacted 91 randomly selected school classes in Year 8 from four counties in Sweden. The counties were selected in a way that ensured the greatest possible geographic spread and the representation of a large city (Stockholm). The objective was to survey the attitudes of the 2,000+ adolescents towards the subject of physical education and their leisure-time sports activities. Since then, follow-up contact and information gathering has been conducted on six additional occasions, primarily via questionnaires sent by post, and most recently in 2006/2007. The project has been successively reported (Engström 1974, 1979, 1980, 1986, 1990, 2004 and 2008). In this chapter, the follow-up period is around 38 years, thus focusing on individuals between the ages of 15 and 53. The total number of requests in 2007 was 1,979 men and women. A total number of 1,518, i.e. 77 per cent, responded to and returned the questionnaire.

Exercise habits and social position

As mentioned above, several investigations have highlighted an association between socio-economic conditions and exercise habits. Definitions of exercise, e.g. the criteria, have varied however. My definition, regarding physical activity level, corresponds with the American Heart Association's recommendations (Haskell *et al.*, 2007): 'moderate-intensity activity aerobic (endurance) physical activity for a minimum of 30 min on five days each week or vigorous-intensity aerobic physical activity for a minimum of 20 min on three days each week. Combinations of moderate- and vigorous-intensity activity can be performed to meet this recommendation'. Two of the questions in my questionnaire were combined; one regarding engagement in strenuous exercise, such as rapid walking, jogging, swimming, working out or other equivalent forms of exercise once a week or more; and the other relating to various forms of physical activity, regardless of whether it is by exercise, work etc., in line with the American Heart Association's recommendations. Here it should be noted that 'exercisers' are those who engage in exercise activities every week and at the same time fulfil the physical activity criteria. Those who belong to the group of non-exercisers do not meet these criteria. This group includes those who are reasonably physically active but do not report exercise activities and those who exercise but do not reach the required level of physical activity. One implication of these criteria is that there are those who are sufficiently physically active (e.g. at work) but nevertheless belong to the non-exercisers group. Consequently, my intention is to describe those who both *deliberately* choose to exercise and whose physical activity is at a sufficiently high level.

My data provides two opportunities for social qualification, namely level of education and self-reported class. In the first case, the individuals reported their highest degree of education from nine-year compulsory school up to university education, and in the second case estimated which social class they belonged to. In order to answer my first research question, a multiple logistic regression analysis was carried out. This showed that both variables, even when adjusted for one another, had a significant association with later exercise habits. The results indicate that these variables measure different aspects of social position, i.e. express different possessions of capital. Social position contains cultural as well as economic capital. If level of education points to a possession of cultural capital, it could be inferred that reported class relation reflects economic capital. These two indicators of social position can therefore be combined to acquire a more significant measurement of social position. If these two variables are merged and the new variable is subdivided into five categories, the following association between the constructed variable of social position and exercise habits is gained (see Figure 7.1).

The relationship between social position and exercise habits is obviously very strong. By using both education level and self-reported class affiliation, a much stronger association is gained than by using only one of these variables.

The impact of childhood and adolescence

In an earlier analysis of the present empirical data (Engström, 2008), I found that the scope of sports activities during adolescence was significantly related to exercise habits in middle age. This concurred with the findings of other researchers. However, an important observation was that this relationship only existed if no variables indicating habitus with a taste for physical training were involved in the analysis. Interestingly, if Physical Education (PE) grades and breadth of sport

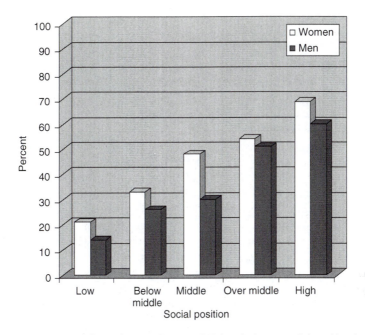

Figure 7.1 Percentage of exercisers at the age of 53 in relation to social position based on educational level and self-reported class.

experiences were involved in the analysis, there was no connection between scope of sports activities and later exercise engagement. Breadth of sport and PE grades were consequently the most crucial indicators of habitus with a taste for physical training, with significance for exercise habits in middle age.

Does the association between these indicators and later exercise habits still exist if a considerably higher demand is made for physical exercise? A multiple logistic regression analysis was undertaken, where the dependant variable was exercise at the age of 53 (see criteria above) and the independent variables, mutually adjusted, were membership of a sports club, scope of sporting activity, experience of various sports and the grade achieved in PE at the age of 15. The analysis showed that with all other variables under control, neither membership nor scope of activity had any significant relationship to exercise habits 38 years later. Neither had experiences of, for example, team ball games, individual ball games or swimming. On the other hand, experiences of (1) skiing, (2) athletics, cross country running, orienteering and (3) gymnastics, dancing and ballet, turned out to be significantly related to exercise habits 38 years later. In addition to that, PE grade was strongly associated with exercise later in life.[1]

By measuring experiences in the three sport areas mentioned above, a new variable, sport breadth, was created. Experience across each sport area was allocated points, with one point per sport area to give a total of experience: no experience =

0 points, experience from one area = 1, experience from two areas = 2, etc. When the value of this new variable was added to the grade achieved in PE (value 1 to 5) another new variable, named habitus with taste for physical training, was created. This variable was then transferred to a scale of 1 to 6, where 1 indicated a very weak taste for physical training and 6 a very strong one. It should be noted that this type of habitus cannot be regarded as a general expression for habitus with taste for physical training, but rather demonstrates which variables in this material were the most significant indicators for later exercise habits (see Figure 7.2).

The association between habitus with a taste for physical training at the age of 15 and exercise habits at the age of 53 is statistically significant for both men and women. My second question was 'Since exercise in middle age is characterised by a logic in which physical training is central, does a habitus imprinted during childhood and youth and in harmony with this logic have a greater significance than a logic based on competition and ranking?' According to my results, there is no doubt that a special kind of sport experience (especially characterised by versatility) has a strong relationship to exercise habits in middle age in contrast to experiences from club sports, where the main content is competition.

In research question three, I explored the position regarding cultural capital, acquired during childhood and adolescence, in relation to later exercise habits. I have earlier confirmed that theoretical subject grades at the age of 15 and the

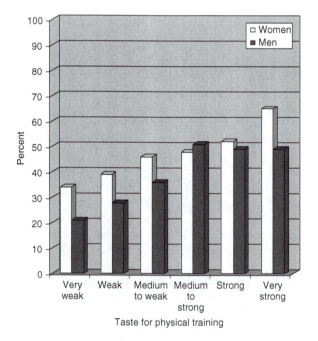

Figure 7.2 Percentage of exercisers at the age of 53 in relation to taste for physical training at the age of 15.

socio-economic status of the father, as indicators of cultural capital, were clearly associated with exercise habits at the age of 53 (Engström, 2008). This relationship still remains, even with more strenuous demands on physical activity. A five-grade scale was established for grades/results in theoretical subjects in combination with socio-economic status. Number 1 signified the lowest cultural capital and number 5 signified the highest cultural capital. As can be seen in Figure 7.3, the connection between cultural capital at the age of 15 and exercise habits at the age of 53 was very strong, and can be compared to the association between habitus with a taste for physical training and exercise habits.

A further analysis proved that both habitus with a taste for physical training and cultural capital, when adjusted for one another, were strongly associated with later exercise habits. A combination of these two variables thus allows optimised opportunity to predict who would become an exerciser later in life. If a class division of this new variable into five groups is made and this variable is related to exercise habits 38 years later, the extent of the association is striking. Since there are only minor differences between men and women, they are reported together (see Figure 7.4).

Anyone with a weak taste for physical training and low cultural capital (as defined in this chapter) at the age of 15 had very little chance of being an exerciser at the age of 53. Around 20 per cent in this group were active, compared to those with a strong taste for physical training and a high cultural capital, where about 70 per cent were active. In other words, in terms of (1) breadth of sport experiences;

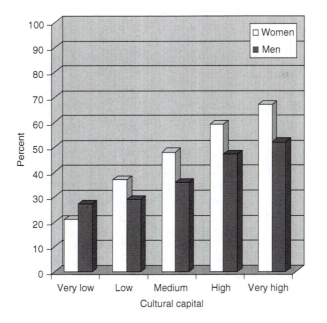

Figure 7.3 Percentage of exercisers at the age of 53 in relation to cultural capital at the age of 15.

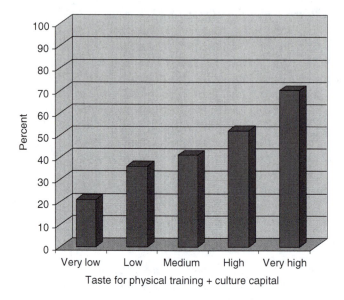

Figure 7.4 Percentage of exercisers at the age of 53 in relation to a combination of taste for physical exercise and culture capital.

(2) grade in PE; (3) father's occupation; and (4) grades/results in theoretical subjects at the age of 15, in this cohort there is a very good chance of making a reliable prediction of exercise habits almost 40 years later. Note, however, that neither membership of a sports club nor scope of sports activities during adolescence had any impact on these relationships.

How might we best understand the associations between cultural capital and sporting experience from childhood and adolescence on the one hand and exercise habits almost 40 years later on the other? Using multiple logistic regression analysis, the impact of taste for physical training and cultural capital on exercise habits with control for social position at the age of 53 was analysed. The results showed that influence from cultural capital disappeared, while influence from taste for physical training remained. My interpretation of this finding is that cultural capital at the age of 15 predicts social position in middle age. However, taste for physical training, as it has been defined here, still had a significant impact on exercise habits, although not to the same extent as social position.

Discussion and implications

In the encounter between the logic of practice and previously incorporated sport experiences, or habitus, it can be decided whether you like the practice or not. In other words, the habitus of those who exercise is in harmony with what is understood as meaningful in life, at the same time as this lifestyle serves as a social marker.

The most common exercise activities (walking, jogging and various gym activities) contain physical training without competition, often with health and bodily appearance as motives, which is why, according to Bourdieu (1978), they do not appeal to the lower social groups to the same extent as to the middle class with good access to cultural capital.

> But physical culture and all the strictly health-oriented practises such as walking and jogging are also linked in other ways to the dispositions of the culturally richest fractions of the middle classes and the dominant class . . .
>
> But also, because they can be performed in solitude, at times and in places beyond the reach of the many, off the beaten track, and so exclude all competition (this is one of the differences between running and jogging), they have a natural place among the ethical and aesthetic choices which define the aristocratic asceticism of the dominant fractions of the dominant class.
>
> (Bourdieu, 1978, p. 214)

My results support Bourdieu's thesis that the taste for sport can be read socially. However, it is not the social position per se that influences the choices, but those who have the same social position often share similar experiences and therefore develop similar habitus. This should not be regarded as a problem as long as this remains a cultural expression. Physical exercise, however, does have an impact on people's health. Social structure and disparity in living conditions will consequently mean that those who belong to the lower social classes have more restricted choices in terms of physical activity, which in turn will have a negative impact on their health and quality of life.

The results I have presented in this chapter indicate that experience of diverse sport patterns and grade in PE (with a diverse content) during childhood and adolescence has a significant impact on later exercise habits. Competitive activities appear to have no impact in this context. This leads me to the conclusion that physical education in school is of central importance, and should have a different emphasis than that for sports activities in clubs, with a content characterised by competition and ranking. PE should therefore offer a broader content with various logics for physical activity, such as physical training, learning and playing. The learning opportunities should be both broadened and deepened. This is particularly important when it comes to basic knowledge and skills, physical literacy; a movement foundation that constitutes essential prerequisites for active participation in a wide range of activities during one's lifetime (Whitehead, 2001; Bailey *et al.*, 2009).

I do not claim that differences in activity between the social classes will disappear if more resources are directed towards PE and more children and youth devote their time to sports activities. Differences in taste for various activities would still be markers for identity and class belonging. My point is, rather, that increasing the opportunities for as many as possible to find an activity they like and in which they are interested, would enable more people to be active.

Many environmental changes could also be made to increase physical activity, e.g. woodland paths, pedestrian precincts, cycle tracks and attractive stairs (not emergency exits). Other urgent measures include the improvement of children's environments, e.g. playgrounds, schoolyards and, not least, the route to and from school. However, whatever measure is taken to increase people's physical activity, it will not hide the fact that sports activities will continue to be socially and culturally impregnated.

Note

1. Of 90 lessons per year, the average number of lessons in gymnastics was around 30, ball games: 25, track and field: 15, swimming: 4, dancing: 4, ice-skating: 3, orienteering: 3 and others: 6. In other words, there was a wide variety of sporting experiences.

References

Andersen, L. B., Harro, M., Sardinha, L. B., Froberg, K., Ekelund, U., Brage, S. and Andersen, S. A. (2006). Physical activity and clustered cardiovascular risk in children: a cross-sectional study (The European Youth Heart Study). *The Lancet, 368*(22), 299–304.

Bailey, R., Armour, K., Kirk, D., Jess, M., Pickup, I. and Sandford, R. (2009). The educational benefits claimed for physical education and school sport: an academic review. *Research Paper in Education, 24*(1), 1–27.

Bourdieu, P. (1978). Sport and social class. *Social Science Information, 17*(6), 819–840.

Bourdieu, P. (1984). *Distinction. A Social Critique of the Judgement of Taste.* London: Routledge & Kegan.

Bourdieu, P. (1990). *The Logic of Practice.* California: Stanford University Press.

Carnethon, M. R., Gidding, S. S., Nehgme, R., Sidney, S. Jacobs, D. R. and Lieu, K. (2003). Cardio respiratory fitness in young adulthood and development of cardiovascular disease risk factors. *Journal of the American Medical Association, 290*(23), 3092–3100.

Cole, R., Leslie, E., Bauman, A., Donald, M. and Owen, N. (2006). Socio-demographic variations in walking for transport and for recreation or exercise among adult Australians. *Journal of Physical Activity and Health, 3*, 164–178.

Engström, L.-M. (1974). Physical activities during leisure time. *International Review of Sport Sociology, 2*(9), 83–98.

Engström, L.-M. (1979). Physical activity during leisure time. A strategy for research. *Scandinavian Journal of Sport Science, 1*(1), 32–39.

Engström, L.-M. (1980). Physical activity of children and youth. *Acta Paedriatrica Scand. Suppl., 283*, 101–105.

Engström, L.-M. (1986). The process of socialisation into keep-fit activities. *Scandinavian Journal of Sports Sciences, 8*, 89–97.

Engström, L.-M. (1990). Exercise adherence in sport for all from youth to adulthood. In P. Oja and R. Telama (Eds), *Sport for All.* Proceedings of the World Congress on Sport for All, held in Tampere, Finland, 3–7 June. Amsterdam: Elsevier, 473–483.

Engström, L.-M. (2004). Social change and physical activity. *Scandinavian Journal of Nutrition, 48*(3), 108–113.

Engström, L.-M. (2008). Who is physically active? Cultural capital and sports participation from adolescence to middle age – a 38 year follow-up study. *Physical Education and Sport Pedagogy, 4*, 319–343.

Haskell, W. L., Lee, I.-M., Pate, R. R., Powell, K. E., Blair, S. N., Franklin, B. A., Macera, C. A., Heath, G. W., Thompson, P. D. and Bauman, A. (2007). Physical activity and public health: updated recommendation for adults from the American College of Sports Medicine and the American Heart Association. *Circulation*, 116, 1081–1093.

Mäkinen, T., Borodulin, K., Laatikainen, T., Fogelholm, M. and Prättälä, R. (2009). Twenty-five year socioeconomic trends in leisure-time and commuting physical activity among employed Finns. *Scandinavian Journal of Medicine & Science in Sport*, 19, 188–197.

Pedersen, B. K. and Saltin, B. (2006). Evidence for prescribing exercise as therapy in chronic disease. *Scandinavian Journal of Medicine & Science in Sports*, 16. Suppl. 1, 3–63.

Scheerder, J., Vanreusel, B. and Taks, M. (2005). Stratification patterns of active sport involvement among adults: social changes and persistence. *International Review for the Sociology of Sport*, 40(2), 139–162.

Scheerder, J., Vanreusel, B., Taks, M. and Renson, R. (2002). Social sports stratification in Flanders 1969–1999: intergenerational reproduction of social inequalities? *International Review for the Sociology of Sport*, 37(2), 219–246.

Scheerder, J., Thomis, M., Vanreusel, B., Lefevre, J., Renson, R., Van den Eyende, B. and Beunen, G. P. (2006). Sports participation among females from adolescence to adult-hood: a longitudinal study. *International Review for the Sociology of Sport*, 41(3–4), 413–430.

Seefeldt, V., Malina, R. M. and Clark, M. A. (2002). Factors affecting levels of physical activity in adults. *Sports Medicine*, 32, 143–168.

Shilling, C. (1993). *The Body and Social Theory*. New Delhi: SAGE Publications Ltd.

Stempel, C. (2005). Adult participation in sports as a cultural capital: a test of Bourdieu's theory of the field of sports. *International Review for the Sociology of Sport*, 40(4), 411–432.

Tammelin, T. (2005). A review of longitudinal studies on youth predictors of adulthood physical activity. *International Journal of Adolescence Medicine and Health*, 17(1), 3–12.

Telama, R., Yang, X., Viikari, J., Välimäki, I., Wanne, O. and Aitakari, O. (2005). Physical activity from childhood to adulthood: a 21-year tracking study. *American Journal of Preventive Medicine*, 28(3), 267–273.

Whitehead, M. (2001). The concept of physical literacy. *European Journal of Physical Education*, 6, 127–138.

Wilson, T. C. (2002). The paradox of social class and sports involvement: the roles of cultural and economic capital. *International Review for the Sociology of Sport*, 37(1), 5–16.

8 Muslim women's experiences of sport

Maryam Koushkie Jahromi

Introduction

Physical education and sport are very important for development of physical skills and promoting physical activity among children and young people (Sallis *et al.*, 1997). They also play a role in preventing many cardiovascular, psychological and musculoskeletal diseases in young and old people (Astrand *et al.*, 2003). There are three main benefits of childhood and youth physical activity (Blair *et al.*, 1989):

1 direct improvement of quality of life;
2 direct improvement of adult health status by, for example, delaying the onset of chronic disease;
3 increased likelihood of maintaining adequate activity through childhood, thus indirectly enhancing adult health status.

While participating in sport and physical activity is recommended for all people, some factors such as culture and religion can influence participation.

Some psychologists believe that religion not only influences the individual psychologically, but also affects him or her socially and culturally (Spilka *et al.*, 2003). Anthropologists also suggest that religion can affect one's social interrelationships (Howard, 1986). Islam is the second largest and fastest growing religion in the world (Lucas and Block, 2008), with between 700 million and 1.2 billion followers worldwide (ReligiousTolerance.org, 2003).

Mohammad is the prophet of Muslims (followers of Islam), and all recommendations and guidelines for Muslims can be found in the Quran, the holy book of Muslims and Miracle of the prophet. Muslims comprise two main groups, Sunnis and Shiites, each having distinct ideological characteristics (Nasr, 1966). Islam is a simple and uncomplicated religion, providing individuals with maximum freedom, without encroaching on the freedom of others (Shakir, 2005). It requires one to believe in one God and do good; to keep up prayers and help disadvantaged people; to fast during Ramadan; and to perform other recommendations of God outlined in the Quran.

'There is no compulsion in religion' (Quran 2:256), and there are no harsh or hard rituals, nor unreasonable dogmas in Islam. Islam emphasises that all human beings and all races have no superiority over each other – only their humanity and performance of their duties to Allah (Muslim name for the one and only God) (Shakir, 2005). Islam does include different groups. Researchers have named four categories: Traditionalism; Modernism; Secularism; and Fundamentalism, according to how Muslims behave and interpret their religion and how it functions in society (Hjaerpe, 1983). The different behaviours and attitudes mean that Islamic influences in Islamic states like Iran and Saudi Arabia are much more obvious and powerful than in secular states like Turkey and Egypt (Vogt, 1995).

The Quran is the common point for all Muslims. In this chapter, criteria and recommendations for Muslim women living and playing sport have been extracted from the holy Quran. Some scholars and researchers believe that there is a very close relationship between sport and religion (Macdonald and Kirk, 1999). The purpose of this chapter is to introduce women's sport status in Islamic beliefs through a summary of experiences of Muslim women's sport in different Islamic and non-Islamic countries.

The status of women in Islam

Islam is not just a belief system, an ideology or a religion in the usual sense that these words are understood. Rather, it is a total way of life, a complete system governing all aspects of man's existence, both individual and social (Hanifa, 1974). Several years of tensions and conflict between the 'Christian West' and the 'Islamic East' have given rise to misconceptions and misinterpretations about Islam (Clarke and Humber, 1997). The role and life of Muslim women demonstrate the tensions in which these misconceptions about Islam have persisted (Aboudeh, 1993). There are growing challenges in the media which support Islamophobia in the West, which in turn can influence women's opportunities in different communities (Allen and Nielsen, 2002). Islam considers the human rights of women by introducing and admiring women who have been successful and selected politically, socially or personally. According to Islam, existence, with all its contrasts and differences, is a unified and interrelated divine system. Men and women are complementary to one another and enjoy equal status (several verses in Quran). Therefore, equality between men and women is represented in Islamic rules. According to the Quran, there is no superiority between men, or between different races, except for their humanity and spiritual preferences (Quran 49:13, 4:1, 16:97).

There are many other parts of the Quran that stress the similarity of men and women. Those differences defined in the progressive laws of Islam for men and women are based on roles played and responsibilities assumed by them. In fact, the rights and privileges specified for women in Islam arise from their natural permanent requirements. Because of women's physical characteristics and their role in creation, some of the laws in Islam give special privileges to them. Some ideologists such as Motahari and Javadi Amoli in Iran believe that seeing women and men as equal in all aspects is, indeed, a discriminatory approach towards women and tends to violate some of their natural rights. Thus, they argue, it is best for women to participate in development with due consideration to their physical and spiritual needs (Motahhrai, 1995; Javadi Amoli, 1991; Baiat, 2002).

Men and women equally should endeavour to fulfil ideals through the advancement of knowledge, promotion of understanding, safeguarding of human integrity, enjoyment of the gifts of life, benefiting from individual and social freedoms and the creation of a better world to live in (Motahhrai, 1995). According to the Quran, women, like men, can make decisions and have wealth without having any need for other people (Quran 4:32).

In the Quran, there are two examples of independent women: Assieh, who could understand the truth even though the Fharao was her husband; and Luts' wife who, although the wife of the messenger, lived in humility.

The Quran considers it a good thing to look at previous generations and many prominent characters can be found in the Quran, each with special characteristics, for example: Mary, mentioned for her spiritual and moral high status; Belquis, for her high knowledge; Zoleikha, for her love and kindness, even if she made a mistake; Sarah, for accompanying her husband Abraham; Hadjar for her patience and resistance; and there was the constant presence of women in Moses' critical and crucial moments. Each is recognised as having special characteristics and different powers of understanding (Gorji, 2008).

One of the subjects raising different interpretations in various religions and even between different branches of Islam is that of covering and dressing modestly (i.e. hijab). Some Muslims see hijab as a symbol of identity, some as a symbol of honour, and some as repressive imposition. Choosing the way to practise hijab is not the same in all countries, for example in French schools, wearing hijab is banned, while having an Islamic dress code in public places is necessary in Iran (Benn, 2008). According to some passages of the Quran, for girls after puberty, and Muslim girls, it is recommended they be segregated from the opposite sex or cover all of their bodies except their hands and face (Quran 24:30–31, 33:59), yet there are other interpretations about veiling in different Islamic branches and countries.

Islamic practices and the lives of Muslims, including Muslim women, have been under scrutiny, especially since 11 September 2001. Many accusations have been made against Muslims, and all Muslims suffer in this process. Muslim women have been negatively portrayed or have been neglected in this process (Benn, 2008). Sometimes, there are misunderstandings by non-Muslims, when they either find Muslim women's dress threatening or believe Muslim women are oppressed and made subservient through it. But Muslim women who choose to wear hijab see it as carrying out the duties of the Islamic code of dressing. The media have particularly attacked Muslim women and their dress, and for the Muslim community, it is a logical step to defend their rights. For Muslim women, modesty is an important attribute. Muslims see modesty in terms of humility, a positive attribute that provides Muslim women with the freedom of obligation from conforming to Western styles and fashion and liberation from the male gaze (Zaman, 1997). However, Muslim females are not a homogeneous group and there are differences in how they choose to resolve religious and other cultural demands.

For example, some choose to adopt the hijab and Islamic dress, while others do not (Benn, 2008); and these differences can transmit to their daily lives, including their participation in sport and physical activity.

Islam and women in sport

The factors affecting Muslim women's participation in physical education and sport are complicated, but can be grouped into two types: barriers and facilitators which all women face (Muslim and non-Muslim) and restrictions related to religious or cultural beliefs. This chapter will address the second factor. Stodolska and Livengood (2006) indicated that the effects of Islam on leisure behaviour reveal the emphasis on strong family ties and on leisure with the family; supervising children to pass traditional moral values to subsequent generations; the requirement of modesty in dress, speech and everyday behaviour; as well as the restrictions from mixed-gender interactions, eating Halal food and avoiding alcohol. Despite the value of physical education and physical activity (Astrand *et al.*, 2003), there are various views in the world about Islamic attitudes towards women's sport. While according to some people, religion is a barrier for women's sport participation in the West (Balboul, 2000), research on the Quran and Islamic recommendations indicate that misinterpretations, culture and traditions are barriers to Muslim women's sport participation (Zaman, 1997). In the Quran, being physically fit and strong has been mentioned as one of the superior characteristics of some prophets or every human (Quran 2:247, 28:26); and the Quran makes references to health, instructing Muslims to take special care of their bodies (Walseth and Fasting, 2003).

There is evidence that the prophet Mohammad encouraged both his son and daughter to participate in physical activity; and he even participated in races with his wife Aishe, indicating that there were no differences in views of men and women participating in physical activity (Sfeir, 1985).

The prophet Mohammad himself prayed for God's protection against laziness and incompetence. He recommended physical activity and exercise and participation in horse-riding, swimming, archery, wrestling, running and mountaineering (Zaman, 1997). Islam has recommended exercise as part of a daily programme for Muslims. The prayers which are performed daily, at five different times, consist of synchronised body movements. The Quran says (77:22) bow down and prostrate yourselves and worship your Lord. During prayers, Muslims have to stand still, bow, kneel and prostrate. The movements are controlled and synchronised and exercise most of the large and small muscle groups in the body (Zaman, 1997). The daily prayers for Muslims can be considered as worshipping God by body and mind. Islam emphasises human body health as well as the spirit and mind; and in no part of the Quran has it been mentioned that men and women are different in being healthy or strong. Some current interpretations thus deserve to be reviewed.

Islam and physical education have some common features: control of the body, in time and space; in rituals and cleanliness; in dress; in the control of diet; and pursuit of a healthy body. However, both emphasise the nature of masculinity and femininity, and sport has been attributed to male domains, in which there has been an imbalance of power between the sexes (Benn, 1996). According to many researchers and scholars, Islam not only observes the same imbalance, but also supports participation of Muslim women in physical activity (Pfister, 2003). After studying Islamic sources and authorities, Daiman (1995) arrived at the conclusion that sport ought to be obligatory for women on health grounds. Walseth and Fasting (2003) found that some women, who most strongly emphasised that participating in sport activities was an obligation for them, were supporters of fundamentalist Islamic interpretations.

According to SalamIran (www.salamIran.org), the official website of the Iranian Embassy, sport plays an important role in women's lives because it helps them perform their maternal duty and nurture the new generation in the best manner, within the sphere of greater Islamic systems. The need for and importance of women's sport and physical education is quite obvious, because women account for around half of the population. Specific programmes should be prepared to promote physical health and sporting ability and to stimulate women's interest in sports (Women Sports Organization, 1998). It is an important interpretation of the role of women in terms of their duties as wives and mothers.

Experiences of Muslim women in sport

Several researchers have focused on Muslim women's participation in physical education and sport. Two separate studies found that Asian and Western European Muslims placed low value on physical education and sport (Fleming, 1994; De Knop *et al.*, 1996). In some countries, Muslim women have even encountered barriers to education (Jawad, 1998). Cultural practices of Islam and physical education may contradict each other, for example in dress codes for women, mixed/single-sex gymnasiums, attitudes towards the body related to privacy and modesty, Ramadan, swimming and dance activities. The Islamic requirements for modesty and privacy are not congruent with short skirts, shorts and T-shirts, public changing and showering situations. During the holy month of Ramadan, many Muslims fast from sunrise to sunset and it is difficult to participate in physical education and sporting activities. Swimming is sometimes problematic because of the mixed-sex, public nature of swimming pools. Some curriculum subjects like dance and music are not recommended by some Islamic groups (Benn, 1996; McDonald and Hayes, 2003) and dancing by women in front of men is not allowed, according to some Islamic recommendations (Stodolska and Livengood, 2006).

A study by Zaman (1997) of Muslim girls and young women from a school located in the East End of London indicated that, although for some Muslim girls 'physical education is a part of their religion, because in Islam looking after body is necessary for all Muslims and physical activity is the best way for taking care of body and health, so taking part in physical education is obeying Islam', some other girls 'believe no connection between Islamic faith and physical education, but state that if exercise is a part of Islam their try for physical activity will be more' (pp. 55–57). According to many Islamic scholars, holistic (mind, body and soul) health is a responsibility for every Muslim, and there is extensive guidance for maintaining well-being. Islam regards the human as a whole – spirit, mind and body. The human body is not perceived as a temple, but as a manifestation of respect and love for God, and it is the duty of all men and women to look after themselves (Zaman, 1997). In Walseth's study (2005), some Muslim women emphasised that the reason for participating in sport is the recommendation of Islam to maintain health. However, some women who restricted themselves within ethnic identities were not interested in sport. When one Pakistani woman was asked about going jogging, she answered that she is not the kind of woman who goes jogging and that it is suitable for young female Norwegians, not Pakistanis. In other examples, some young Pakistani women who participate in sport have often experienced being penalised by those who guard ethnic boundaries. It may be that participation in sport activities causes time out of the home and perceptions of women undertaking male-like behaviours (Walseth, 2005). This indicates the influence of culture rather than religion on sport participation.

Due to Muslim women's dress code, in many countries, their participation in sport at certain facilities is impossible or limited. In these countries, physical education may take place in mixed-sex environments and with short skirts or coverings which are not acceptable to the Islamic dress code (Benn, 2000). It has been observed that in England, young Muslim women can face particular problems for participation in physical education and sport because of their religion (Benn, 2002).

Carroll and Hollinshed (1993) tried to identify the influence of religious beliefs of Muslim girls on their experiences of physical education. Problems included inadequacy of clothing for physical education, truancy due to communal showers, participation in sporting activities during fasting month of Ramadan and coming home late (for daughters) from school after extracurricular activities at school. Sfeir (1985) expressed that Muslim women in the West can participate in a sport only within a secular context, and not as a Muslim.

In European countries, Muslim women may experience different problems related to participating in physical education and sport. A comparative study indicated that for British women, religious identity and consciousness of Islamic requirements were more obvious than for Greek women. Greeks encountered fewer problems with physical education and appeared more closely assimilated into the dominant culture (Dagkas and Benn, 2006).

Mixed-sex gymnasia have presented problems for some Muslim pupils. A study on immigrant Muslims in the United States indicated that Muslim parents do not allow their daughters to swim at public beaches and, for that reason, they have installed private pools at their homes (Stodolska and Livengood, 2006).

Palmer (2009) investigated the ways in which a group of young Muslim refugee women in Adelaide, South Australia, experienced playing in a soccer team as a way that both affirms and challenges many of the traditions of Islam. In this study, different veils of Muslim women indicated the different interpretation of Islam. It was crucial for Muslim women who wore hijab to play in a setting entirely away

from the male gaze. It was particularly problematic for them at the final Refugee
Week competition itself, when the men came to watch the young women compete. But some Muslims who did not wear hijab did not mind playing in such settings. In some cases, parental disapproval, rather than their own religious beliefs,
prohibited them from playing in such settings. Some of the players who played
with covering expressed anxiety at having to play and train in clothes that were
oppressively hot and restricted their movement. Such tensions between the perceived oppression of women and respect for the religious beliefs are common in
debates about Muslim women in the West. Many Westerners consider the action
of covering one's body to be oppressive, but, for many Muslim women, the hijab
protects their bodies and their 'moral safety' (Nakamura, 2002). We can consider
this as symbolic of Islamic and secular ideologies (Hargreaves, 2007).

Fasting during Ramadan can contradict participation in sport activities. Short-
age of energy and dehydration may limit capacity for physical activity and
swimming during fasting may not be allowed in case swimmers accidentally
swallow water. In a study by Dagkas and Benn (2006), one student said:

> Swimming during Ramadan . . . my father had to go to the school again to ask
> for me to be excluded. It was a struggle. I did think sometimes 'why am I bat-
> tling with them? They are going to think I am a troublemaker with a problem
> with everything' . . . but I am not like that, I just want to have what the others
> have, as well as being Muslim.

Some Greek students participated in physical education (but not swimming) during fasting and observed no complications, however, some girls did experience
difficulties. Some students also complained about a lack of knowledge among
their teachers about Islamic requirements for Muslim girls, while some students
admired their teachers for their understanding (Dagkas and Benn, 2006).

Considering the different levels of competition – recreational, national championships and international championships – dress code is one of the major problems facing Muslim women who want to participate in international competitions
(Hargreaves, 2000). Many Muslim women have been marginalised for their dress
(Henry et al., 2003). Yet different interpretations of Islamic requirements by
individuals and governments across the world mean that there are different
experiences of Muslim women in international competitions (Benn and Ahmad,
2009). In Morocco in 1984, a female gold medallist was heralded as triumphant
in Algeria, while in 1992 a female Olympic medallist received negative feedback
after returning home and was even exiled because she did not wear Islamic coverings for her competition (Hargreaves, 2000).

In higher level international competitions such as the Olympic Games, Muslim
women are invisible (Hargreaves, 1994). The Olympic Games and some other
international competitions are Westernised and require mixed-sex competition or
spectators, some with special dress codes that conflict with Islamic requirements.
For some women, observing their religious identity by observing their hijab
during sport participation is much more important than participating at high

levels of sport. There are, however, about 23 international sports federations that have accepted participation by Muslim women with Islamic dress, while others continue to exclude covered Muslim women in competitions.

Many women in countries such as Iran (before the Islamic Revolution) had to be represented in Western style and many Muslim girls could not participate in physical education or sport activities. In Iran, Islamic feminists have tried to increase opportunities for Muslim women to take part in sport in different ways. In the Islamic Republic of Iran, a cultural movement developed practices with cultural and Islamic characteristics, suitable for Muslim women. Women's competitions in the presence of men were stopped and gymnasia were sex segregated. To assist in progressing women in sport, a position was defined in government for women's sport management and for Muslim women's participation in international competitions, wherever possible, special clothes were designed.

In Iran, it was decided several years ago to call Muslim and later non-Muslim women together to a four-yearly competitive meeting that would enjoy an Islamic ambience, with the aim of setting standards for cultural and sport competition for Muslim women. This was a global event for all sports and at all levels of competition. This event was not at all meant to provide grounds to challenge other world or Olympic competitions, but rather to provide an organised women's sporting competition, while observing Islamic values. International events, including Islamic competitions for women, were organised by the Islamic Federation of Women's Sport (www.IFWS.org), which was founded on 21 October 1991. The Federation was supported by international organisations such as the International Olympic Committee (IOC), the Olympic Council of Asia (OAC) and cooperated with the Muslim Countries Federation (ICWSF, 2008).

Although the women's movement has caused improved opportunities for Muslim women's sport participation (David, 2005), according to Hargreaves it has resulted in the exclusion of Muslim women from international sport competitions because of their religious observances 'which is neglecting their human right'. It is challenging secular sport structures (2000).

A great step was taken in February 2008 regarding respect for Muslim women's dress code in sport. The International Association of Physical Education and Sport for Girls and Women (IAPESGW) organised an event at the Sultan Qaboos University in Oman, at which a declaration, 'Accept and Respect', was agreed to by 16 scholars from Europe, the Middle East and Far East countries, Bahrain, Bosnia and Herzegovina, Denmark, Egypt, Iran, Iraq, Malaysia, Morocco, Oman, South Africa, Syria, Turkey, United Arab Emirates and the United Kingdom. The declaration affirms the value of physical education and sport in the lives of all people, including Muslim women, supports Islamic recommendations for women's participation in sport and respect for Muslim dress codes by international sport federations and national governments (IAPESGW, 2008). The declaration has been presented in different places, including the IOC Women and Sport World Conference in Jordan, 2008; the International Convention on Science, Education and Medicine in Sport in China, 2008 and the IAPESGW Congress in South Africa, 2009.

Refugee Muslims encounter different problems in regard to participation in sport. Palmer (2005) has noted some of the practical issues such as transport and cost that frequently act as barriers to participation in sport for refugee communities in Australia, which increasingly includes groups from Muslim countries who have re-settled in the West.

Future directions

There is a variety of factors that inhibit Muslim women from taking part in physical education, physical activity and sport. All available documents indicate that Islam does not oppose Muslim women's participation in physical activity; but many misinterpretations, cultural interpretations, gymnasium situations and policies of international events act as barriers. The first step is to recognise these barriers, and to introduce genuine religious recommendations to overcome them. Challenging misinterpreted cultures about Muslim women's sport participation by informing families can be useful. The circumstances under which women's sports are practised internationally, or in many secular countries, can prevent Muslims taking part in many opportunities for physical activity or competition. There are many Muslim women who are prevented from taking part in world and Olympic events due to retaining Islamic cover. To increase participation of Muslim women in sport, Muslim values should be considered when organising sport facilities and competitions. The Accept and Respect Declaration recommends that international sports either try to modify available laws regarding women's sport dress codes, to embrace or respect Muslim dress codes, or consider holding events for women (e.g. swimming and gymnastics) with suitable dress. Training women as coaches and referees is also very important for developing Muslim female athletes, as is holding courses in single-sex contexts.

Prejudice and discrimination against Muslim women who have accepted Islamic dress (Dagkas and Benn, 2006) must be challenged. Favourable and informed views and attitudes about Islam can positively influence policy-makers and hence improve cooperation with Muslim women's sport. Muslim women's involvement and collaboration in sport's organisational decision-making can also be important, as can conducting scientific research to explore the special needs of all women, including Muslims, for participating in physical activity, physical education and sport.

References

Aboudeh, L. (1993). Post colonial feminism and the veil: thinking the difference. *Feminist Review, 43*, 26–37.

Allen, C. and Nielsen, J. (2002). *Summary report on islamophobia in the EU after 11 September 2001*. Commissioned by the European Monitoring Centre on Racism and Xenophobia (EUMC). University of Birmingham, Centre for the Study of Islam and Christian-Muslim Relations.

Astrand, P. O., Rodahl, K., Dahl, H. A. and Stromme, S. B. (2003). *Textbook of work physiology: physiological bases of exercise*. Canada: Human Kinetics.

Baiat, A. (2002). *Culture of terms (Persian)*. Tehran: Andishe.

Balboul, L. (2000). Sporting females in Egypt: veiling or unveiling – an analysis of the debate. In S. Scraton and B. Watson (Eds), *Sport, leisure identities and gendered spaces*, Vol. 67 (pp. 74–85). Eastbourne: LSA Publication.

Benn, T. (1996). Muslim women and physical education in initial teacher training. *Sport, Education and Society, 1*(1), 5–21.

Benn, T. (2000). Towards inclusion in education and physical education. In A. Williams (Ed.), *Primary school physical education: research into practice* (pp. 118–135). London: Routledge.

Benn, T. (2002). Muslim women in teacher training: issues of gender, 'race' and religion. In D. Penney (Ed.), *Gender and physical education* (pp. 57–79). London: Routledge.

Benn, T. (2008). Evidence and influence, making a difference for girls and women in physical education and sport. *International Convention on Science Education and Medicine in Sport* (p. 313). Guangzhou, China.

Benn, T. and Ahmad, A. (2009). *Alternative visions: international sporting opportunities for Muslim women and implications for British sport youth*. London: Routledge.

Blair, S. N., Clark, D. G., Cureton, K. J. and Powel, K. E. (1989). Exercise and fitness in childhood: implications for a lifetime of health. In C. V. Gisolfi and D. R. Lamb (Eds), *Perspectives in exercise science and sports medicine, vol 2, exercise and sport* (pp. 401–430). New York: McGraw-Hill.

Carroll, B. and Hollinshed, G. (1993). Ethnicity and conflict in physical education. *British Educational Research Journal, 19*(1), 59–76.

Clarke, G. and Humber, S. B. (1997). *Researching women and sport*. Chippenham: Antony Rowe Ltd.

Dagkas, S. and Benn, T. (2006). Young Muslim women's experiences of Islam and physical education in Greece and Britain: a comparative study. *Sport, Education and Society, 11*(1), 21–38.

Daiman, S. (1995). Women in sport in Islam. *ICHPER SD Journal, 32*(1),18–21.

David, P. (2005). *Human rights in youth sport: a critical review of childrens rights in competitive sports*. London: Routledge.

De Knop, P., Theeboom, M., Wittock, H. and De Martelaer, K. (1996). Implications of Islam on Muslim girls sport participation in western Europe. *Sport, Education and Society, 1*(2), 147–164.

Fleming, S. (1994). Sport and South Asian youth: the perils of false universalism and stereotyping. *Leisure Studies, 13*(4), 1–20.

Gorji, M. (2008). *The holy Quran attitudes towards women's presence in the history of prophets (Persian)*. Tehran: Alhoda International Publication and Distribution and Institute for Women Studies and Research.

Hanifa, S. (1974). *What every Muslim should know about Islam*. Lahore press, Lahore.

Hargreaves, J. (1994). *Sporting females: critical issues in the history and sociology of women's sport*. London: Routledge.

Hargreaves, J. (2000). The Muslim female heroic: shorts or veils? In J. Hargreaves, *Heroines of sport: the politics of difference and identity* (pp. 46–77). London: Routlege.

Hargreaves, J. (2007). Sport, exercise and the female Muslim body: negotiating Islam, politics and male power. In J. Hargreaves and P. Vertinsky (Eds), *Physical culture, power and the body* (pp. 74–100). London: Routledge.

Henry, I., Amara, M. and Altauqi, M. (2003). Sport, Arab nationalism and the pan-Arab games. *International Review for the Sociology of Sport, 38*(3), 295–310.

Hjaerpe, J. (1983). *Politisk Islam, studier i muslimsk fundamentalisme*. Alvsjo: Skeab Forlag.

Howard, M. C. (1986). *Contemporary cultural anthropology*. Boston: Little, Brown and Company.

IAPESGW (2008). *Accept and respect.* Retrieved 4 January 2011, www.vagacms.co.uk/content/showcontent.aspx?contentid=1460.

Islamic Countries Women Sport Federation (ICWSF) (2008). Retrieved from http://www.IFWS.org

Javadi Amoli, M. (1991). *Women in Islam (Persian).* Tehran: Rajaea Press.

Jawad, H. (1998). *The rights of women in Islam.* London: Macmillan.

Lucas, M. D. and Block, M. E. (2008). What adapted physical education teachers should know about Islam. *Palaestra, 24*(2).

Macdonald, D. and Kirk, D. (1999). Pedagogy, the body and Christian identity. *Sport, Education and Society, 4*(2), 131–142.

McDonald, I. and Hayes, S. (2003). 'Race', racism and education: racial stereotypes in physical education and school sport. In S. Hayes and G. Stidder (Eds), *Equity and inclusion in physical education and sport* (pp. 153–168). London: Routledge.

Motahhrai, M. (1995). *Women's rights in Islam (Persian).* Tehran: Iran Publisher.

Nakamura, Y. (2002). Beyond the hijab: female Muslims and physical activity. *Women in Sport & Physical Activity, 11*(1), 21–48.

Nasr, S. H. (1966). Sunnism and Shiism. In S. Nasr (Ed.), *Ideals and realities of Islam* (chapter 15). London: George Allen and Unwin Ltd.

Palmer, C. (September 2005). *A world of fine difference: sport and newly arrived young refugee women in Adelaide, South Australia.* Paper presented to Department of Gender Studies, University of Otago, Dunedin, New Zealand.

Palmer, C. (2009). Soccer and the politics of identity for young Muslim refugee women in South Australia. *Soccer & Society, 10*(1), 27–38.

Pfister, G. (2003). Women and sport in Iran: keeping goal in hijab. In T. Hartman and G. Pfister (Eds), *Sport and women: social issues in international perspectives* (pp. 207–223). London: Routledge.

ReligiousTolerance.org (2003). *Islam, the second largest religion . . . and growing.* Retrieved 3 September 2003, www.religioustolerance.org/islam.htm.

Sallis, J., McKenzie, T., Alcaraz, J., Kolody, B., Faucette, N. and Hovell, M. (1997). The effects of a 2-year physical education (APARK) programme on physical activity and fitness of elementary school children. *Amerian Journal of Public Health, 87*, 1328–1334.

Sfeir, L. (1985). The staus of Muslim women in sport: conflict between cultural tradition and modernization. *International Review for the Sociology of Sport, 30*, 283–306.

Shakir, M. (2005). *Translation of the glorious Quran.* Qum: Ansarian Publisher.

Spilka, B., Hood, R. W., Hunsberger, B. and Gorstich, R. (2003). *The psychology of religion.* New York: The Guilford Press.

Stodolska, M. and Livengood, J. S. (2006). The influence of religion on the leisure behaviour of immigrant Muslims in the United States. *Journal of Leisure Research, 38*(3), 293–320.

Vogt, K. (1995). *Islams hus, verdensreligion pa fremmarsj.* Oslo: Cappelens Forlag.

Walseth, K. (2005). Young Muslim women and sport: the impact of identity work. *Leisure Studies, 25*(1), 75–94.

Walseth, K. and Fasting, K. (2003). Islam's view on physical activity and sport. *International Review for the Sociology of Sport, 38*(1), 45–60.

Women Sports Organization (WSO) (1998). *The embassy of Islamic Republic of Iran, Ottawa.* Retrieved from www.Salamiran.org/women/organizations/wso.html.

Zaman, H. (1997). Islam, well being and physical activity: perceptions of Muslim young women. In C. Clarke and B. Humberstone (Eds), *Researching women and sport* (pp. 50–65). London: Macmillan.

9 Engagement of people with disabilities in sport across the life span

Howard L. Nixon II

Introduction

This chapter focuses on the engagement of people with disabilities in sport across the life span. The relatively limited mainstream media coverage of persons with disabilities in sports, the relatively limited involvement of persons with disabilities in community sports programmes and the belief that disability typically implies poor health and an inability to engage in vigorous physical activity might seem to minimise the relevance or significance of examining people with disabilities in sport. However, statistics about the incidence of disability in populations around the world and facts about the capabilities of people with disabilities constitute a strong argument for considering persons with disabilities in a general examination of engagement in sport and physical activity across the life span. According to the United Nations (2009), persons with disabilities are the world's largest minority, with approximately 10 per cent of the world's population living with a disability and with relatively more people with disabilities being poor and living in poorer countries. According to a review of data from the 2008 United States (US) American Community Survey (Brault, 2009), it was conservatively estimated that nearly 13 per cent of the civilian non-institutionalised population five years old and older in the US had a disability. Disability rates in this population increased with age, ranging from 5.2 per cent for those 5–17 years old to 38.1 per cent for those 65 years old and older. Being disabled implies having some limitations, but these limitations do not necessarily prevent people from engaging in sports and other vigorous physical activities.

Even among un-athletic children and young adolescents, participation in some type of sport is a common experience of childhood and adolescence in the US and other countries. For example, according to one estimate, approximately 40 million boys and girls between the ages of five and 18 participate in some type of organised sport (Nixon, 2008, p. 186). While there is a precipitous decline in organised sports participation in the US as able-bodied youths progress through adolescence and into adulthood (Nixon, 2008, pp. 211–212), there is no evidence that sports participation is a common experience for people with disabilities at any age. The purpose of this chapter is to look at the engagement of people with disabilities in sport across the life span by focusing on the types of contexts in which people with disabilities participate in sport; the general patterns of sports participation for people with disabilities across the life span; major factors explaining the participation or non-participation of people with disabilities in sport; reasons why they participate or do not participate in sport; and why it might be important to make sports opportunities available for people with disabilities. Our focus here will be limited to organised and competitive sports participation because it is beyond the scope of this chapter to try to cover the broader topic of participation in physical activity in general. The discussion will emphasise social and cultural factors, reflecting my background as a sociologist (see Nixon, 2000, 2006).

Definitions

We will begin the discussion with some important definitions. Although they are sometimes used interchangeably, distinguishing among the terms 'impairment', 'disability' and 'handicap' allows us to gain valuable sociological insights about the experiences of people with disabilities in society and sport (see Nixon, 2000). I will define an *impairment* as a biomedical condition that underlies a disability or handicap, and the various types of impairments include physical, organic, sensory, intellectual, mental, emotional, learning and speech conditions. An impairment may be due to a disease, defective gene, accident or injury. A *disability* exists when an impairment limits a person's ability to use certain skills, perform certain tasks, or participate in certain activities or roles. When we refer to a person's level of disability, we are usually referring to some restriction in their functional ability to carry out the routine tasks or activities of everyday life. People with a particular impairment may be disabled to differing extents as a result of different levels of motivation and compensatory abilities and the extent to which roles, tasks, activities and interaction settings are structured to accommodate or compensate for the impairment. For example, the visual disability of a wrestler who is blind is substantially minimised by a rule that requires physical contact between wrestlers during the entire match. Thus, disability is situational, and how much a person is disabled depends on how a role, interaction or situation is organised and how much it requires abilities or skills a person does not possess. When I refer to participants with disabilities, I am referring to people who are impaired and can be classified in terms of a 'permanent disability' of some sort in their everyday lives. People with disabilities may be involved in sports with tasks or interaction requirements that are *matched* or *mismatched* with their type or level of athletic interest, motivation, ability and performance skills (Nixon, 2007). Mismatching in settings without any accommodations is a reason why people with disabilities may become frustrated by a particular sport, or sports in general, or why other people might see them as generally incapable of organised sports participation.

A *handicap* reflects a social process of relegating a person to an inferior status on the arbitrary basis of being impaired or disabled. Along with experiencing a diminished status as a result of being impaired or disabled, a person who is handicapped will become a discredited person with a 'spoiled identity', and in this sense, being handicapped also implies being *stigmatised* (Goffman, 1963). The negative stereotypes or labels and discriminatory treatment experienced by people with impairments and disabilities, merely because they are impaired or disabled, are defining elements of the societal process of *handicapism*, which is like sexism and racism. Like sexism and racism, it reflects basic inequalities in society and is unfair because it is arbitrary and biased. In our consideration of the reasons for the sports participation patterns of people with disabilities, we will gain a clearer idea of how handicapism has influenced these patterns. In the next section, we will consider the types of contexts in which people with disabilities have participated in sport.

Contexts of sports participation

When people with disabilities participate in organised and competitive sports, they generally participate in *disability sports*. These sports are organised for people with disabilities and usually are separate or segregated from the mainstream of society. Wheelchair sports are among the most popular and researched disability sports and have various forms, including basketball, track and field, road racing, tennis and even football. Events are organised in these and other disability sports at the local, state, national and international levels. In the case of marathons, a wheelchair competition is embedded into the larger event, with wheelchair athletes competing against each other. There is also the Paralympic Games, sponsored by the International Paralympic Committee, whereby athletes with differing disabilities compete in a variety of events every four years.

Disability sports can be contrasted with *able-bodied* or *mainstream sports*, which are organised for people without disabilities. It is unusual to see athletes with disabilities compete against able-bodied athletes in mainstream sports and even more unusual to see able-bodied athletes in disability sports. *Integrated sports* include athletes with and without disabilities competing against each other and they occur less often as sports become more competitive. *Segregated sports* involve only able-bodied participants or only participants with disabilities. Over the past decade, the concept of '*inclusion*' has gained increasing attention in the literature about sport and disability (e.g. Fay *et al.*, 2000; Legg and Steadward, 2002; Wolff and Hums, 2003). It refers to situations where people with disabilities are involved, accepted and respected at all levels of the sports competition or organisation and it implies that people with disabilities can participate in a sport without being handicapped. I assume that eligibility or classification systems that *match* the characteristics of people with the requirements of particular sports promote inclusion. *Fairness* exists for people with disabilities when they have an equivalent range of choices as their able-bodied counterparts to pursue sports opportunities that match their motivation, interest, abilities and skills.

Sports participation patterns for people with disabilities

Evidence of national patterns of sports participation for people with disabilities is scarce. In the US, the Harris Interactive polling organisation recently conducted a study of sports and employment patterns for American adults aged 18 and older (Krane and Orkis, 2009). It included data from a cross-section of 704 adults with disabilities and from samples of approximately 200 participants in Disabled Sports USA and 200 military service members who were disabled and involved in the Wounded Warriors sports rehabilitation programmes sponsored by Disabled Sports USA. The Harris data revealed that about 22 per cent of those in their general sample of adults with disabilities reported they were currently participating in a sport *or* physical activity *or* exercise more than four times a month (Krane and Orkis, 2009). These data suggest a fairly low rate of regular participation specifically in sports.

No recent data about sports participation of young people with disabilities in the US exist, but we can assume that recent groundbreaking legal battles in states such as Maryland to gain equitable access to physical education and interscholastic athletics for students with disabilities (see Lakowski, 2008) reflect patterns of limited opportunity and participation for students with disabilities. In Maryland, a prominent case that helped propel the passage of the 2008 *Maryland Fitness and Athletics Equity for Students with Disabilities Act* involved a high school student and Paralympic wheelchair athlete, Tatyana McFadden, who went to court to be able to compete alongside her able-bodied team mates in interscholastic track meets for Atholton High School in Howard County, Maryland. She had faced resistance from school and athletic officials in her school district. As in the case of the struggle to achieve gender equity in sport, efforts to achieve equity for students with disabilities clearly imply the existence of significant opportunity and participation gaps between students with and without disabilities. Existing evidence does not permit a precise estimate of the size of these gaps, but evidence from studies commissioned by Sport England (2002) validates the existence of a participation gap for adults as well as youths in England. Since the British government plays a more active role than the US government in organising sports for its citizens, it is likely that the participation gap in the US will be at least as large as it is in England.

Sport England is a government agency responsible for developing and promoting community sports programmes in that country. A study conducted in 2000–2001 focused on people aged 16–59, disability and participation in physical activity and sport (Sport England, 2002). Another study was conducted in 2000 and focused on disability and sport patterns for young people aged 6–16 in England and Scotland (Sport England, 2001). This latter research was combined with a similar study in 1999 of the general population of English students aged 6–16.

In the Sport England studies, 'sport' was defined broadly to include competitive and non-competitive physical activities rather than just organised competitive sports, which means that the general participation statistics overestimated the participation rates in organised competitive sports. We need to be careful in making global generalisations from surveys from one or two countries, however, the Sport England data documents patterns that are often assumed about sports participation of people with disabilities. First, the data reveal low rates of participation in organised and competitive sports programmes for people with disabilities. Second, the data show that involvement in sport and physical activity is substantially less in all age groups for people with disabilities than for their non-disabled counterparts. Third, the data indicate that among adults with disabilities, sports participation is less for women, minorities and the less affluent.

The adult Sport England (2002) study also showed that, in general, adults with disabilities rarely participated in more than three physical activities or sports and having more disabilities decreased the number of activities in which these people participated. Participation rates were higher for males with disabilities than for their female counterparts and sports participation rates steadily declined with age. Among people with disabilities, participation rates were also significantly higher for professionals than for unskilled and skilled blue-collar workers and for whites than for members of other racial and ethnic groups, such as blacks, Indians and Pakistanis. Less than 1 per cent of the people with disabilities in this survey were members of a sports club for people with a disability and among those who had participated in a physical activity in the previous four weeks, 12 per cent had competed in that activity in the previous 12 months.

Major findings of the youth survey (Sport England, 2001) were significant gaps in participation rates between young people with disabilities and the general population of students in various sports contexts, including formally organised or informal after-school sports activities, extracurricular sports organised by the school, and sports club activities not organised by schools. Perhaps reflecting a greater emphasis on gender equity in sports for the younger generation, there was no gender difference in participation rates for students with disabilities in extracurricular school sports. Paralleling a pattern in the general population, older students (11–16 years old) with disabilities were more likely than their younger counterparts (6–10 years old) to participate in extracurricular sports organised by the school. Fewer students with disabilities than students in general enjoyed being involved in sport and exercise in their leisure time.

While participation rates are relatively low for people with disabilities of all ages and from all types of backgrounds, those who participate in organised sports in the US are most likely to be involved in these activities in segregated programmes organised for people with disabilities. The relative prevalence of this type of segregated sports participation is reflected in the predominant emphasis in sport and disability research on athletes in disability sports. The Harris poll (Krane and Orkis, 2009) showed that adults in the US with disabilities were aware of the existence of many organisations that sponsored sports for people with disabilities, with Special Olympics the best known, recognised by 86 per cent of the sample. Others such as Wheelchair Sports USA and US Paralympics were recognised by more than 25 per cent of this population, but relatively few people (11 per cent or less) were aware of most of the other disability sport organisations. Disabled Sports USA, which sponsored the Harris poll, was established by disabled Vietnam War veterans to provide a variety of sports rehabilitation programmes for veterans injured in war. Although this organisation has a network of regional chapters across the nation, it was recognised by only 7 per cent of the sample of adults with disabilities. It is encouraging that many organisations have emerged over the past several decades to provide sports opportunities for people with disabilities and that a few have significant name recognition, but it is also true that many people with disabilities are unaware of most of these disability sport organisations.

Despite limited public awareness, some disability sport organisations are achieving impressive progress in expanding sports involvement and skills of people with disabilities. An example is the National Ability Center in Utah, which has pursued a mission of developing 'ability through integration, public awareness, and education' by offering sports training opportunities in integrated and adapted settings (see www.discovernac.org). Its emphasis is on mixing people with and without disabilities in an environment where ability is emphasised. Over the first 20 years of its existence, between 1986 and 2006, the number of athletes with disabilities that it trained increased from less than 50 to over 10,000 (http://usa.usembassy.de/sports-numbers.htm). Although its numbers are still relatively small, its rate of growth is impressive and suggests that well organised programmes can increase sports involvement and skills of people with disabilities. The success of these kinds of organisations can be at least partially explained by their effectiveness in building partnerships with disability and mainstream sport organisations, schools and government agencies. The National Ability Center, for example, has partnerships with the Paralympics, Disability Sport USA and the Federal Americorps volunteer programme. Its programmes provide a model for those interested in inclusion. In the next section, we will consider the factors affecting whether or not and how people with disabilities become involved in sport.

Explaining sports participation patterns for people with disabilities

During the school years, families and schools often discourage children and youths with disabilities from having a serious interest or any interest in active formal or informal sports participation. Parents worry, and even when they encourage their child's involvement in sports, they face many obstacles that handicap their child, including ignorance, insensitivity, resistance and a lack of appropriate accommodations (Nixon, 1988). A study of elite female wheelchair athletes found that people who might be expected to encourage sports involvement, such as physical education teachers, often do not, as a result of their lack of awareness and inadequate training (Ruddell and Shinew, 2006). These elite athletes eventually developed relationships with peers and coaches in wheelchair sports, which encouraged their own participation, but they were frustrated that they were not exposed to the sport earlier and that the opportunity to participate was not advertised to more people who might be interested.

Parents of children with disabilities are often most comfortable with sports that are organised to be unthreatening and over which they have some control (Castaneda and Sherrill, 1999). Parents may find that as their child gets older, the social and functional differences between their child who is disabled and non-disabled peers are, or appear, greater. As a result, they may become less concerned about pushing their child into integrated community sports programmes as they get older. For example, a study in Hong Kong of parents of children with intellectual disabilities who were looking for sports opportunities for their children initially wanted their children to be involved in integrated sports (Tsai and Fung, 2009). However, as a result of rejection by staff members and participants, they soon gave up their quest. Parents were more successful in finding integrated opportunities when they found supportive and trained staff and their children had more social skills. The Special Olympics has appealed to parents of children with developmental or intellectual disabilities because this organisation has a well-established reputation for providing a wide range of appropriate sports opportunities within a supportive social network and for encouraging parental involvement in various types of volunteer roles (Goodwin *et al.*, 2006). It appears that once an individual becomes involved in Special Olympics, the involvement is likely to continue. A recent national survey of Special Olympics participants in the US revealed that they had participated for an average of 11 years and 73 per cent had been involved for six years or more (Harada and Siperstein, 2009).

People with disabilities are handicapped in their access to sport because key people in their social networks, such as parents, physical educators, rehabilitation specialists, sports organisers, coaches, teachers and even friends, underestimate their sports abilities and interest and place little value on finding out about relevant sports opportunities. In addition, factors that limit sports opportunities in the general population, such as low socioeconomic status and inadequate funding of school and community recreational programmes, further restrict access to sport for people with disabilities (Crawford and Stodolska, 2008). Girls and women also face the 'dual disability' in sport of being female and being disabled in a world that has been organised to favour males and able-bodied people (Anderson *et al.*, 2008). The obstacles to sports participation for people with disabilities tend to be highest when these activities are in the mainstream and involve able-bodied athletes, are intensely competitive and are viewed seriously in society (Nixon, 2007).

While the mass media have historically paid very little attention to sports participants with disabilities, elite disability sports events such as the Paralympics have received more mainstream media coverage in recent years. This coverage, however, has not yet been 'normalised' with the same amount of critical analysis we expect to see in coverage of big-time mainstream sport (Howe, 2008). The mainstream media may be cautious about such criticism for fear of being labelled insensitive and elite disability sports organisers may want to 'manage' media coverage to try to assure favourable reactions from the public and commercial sponsors. Athletes with disabilities may be most encouraged by the specialised disability sport media (see Ruddell and Shinew, 2006), but limited circulation restricts the reach of these media to people who might be interested in them.

The mass media can create role models that encourage people to participate in sport. However, there has been some controversy about the images of elite athletes with disabilities that the mainstream media tend to portray (Hardin and Hardin, 2003; Berger, 2008). The idea that these athletes are superheroes or 'supercrips' with superhuman motivation, perseverance and ability sets them apart from ordinary people with disabilities in ways that could make success in sport seem unattainable for the average person with a disability. In general, the mass media tend to idealise the bodies of star athletes, which is a problem for elite athletes with disabilities as well as for more ordinary people with disabilities who might be interested in sport. As a number of scholars have noted (e.g. DePauw, 1997; Berger, 2008), the impaired or disabled body tends to conflict with idealised images of the athletic body. The challenge for people with disabilities is to find or create structures for physical activity and sport that minimise issues about the body that participants should have and instead emphasise the capabilities and achievements of the bodies that the participants actually have. The importance of meeting this challenge should be evident in the next section, which will consider benefits of sports participation for people with disabilities.

Benefits of sports participation for people with disabilities

With all of the attention in the media about obesity and health problems related to inactivity, it is obvious that being physically active in sports could have health benefits for people with disabilities, as long as participants do not push their bodies too hard and get injured or risk their health with drugs and other performance-enhancing substances (Nixon, 2000). The International Paralympic Committee (www.paralympic.org) has argued that organised sport is important for people with disabilities because it promotes their health by increasing body and health awareness, by helping to control weight and by increasing mobility through physical fitness. It has also been proposed that participation in organised sports teams can be the basis for positive interactions with teachers, coaches and peers, which may challenge negative and handicapping stereotypes and contribute to a more positive self-image (Blauwet, 2005). The Harris poll (Krane and Orkis, 2009) cited earlier found that adults with disabilities involved in Disabled Sports USA programmes were more likely than adults with disabilities in general to report that they were physically active, in very good or excellent health, employed, and satisfied with life and that they enjoyed socialising and had a strong support network. Taken together, these findings suggest that participation in organised sports sponsored by disability sport organisations contributes to a better quality of life for people with disabilities (Giacobbi *et al.*, 2008). Furthermore, to the extent that organised sports participation increases the employability and employment of adults with disabilities, it improves the economy and tax base of communities and nations by making these people less dependent on government assistance and more able to be economically productive. These economic generalisations are likely to be most valid in communities and nations that are less economically developed (Blauwet, 2005).

The survey of Special Olympians and their families showed that subjects recognised the benefits of involvement in disability sport organisation programmes, such as the Special Olympics (Harada and Siperstein, 2009). For example, the athletes and their families referred to the fun, friendship, challenge, sense of competence, achievement, respect, and health and fitness benefits that the athletes gained from involvement in the Special Olympics. A few Special Olympians had dropped out because they wanted to avoid negative stereotypes or perceptions of being 'different' as participants in a segregated sports setting, but other research has shown that athletes with disabilities like participating in disability sport because it gives them a chance to compete and interact with other people who understand what it means to be an athlete with a disability. For example, a study of a small group of national level wheelchair rugby players (Goodwin *et al.*, 2009) showed that these athletes gained a positive identity, a feeling of independence and a shared emotional connection to other athletes in their sport.

Even though these elite wheelchair athletes could be seen as 'supercrips' who defied societal stereotypes, they were more interested in talking to researchers about the benefits of community and self-confidence they gained from their sports participation than about how they were defying handicapism by excelling at their sport. The documentary film *Murderball*, which brought full-contact quadriplegic wheelchair rugby into the public eye, conveyed a message similar to Goodwin *et al.*'s (2009) research results. The athletes in the film competed at the international level. They expressed pride in their accomplishments but also a desire to be treated as ordinary people. Although they did not want to be treated as 'supercrips', they expected to be respected as elite athletes, just as elite able-bodied athletes are.

Conclusion

The idea that people with disabilities are likely to benefit most from sports participation that matches their sport interests, motivation, ability and skills is not really a new insight, since it applies to able-bodied sports participants as well as to participants with disabilities. We have seen that there are many types of sports that people with disabilities could pursue in integrated or segregated settings and many different ways that those sports could accommodate people with disabilities (Nixon, 2007), from relatively casual competition where participation is open to all kinds of people with and without disabilities and where everyone is treated as a winner, to intensely competitive and elite settings where winning is paramount to the competitors. One size definitely does not fit all. Like their non-disabled counterparts, people with disabilities have a wide range of sports interests, motivation and abilities, which may vary according to their type and severity of impairment, their disability history and the types of people and experiences that have influenced their desire to participate in physical activity and sport. Fairness implies that people with disabilities have the same range of choices that able-bodied people have.

In trying to maximise the number, diversity and quality of sports opportunities for people with disabilities across the life span, it is especially important to remove the structural, cultural, situational, interpersonal and personal barriers that limit their choices and discourage participation. People with disabilities will not become interested in sport or be able to benefit from these activities throughout their lives unless people generally realise that being physically active and even competitive in sports is as beneficial to people with disabilities as it is to non-disabled people. When people with disabilities have access to appropriate sports that match their interests, motivation, ability and skills, the evidence indicates that they will generally enjoy them and that this enjoyment is a strong predictor of their desire to stay involved (Martin, 2006).

In future research, we need to expand the scope of our knowledge about sport and disability around the world. More specifically, we need to increase our understanding of the obstacles to sports participation across the life span for people with disabilities and of the ways people have been able to organise sports for males and females with disabilities of varying ages and social backgrounds to match their interests, motivation and abilities and enable them to develop their skills, be respected and have fun. Important applied research is needed to show how sports of various types can be made more accessible in schools and in the community for people with disabilities. This research could also shed light on broader access issues for other people of minority or disadvantaged status, who have also been handicapped in sport as a result of their status.

References

Anderson, D. M., Wozencroft, A. and Bedini, L. A. (2008). Adolescent girls' involvement in disability sport: a comparison of social support mechanisms. *Journal of Leisure Research*, *10*, 183–207.

Berger, R. J. (2008). Disability and the dedicated wheelchair athlete: beyond the 'supercrip' critique. *Journal of Contemporary Ethnography*, *37*, 647–678.

Blauwet, C. (2005). Promoting the health and human rights of individuals with a disability through the Paralympic Movement. Bonn, Germany: International Paralympic Committee. Retrieved 29 May 2009, from www.paralympic.org/release/Main_Sections_Menu/Development/Development_Programmemes/Symposium.

Brault, M. W. (2009). Review of changes to the measurement of disability in the 2008 American Community Survey. U.S Census Bureau. Retrieved 22 November 2009, from www.census.gov/hhes/www/disability/2008ACS_disability.pdf.

Castaneda, L. and Sherrill, C. (1999). Family participation in Challenger Baseball: critical theory perspective. *Adapted Physical Activity Quarterly*, *16*, 372–388.

Crawford, J. L. and Stodolska, M. (2008). Constraints experienced by elite athletes with disabilities in Kenya, with implications for the development of a new hierarchical model of constraints at the societal level. *Journal of Leisure Research*, *40*, 128–155.

DePauw, K. P. (1997). The (in)visibility of DisAbility: cultural contexts and sporting bodies. *Quest*, *49*, 416–430.

Fay, T. G., Hums, M. A. and Wolff, E. A. (2000). Inclusion of sport for athletes with disabilities into non-disabled sport organizations: a comparative analysis of three case studies. Presented at the Annual Meeting of the North American Society for Sport Management, June, Colorado Springs, CO.

Giacobbi, P. R., Stancil, M., Hardin, B. and Bryant, L. (2008). Physical activity and quality of life experienced by highly active individuals with physical disabilities. *Adapted Physical Activity Quarterly*, *25*, 189–207.

Goffman, E. (1963). *Stigma: notes on the management of spoiled identity*. Englewood Cliffs: Prentice Hall.

Goodwin, D. L., Fitzpatrick, D. A., Thurmeier, R. and Hall, C. (2006). The decision to join Special Olympics: parents' perspectives. *Adapted Physical Activity Quarterly*, *23*, 163–183.

Goodwin, D., Johnston, K., Gustafson, P., Elliott, M., Thurmeier, R. and Kuttai, H. (2009).

It's okay to be a quad: wheelchair rugby players' sense of community. *Adapted Physical Activity Quarterly*, *26*, 102–117.

Harada, C. M. and Siperstein, G. N. (2009). The sport experience of athletes with intellectual disabilities: a national survey of Special Olympics athletes and their families. *Adapted Physical Activity Quarterly*, *26*, 68–85.

Hardin, B. and Hardin, M. (2003). Conformity and conflict: wheelchair athletes discuss sport media. *Adapted Physical Activity Quarterly*, *20*, 246–259.

Howe, P. D. (2008). From inside the newsroom: paralympic media and the 'production' of elite disability. *International Review for the Sociology of Sport*, *43*, 135–150.

Krane, D. and Orkis, K. (2009). Sports and employment among Americans with disabilities. Harris Interactive. Retrieved 28 May 2009, from www.harrisinteractive.com.

Lakowski, T. (2008). Victory! Maryland blazes the trail for students with disabilities. East Meadow, NY: Women's Sports Foundation. Retrieved 29 May 2009, from http://womanssportsfoundation.org.

Legg, D. F. H. and Steadward, R. D. (2002). Inclusion of athletes with disability within sport. *International Council for Sport Science and Physical Education Bulletin No. 35*.

Martin, J. J. (2006). Psychosocial aspects of youth disability sport. *Adapted Physical Activity Quarterly*, *23*, 65–77.

Nixon II, H. L. (1988). Getting over the worry hurdle: parental encouragement and the sports involvement of visually impaired children and youths. *Adapted Physical Activity Quarterly*, *5*, 29–43.

Nixon II, H. L. (2000). Sport and disability. In J. Coakley and E. Dunning (Eds), *Handbook of sports studies* (pp. 422–438). London: Sage Publications.

Nixon II, H. L. (2006). Disability sport. In G. Ritzer (Ed.), *Encyclopedia of sociology* (pp. 1171–1174). Oxford: Blackwell Publishing Ltd.

Nixon II, H. L. (2007). Constructing diverse sports opportunities for people with disabilities. *Journal of Sport & Social Issues*, *31*, 417–433.

Nixon II, H. L. (2008). *Sport in a changing world*. Boulder: Paradigm Publishers.

Ruddell, J. L. and Shinew, K. J. (2006). The socialization process for women with disabilities: the impact of agents and agencies in the introduction to an elite sport. *Journal of Leisure Research*, *38*, 421–444.

Sport England (2001). *Disability survey 2000: young people with a disability in sport*. London: Sport England. Retrieved 29 May 2009, from www.sportengland.org.

Sport England (2002). *Adults with a disability and sport: national survey 2000–2001*. London: Sport England Information Centre. Ref. no. 2161. Retrieved 29 May 2009, from www.sportengland.org.

Tsai, E. H-L. and Fung, L. (2009). Parents' experiences and decisions on inclusive sports participation of their children with intellectual disabilities. *Adapted Physical Activity Quarterly*, *26*, 151–171.

United Nations (2009). Persons with disabilities. Retrieved 22 November 2009, from www.un.org/en/globalissues/disabilities/index.shtml.

Wolff, E. A. and Hums, M. A. (2003). Sport without disability: understanding the exclusion of athletes with a disability. Presented at the Annual Conference of the North American Society for the Sociology of Sport, November, Montreal, Canada.

Part IV

Sport and physical activity during older adulthood

10 Psycho-social perspectives on the motivation and commitment of Masters athletes

Bradley W. Young

Introduction

'Masters' athletes are individuals who participate in organised sport, usually beginning at 35 years of age, with participants older than 55 referred to as 'Seniors'. Masters sport is distinguished from exercise because it is rule-governed and has varying degrees of inherent competition. Some Masters appreciate being referred to as 'athletes' whereas others are reluctant to be labelled as such, however, they all typically acknowledge that they engage in practice or training to prepare themselves for a sport event. Events usually require formal registration of some type to jamborees, tournaments or adult leagues which may be inclusive and recreationally competitive on a local level. Participants may register for inclusive yet incrementally more competitive events such as Masters or Seniors *Games* that occur at regional, national or international levels. Finally, there are a host of *Championships* that occur from local to international levels which are exclusive in that athletes must first qualify in order to participate, and thus they entail comparatively higher degrees of competition. Generally, Masters events are more exclusive in nature than Seniors events.

Preparation for these competitive events engenders a regular pattern of involvement in goal-oriented activities for skill acquisition, at intensities and durations that easily satisfy guidelines for physical activity and healthy aging. The remarkable depth and extent of this involvement is illustrated by the fact that swimmers in their fifties typically train on average from five to 11 hours per week, with lower levels typically corresponding to regional-level athletes and the highest amounts relating to international-level status (Weir *et al.*, 2002; Young *et al.*, 2008a). National-level runners in their fifties train between seven and nine hours per week, average 48 weeks of training yearly, and have been seriously involved for 29 years of life (Starkes *et al.*, 1999; Young *et al.*, 2008b), and it is not uncommon for some to have trained for over 15 years consecutively (Young and Starkes,

Acknowledgements: writing of this chapter was supported by a Strategic Initiative Grant from the Social Sciences and Humanities Research Council of Canada and Sport Canada. The author would like to thank Alexandre Dumas and Isabel Theberge for their comments on an earlier draft of this manuscript.

2005). Though there are exceptions, practice amounts generally correspond to skill group in that international-level participants typically are more heavily engaged and have trained more continuously compared to national, state/provincial and local-level participants.

Masters have a unique motivation to do sport at life stages when most others either have dropped out, are under-committed to sport, or are unable to commit because social circumstances and life demands constrain such opportunities. Yet, Masters are engaged because they have remained continuously invested in the domain or have resumed sport after time away (Harada, 1994). As such, emerging research seeks to account for the exceptional dedication of Masters. The purpose of this chapter is to review psycho-social research on the motivation and commitment of Masters and to present emerging lines of inquiry in this field. This topic remains under-examined, particularly in light of the fact that Masters are one of the fastest growing sport cohorts worldwide, and considering the potential that studies of Masters hold for informing academics about the psycho-social underpinnings of long-lasting motivation, and how people re-engage into sport after lengthy interruptions. Several directions of research are reviewed with the intent of informing students, researchers, practitioners, sport programmers and policy advisors who seek to sustain the participation of aged athletes by optimising their motivation, or who seek to engage greater numbers of people in Masters sport.

Describing the motivational profiles of Masters

Descriptive research that has largely been atheoretical and reliant on single-item measures still informs much of what we know about this topic. Studies involving samples ranging in age from late thirties to 75 years show that Masters have intrinsic motives such as loving the sport and enjoyment, and extrinsic motives such as obtaining or preserving health, fitness and well-being (Fung et al., 1992; McIntyre et al., 1992; Tantrum and Hodge, 1993). Highly committed adult marathoners endorse mastery motives whereby they focus on improvement and meeting personal challenges rather than social comparison reflecting performance outcomes, and recognise sport as a means to enhance self-esteem (Ogles and Masters, 2003). Amongst certain Seniors Games samples, extrinsic motives specifically relating to appearance and weight loss are also seemingly of less importance (Gill et al., 1996: mean age = 69 years).

The relative importance of competitive, social affiliation and social recognition motives amongst Masters remains unclear, and this may depend very much on the specific nature of the Masters sample that is examined. Adult competitive runners cited social and competitive motives less frequently than health-enhancing motives (Ogles and Masters, 2003). Alternatively, compulsive (i.e. behaviourally-identified as feeling obligated to run) runners in their late thirties cited competition as a motive more frequently than well-being motives (Ogles et al., 1995). Australian Masters Games attendees in their late forties rated 'social motivations' equally important to health-enhancing motives and indicated that they participated in order to interact with like-minded peers, or to meet new people (McIntyre *et al.*, 1992). In contrast, national-level Masters track and field athletes in their early fifties less frequently indicated fellowship and social affiliation reasons compared to 'love of sport', competition, personal challenge and achievement and health-enhancement (Medic *et al.*, 2005a). Highly-involved competitive runners in their thirties place an emphasis on achieving recognisable success (Ogles *et al.*, 1995) and can be strongly motivated to gain social approval and admiration from others (Summers *et al.*, 1983). Overall, the most informative aspect of the body of descriptive work is the breadth or heterogeneity of intrinsic and extrinsic motives, which is attributable partly to variance in the age of samples and the nature of the competitive venue at which they were derived. At the very least, one might conclude that Masters are characterised by health-enhancement and personal challenge motives, however, one should refrain from concluding that Masters are not characterised by competitive motives, or that they are predominantly motivated for social reasons.

Goal orientations and motives for sport

Recent studies have employed multiple-item instruments, multivariate analyses and have been grounded in conceptual frameworks such as Achievement Goal Theory (AGT) (Duda, 2001), Self-Determination Theory (SDT) (Deci and Ryan, 1985) and the Social Motivation Model (SMM) (Allen, 2003). AGT views striving behaviour as a quest to demonstrate physical ability and to perceive oneself as competent while doing sport. SDT contends that Masters will be most self-determined, or intrinsically motivated, when they sense that they are agents of their own actions, that they can skilfully interact in an environment and when they feel that they can develop connected relationships with others. According to SMM, the central energiser of motivated behaviour in sport is the desire to demonstrate social bonds with others.

In a sample of Senior Olympians (mean age = 65 years), Newton and Fry (1998) demonstrated task- and ego-orientation factors coherent with theoretical predictions and findings for younger athletes. Athletes with an ego-orientation use normative references or whether they outperformed others as information by which they judge personal competence, whereas task-oriented athletes judge their competence based on personally-referenced criteria. Ego-orientation corresponded with beliefs that sport success is due to innate ability and is achieved by those who know how to maximise external/deceptive factors, and that sport should enhance one's social status and personal gain. Task-orientation was linked to beliefs that sport success is due to hard work, and that sport is a means for personal improvement and cooperation. Unlike ego-orientation, task-orientation was positively associated with intrinsic motivation (IM). Both task- and ego-orientations were each linked to beliefs that sport should enhance self-esteem and foster competitive inclinations, although task disposition was more strongly linked to esteem enhancement and ego-disposition was more strongly associated with competitiveness. On average, these Senior Olympians demonstrated high task-orientation and moderate-to-low scores for ego-orientation, levels which have been replicated with World Masters Games (Hodge *et al.*, 2008: mean age = 48 years), National Senior Games (Steinberg *et al.*, 2000: mean age = 65 years), and national-level Masters track and field athletes (Medic *et al.*, 2005b: mean age = 54 years). Compared to athletes in their twenties or younger (Duda, 2001), Masters are particularly high in task- and unusually low on ego-orientation. Greater task-orientation is purported to foster an ongoing interest in sport across the life span because it gives individuals a sense of control over their athletic involvement, their effort and enjoyment. Based on a sample of adult co-ed soccer players ranging from 18 to 55 years of age, Etnier *et al.* (2004) proposed that a low task-orientation profile, irrespective of ego scores, puts athletes at risk for dropout.

Kowal and Fortier (2000) examined aspects of SDT and their relations to motivational climates with local Canadian Masters swimmers who were on average in their late thirties. Generally, swimmers were slightly higher than midpoint on an index reflecting a continuum of degrees of self-determined motivation from predominantly intrinsic motivation (high) to extrinsic motivation and amotivation (low). Perceptions of autonomy, competency and relatedness were associated with higher self-determined motivation scores when they were assessed in the immediate training environment. However, when general motivation to be involved in swimming was assessed, only perceived relatedness significantly predicted self-determined motivation. Investigators explained this by suggesting that the atmosphere for their Masters swimmers was not that competitive in that many swimmers competed on a limited basis; this afforded social connectedness a more prominent mediating role for self-determined motivation, with relatively diminished mediating roles for autonomy and competence. Results did support this – swimmers' mean ratings were substantially higher for perceptions of a mastery motivational climate than for an ego-oriented climate, and scores for perceptions of a mastery motivational climate were positively associated with perceived relatedness. Finally, swimmers who perceived an ego-oriented climate reported lower feelings of autonomy.

North American track and field Masters demonstrated a self-determined motivational profile (Medic *et al.*, 2005b). Athletes rated three motives highly – IM to experience stimulating sensations, IM to accomplish and integrated regulation. High integrated regulation, the most self-determined form of extrinsic motivation, was likely because athletes had incorporated various extrinsic sport goals within their self such that they were congruent with their values and needs. Finally, Masters had very low levels of amotivation, likely because they recognised the value in sport activity, were cognisant of their reasons for doing sport and felt that their sporting behaviours were leading to some desirable outcome. These findings are enlightening because high intrinsic motives and self-determined forms of extrinsic motivation, coupled with low amotivation, comprise a profile that is associated with persistence in sport.

Hodge *et al.* (2008) examined the collective relationships between the two goal orientations of AGT and three additional goal orientations advocated by the SMM – social affiliation, social status and social recognition. On average, World Masters Games participants had high social affiliation and task-orientation and a moderately high social recognition orientation. Social status and ego-orientation scores were lower. Investigators used a goal profiling technique based on various permutations of goal orientations to identify five motivational clusters. Two clusters particularly corresponded with dependent measures for IM, enjoyment and commitment. A 'Hi Social' cluster had a very strong social affiliation orientation marked by a desire to successfully establish mutual connections, as well as relatively high scores for social status orientation. A motive to use sport as a means to enhance one's standing is potentially maladaptive in certain cases, however, this particular orientation was likely benign because Masters in this cluster also had high perceived belonging scores, indicating they had satisfied a need for relatedness (Allen, 2003). A 'Hi Achievement' profile reflected a predominant task-orientation as well as high ego-orientation scores. The potentially maladaptive condition engendered by an ego-orientation was likely benign for this cluster because they also had high scores for perceived ability (Duda, 2001). In sum, this study identified two motivational profiles, both associated with adaptive correlates, but each profile was linked to these outcomes via different orientations – one by striving for social connections and the other by striving for mastery achievement. Investigators claimed that findings reflected the fact that participants are motivated when Masters sport represents a sporting and a social occasion. Finally, it is notable that both profiles were associated with moderately high scores for extrinsic motivation. Thus, while adaptive Masters' profiles were associated predominantly with personal mastery goals and intrinsic social motives, it is not possible to entirely discount that they were also linked to competitive goals involving external comparison, and the drive to obtain public acclaim.

Within-Masters differences

Masters' motives appear more heterogeneous than those in younger sporting populations due to the fact that their ages span many decades and that motives change depending on life experiences, family and career demands, and in response to altered expectancies or societal norms with age (Rudman, 1989). An appealing line of inquiry is whether there are differences in adult athletes' motives as a function of age or life stage, gender, or experience.

Age

Male athletes over 50 years of age diminish in competitive orientation as evidenced by the fact that National Senior Games participants had lower ego-orientation scores than middle-aged (31–49 years) and collegiate male athletes (Steinberg *et al.*, 2000). No differences for task-orientation were evident. Other research (Ogles and Masters, 2003) shows that adult participants are enthusiasts who are motivated by the aesthetics of the sport rather than by competition or goal achievement. Runners over 50 years of age took on a broader health orientation and were more concerned about social affiliation than runners in their twenties; however, older runners were no less competitive and equally valued motives related to social recognition and self-esteem enhancement (Ogles and Masters, 2000). Some evidence suggests that marathoners between the ages of 41 and 61 adopt goals to master control over their body in spite of the effects of aging more than younger marathoners (Summers *et al.*, 1983). Individual-sport Masters who were on average in the early fifties showed a more self-determined profile than collegiate-aged athletes, with lower levels of amotivation and extrinsic motivation, which may explain their continued involvement (Medic *et al.*, 2004).

Generally, Masters are less ego-oriented and less competitively-focused and more motivated towards fun as they age. These trends corroborate literature from leisure science which suggests a shift from normatively referenced judgments of competence towards more intrinsic reasons with age (Maehr and Kleiber, 1981). Considering that limited studies have used a rigorous life stage design within exclusive samples of Masters, and several studies showing no age effects for either intrinsic or extrinsic motives (Ashford *et al.*, 1993; Hastings *et al.*, 1995; Tantrum and Hodge, 1993; Toepell *et al.*, 2004), this statement might prove to be oversimplified (also see Dionigi, 2008). This trend has yet to be supported unequivocally with Masters.

Gender

Gender profiling of Masters does bear some similarity to younger sport populations. Males enjoy striving for success in competition more (Gill *et al.*, 1996; Tantrum and Hodge, 1993), whereas females place higher importance on enjoyment (Toepell *et al.*, 2004), health and fitness (Gill *et al.*, 1996; Hastings *et al.*, 1995). Females have lower ego-orientation (Medic *et al.*, 2006a; Newton and Fry, 1998), higher task-orientation (Medic *et al.*, 2005b), and perceive their training climates as mastery-oriented more than males (Kowal and Fortier, 2000). Masters men have greater affinity for extrinsic motives than women who instead pursue intrinsic motives, or more self-determined forms of extrinsic motivation (Medic *et al.*, 2006a).

Acknowledging that gender differences exist, the challenge is identifying whether they differ broadly (e.g. differences on seven motives in Toepell *et al.*, 2004) or on select motives (e.g. difference on only 'IM to know' in Etnier *et al.*, 2004). Females' preference for social affiliation, seen in youth research, is not necessarily as marked with Masters. Finally, a gender by competitive experience interaction may exist, such that gender differences are most evident when recreational participants are examined, and disappear with more committed or higher-level Masters. Etnier *et al.* (2004) suggested that adult sport provides competitive outlets that are attractive for a sub-group of women who might be more ego-oriented compared to other women.

Competitive experience and other factors

Stage of competitive experience (i.e. short/extended, light/intensive involvement) may determine dominant motives more than gender or age (Hastings *et al.*, 1995).

Masters swimmers with substantial lifelong competitive experience, or who were currently competing frequently, stressed achievement motives, whereas novice and less-involved Masters emphasised skill development reasons. Masters swimmers with more than five years of experience judged team work and social affiliation as more important than less experienced swimmers, and the most competent swimmers were more likely to rate 'winning' and 'doing something they are good at' as important motives (Tantrum and Hodge, 1993). Etnier *et al.* (2004) reported no effects of level of competition on the task or ego-orientation scores of adult soccer players.

Evidence suggests that marital status (i.e. unmarried Masters reported more sociability motives), and culture (United States Masters were more extrinsically motivated than Canadians) might influence motives, but parental status might not (Hastings *et al.*, 1995). Higher education levels appear related to greater motivation to participate in adult sport (Kolt *et al.*, 2004) and it is plausible that sport type has an influence, although few studies have examined these questions directly concerning Masters. Finally, Masters who are relatively younger in any five-year competitive registration category (e.g. 45 years old in the 45–49 years grouping) are less amotivated and less task-oriented than relatively older athletes (e.g. age 49 years) against whom they compete (Medic *et al.*, 2005b).

Personal and social factors influencing the sport commitment of Masters

In order to understand how Masters maintain continuity of participation, investigators have begun to examine the conditions that foster commitment. The Sport Commitment Model (SCM) (Scanlan *et al.*, 2003) is a suitable model because it considers personal and social factors that determine commitment, considers costs and benefits associated with the commitment, positions the decision to do sport amongst a constellation of other leisure activities that could also be pursued, and because it has facilitated research on entrapment, persistence and burn-out in youth sport. SCM predicts that an athlete's resolve to continue sport involvement is related to higher perceptions of enjoyment/satisfaction, involvement opportunities, personal investments and a perceived lack of appealing alternative activities. Perceived pressure from significant others, called 'social constraints', as well as 'social support', also influence commitment. Two different types of commitment result from these antecedent conditions – functional and obligatory, with the former predicted to explain persistence in sport (Wilson *et al.*, 2004).

Young *et al.* (2008a) tested functional and obligatory models with World Championship Masters swimmers (mean age = 54 years). Overall, swimmers reported significantly higher functional than obligatory commitment. Scores for satisfaction were highest, personal investments and involvement opportunities were very high and social support was moderately high. Perceptions of involvement alternatives and social constraints were low. Swimmers' functional commitment was positively linked to feelings of satisfaction, the real or anticipated opportunities that they perceived arose from being involved in their sport (e.g. to travel, to achieve personal goals, to defer aging effects) and the personal investments they had already made. Results replicated findings for the functional commitment of similarly-aged national-level Masters runners (Medic *et al.*, 2006b). In swimmers, functional commitment was also associated with athletes reporting an absence of other activities that they could be involved in that would be as worthwhile as sport (Young *et al.*, 2008a). Obligatory commitment was associated with high levels for social constraints and low levels of social support, and high levels of involvement alternatives, involvement opportunities and prior personal investments. Thus, satisfaction and social influences played very different roles depending on commitment type. Satisfaction was essential for functional commitment, suggesting that interventions which maximise athletes' fun and positive affect inherent in the sport are critical for sustaining involvement. Obligatory commitment, which is not necessarily linked to long-term engagement patterns, was critically influenced by social factors. Specifically, interventions that enhance encouragement or endorsement from persons around an athlete and that also sensitise significant others to the pressures that they might place on older athletes might serve to moderate athletes' feelings of obligation, and may facilitate persistent involvement. Results showing the opposite influences of social constraints and social support on obligatory commitment are also apparent in other studies on Masters swimmers (Young and Medic, 2011) and runners (Medic *et al.*, 2006b), and corroborate atheoretical work relating to seriously committed adult runners in their late twenties and thirties (Yair, 1992).

Social support

Social support is associated with sustained coping and behavioural persistence and facilitates adherence and compliance to exercise and physical activity (Carron *et al.*, 1996). Considering the importance that social support has for older casual/recreational exercising populations (Chogahara *et al.*, 1998), and assuming that Masters' frequent, intense and persistent sporting activity present greater demands that must be navigated, it is plausible that the role of social support might be further accentuated with Masters. Several disparate studies support this hypothesis. Golding and Ungerleider (1991) discovered a positive association between perceived social support from friends and frequency of training amongst 50-year-old runners. National-level Masters runners (mean age = 57 years) who either train with a coach, or who are part of a training group, report a more self-determined profile (Medic *et al.*, 2005c) that is beneficial to one's overall motivation, psychological well-being and is a strong predictor of sport persistence. Twenty-three per cent of national-level Masters runners claim that 'training in groups' is a strategy they use to overcome motivational lapses (Medic *et al.*, 2005a).

World Masters championship swimmers acknowledge having the following agents or sub-groups who are potentially supportive in their social network: non-sport colleagues (97 per cent), broader family members (96 per cent), sport community peers (96 per cent), health professionals (93 per cent), training partners (84 per cent), spouse (81 per cent), own children (74 per cent) and a coach

(72 per cent) (Young *et al.*, 2008a). Heavily-involved Masters international-level swimmers reported a significantly greater number of these agents or sub-groups in their network than less-involved swimmers (Piamonte and Young, 2009). These preliminary analyses were structural in nature, and served to identify differences in the number of sources that *potentially* encourage and endorse athletes' sport involvement. Recent research examining the functional aspects of social influence has noted that four particular social agents - one's spouse, own children, training mates, and one's health practitioner, may be influential for creating an adaptive psycho-social climate which promotes commitment amongst international-level Masters swimmers (Young and Medic, 2011).

Barriers to aged sport involvement

Sport for the aged is growing and participation numbers are sufficient for it to warrant consideration as a viable community-intervention to promote healthy aging. Advocates recommend that policy-makers design community initiatives to advance sport programming for older adults, that address barriers to sport participation facing older adults, and advance family sport policies that unite adults and their children in activity (CFLRI, 2009). In the US, Seniors Games initiatives are portrayed as a means to promote healthy and active aging through sport.

Many older adults perceive personal and environmental barriers that may significantly constrain the adoption and maintenance of sport participation (Booth *et al.*, 2002) and may also limit the efficacy of broader-scale community interventions to promote sport (Sallis *et al.*, 1998). A better understanding of specific barriers is thus needed, yet no studies so far have strategically examined perceived barriers of middle-aged Masters, and only two studies have studied this issue amongst already-active Seniors participants. North Carolina Seniors Games participants (Cardenas *et al.*, 2009) experienced few barriers overall, with lack of 'time' and 'self-discipline' emerging as the only notable items. Investigators conducted a series of between-group analyses for each of three factors – 'Community linked' (e.g. lack of equipment, facilities, knowledge), 'Social influences' (e.g. discouragement from friends, lack of company) and 'Intrapersonal' (e.g. fear of injury, self-consciousness) barriers. Individuals with better health had lower barrier scores on each factor than individuals in poor health. Persons aged 55–64 years reported higher community- and social influence-barriers than persons over 65 years. No effects were found for gender, marital status, education level, race or rural/urban location. Finally, having fewer reported barriers was associated with individuals' capability to adopt training as part of a daily routine and their capability to meet recommended daily physical activity requirements for healthy living.

Young *et al.* (2009) explored perceived barriers to increased sport involvement amongst Ontario Seniors Games participants. Males reported higher barrier levels overall. No effects of activity level or age (55–64, 65+ years) were evident. Collapsed across all participants, barrier levels were highest for 'Unavailability of organisational training and competitive opportunities' (e.g. no teams, training mates, coaches, leagues) and 'Family not participating' (i.e. spouse, children).

These barrier factors were rated equally highly and both were higher than factors related to 'Unattractive (e.g. busy) venues and inadequate personal resources' (e.g. money, time), 'Fear of injury and lack of confidence' and 'Unpleasant weather'.

Limits to existing knowledge and future directions

In this section, several recommendations are advanced which may serve to direct future research and which may facilitate quantitative research efforts to resolve equivocal trends and knowledge gaps in the field. Cross-sectional studies have underscored the heterogeneity of Masters' motives. It remains difficult to define the motives and profiles that would best promote continuous involvement in the absence of longitudinal research. Existing Masters research has exclusively used cross-sectional and correlational methods that are restricted in explaining how specific motives change over time or how various personal/social conditions evolve to influence commitment. A better understanding of psycho-social mechanisms driving persistence in sport requires longitudinal approaches that use analyses such as structural equation modelling to study pathways between various antecedents, motivational mediators, and identifiable outcomes. Using longitudinal research, investigators will more likely be able to infer the importance of various motives and profiles based on the effect they have on identifiable outcomes.

It is recommended that identifiable outcomes comprise reliable and valid measures that capture the rich dynamics of sporting behaviour, including amounts of training and competition, as well as self-perception measures that are positive (e.g. happiness, fulfilment, intention to increase involvement) and negative (e.g. tension, restlessness, regret, burn-out, intention to reduce involvement). With the increasing study of social goal orientations, outcomes might also include measures of affiliation, social cohesion and friendship networks. Finally, longitudinal efforts would benefit from the reporting of attrition data and strategies to follow-up with Masters sport dropouts in order to comprehend a fuller profile of long-lasting motivation.

Cross-sectional designs help to identify new between-subject factors (e.g. retirement status) and to clarify within-Masters motivational differences pertaining to gender and competitive level. Rigorous cross-sectional designs are needed to determine age/developmental motivational differences. Researchers who have employed life-stage designs have recognised that results can be confounded by sampling issues, whereby younger participants are selected from competitive sport and older participants from non-competitive fitness programmes (Brodkin and Weiss, 1990). Goal profiling (Hodge and Petlichkoff, 2000) represents a methodological advance because it offers a protocol for collectively analysing several goal orientations, yet enables investigators to disentangle different permutations of social goals and achievement goals. Future efforts might attempt to replicate goal profiling results and endeavour to conduct longitudinal analyses linking different goal profiles with unique patterns of self-perceptions and behaviours.

From a sampling perspective, more research could be conducted with team sport participants, as almost all studies have related to individual-sport Masters in athletics and swimming. Investigators have typically conveniently sampled from elite international- and national-level cohorts, thus future work might examine all competitive levels in order to determine whether trends for serious Masters also generalise to more recreational participants. Moreover, strategic attempts to assess more intermittently-involved participants may help remedy a self-selection sampling bias that likely exists in existing research on more-elite Masters. The inclusion of local, less competitive, intermittent sport participants would enrich our understanding of the psycho-social mechanisms amongst older athletic populations.

From a theoretical perspective, AGT and SMM examine a full complement of motives for sport, and SDT and SCM afford comprehensive studies of motivation and commitment, respectively. It is important, however, for future investigators to report factor analyses for each model to confirm their applicability to older populations. Although the factor structures for AGT and SMM were acceptable amongst Masters (Hodge *et al.*, 2008), Shaw *et al.* (2005) showed a less acceptable fit for SDT factors amongst Seniors. One productive research direction might involve the longitudinal assessment of associations between different perceived motivational climates in Masters' training environments and concurrent measures for attendance, training frequency, perceived competence, autonomy and relatedness. In addition, the role of social influences on Masters' commitment remains under-examined. As in youth sport, there may be segments of the Masters population who are pressured by significant others to continue their involvement, or who feel pressure to maintain a social athletic identity, and such feelings may result in uniquely negative behavioural and psychological outcomes. Future research might examine positive and negative social influences at the level of the specific source to identify agents (e.g. spouse, coach, health professional) who are most encouraging or pressuring and who have the greatest impact on behavioural persistence.

More studies on the perceived barriers of already-active sport participants are needed from a social-ecological perspective, including an examination of how societal ageist stereotypes are a barrier to sport participation by adults. Future work might also assess Masters' barriers as a function of age, gender and retirement status. In concert with surveys of barriers for those who do not participate in sport as adults (CFLRI, 2009) but who may have in youth, this research will possibly produce information that informs community initiatives to sustain current Masters and attract newcomers to Masters sport.

Conclusion

The Masters cohort is an intriguing and rapidly exploding segment of our sporting population that appears to defy what we know about exercise adherence across the life span and our traditional assumptions of decreasing involvement with age. Masters offer evidence of enthusiastic and enduring involvement in sport. Emerging research that is theoretically grounded and multivariate in nature now complements a body of early descriptive research and has served to advance the line of inquiry. This emerging research facilitates the identification of motivational profiles to effectively tease out various clusters by life stage, gender and competitive experience within a very heterogeneous Masters population that reflects both competitive and social orientations in yet indistinguishable proportions. Such research also lends itself well to a better understanding of personal and social factors relating to motivation or commitment, and ultimately to better prediction of long-lasting sport involvement. Finally, there are several methodological steps and future directions that might be considered and potentially accommodated in order to help paint a richer picture of the psycho-social mechanisms that underscore continuity in Masters sport.

References

Allen, J. B. (2003). Social motivation in youth sport. *Journal of Sport and Exercise Psychology*, *25*, 551–567.

Ashford, B., Biddle, S. and Goudas, M. (1993). Participation in community sports centres: motives and predictors of enjoyment. *Journal of Sports Sciences*, *11*, 249–256.

Booth, M. L., Bauman, A. and Owen, N. (2002). Perceived barriers to physical activity among older Australians. *Journal of Aging and Physical Activity*, *10*, 271–280.

Brodkin, P. and Weiss, M. R. (1990). Developmental differences in motivation for participating in competitive swimming. *Journal of Sport and Exercise Psychology*, *12*, 248–263.

Cardenas, D., Henderson, K. A. and Wilson, B. E. (2009). Physical activity and Senior Games participation: benefits, constraints, and behaviours. *Journal of Aging and Physical Activity*, *17*, 135–153.

Carron, A. V., Hausenblas, H. A. and Mack, D. A. (1996). Social influence and exercise: a meta-analysis. *Journal of Sport and Exercise Psychology*, *18*, 1–16.

CFLRI (Canadian Fitness and Lifestyle Research Institute) (2009). *Sport participation in Canada. 2006–2007 Sport Monitor Bulletin 3*. Retrieved April 2009 from www.cflri. ca/eng/statistics/surveys/documents/sport2007_b3.pdf.

Chogahara, M., O'Brien-Cousins, S. and Wankel, L. M. (1998). Social influences on physical activity in older adults: a review. *Journal of Aging and Physical Activity*, *6*, 1–17.

Deci, E. L. and Ryan, R. M. (1985). *Intrinsic motivation and self-determination in human behaviour*. New York: Plenum Press.

Dionigi, R. A. (2008). *Competing for life: older people, sport and aging*. Saarbrücken: VDM Verlag Dr. Müller.

Duda, J. L. (2001). Achievement goal research in sport: pushing the boundaries and clarifying some misunderstandings. In G. Roberts (Ed.), *Advances in motivation in sport and exercise* (pp. 129–182). Champaign: Human Kinetics.

Etnier, J. L., Sidman, C. L. and Hancock II, L. C. (2004). An examination of goal orientation profiles and motivation in adult team sport. *International Journal of Sport Psychology*, *35*, 173–188.

Fung, L., Ha, A., Louie, L. and Poon, F. (1992). Sport participation motives among veteran track and field athletes. *ICHPER Journal*, *29*, 24–28.

Gill, D., Williams, L., Dowd, D. A., Beaudoin, C. M. and Martin, J. J. (1996). Competitive orientations and motives of adult sport and exercise participants. *Journal of Sport Behaviour*, *19*, 307–318.

Golding, J. M. and Ungerleider, S. (1991). Social resources and mood among Masters track and field athletes. *Journal of Applied Sport Psychology, 3,* 142–159.

Harada, M. (1994). Early and later life sport participation patterns among the active elderly in Japan. *Journal of Aging and Physical Activity, 2,* 105–114.

Hastings, D. W., Kurth, S., Schloder, M. and Cyr, D. (1995). Reasons for participating in a serious leisure career: comparison of Canadian and U.S. Masters swimmers. *International Review for the Sociology of Sport, 30,* 101–117.

Hodge, K. and Petlichkoff, L. (2000). Goal profiles in sport motivation: a cluster analysis. *Journal of Sport and Exercise Psychology, 22,* 256–272.

Hodge, K., Allen, J. B. and Smellie, L. (2008). Motivation in Masters sport: achievement and social goals. *Psychology of Sport and Exercise, 9,* 157–176.

Kolt, G. S., Driver, R. P. and Giles, L. C. (2004). Why older Australians participate in exercise and sport. *Journal of Aging and Physical Activity, 11,* 185–198.

Kowal, J. and Fortier, M. S. (2000). Testing relationships from the hierarchical model of intrinsic and extrinsic motivation using flow as a motivational consequence. *Research Quarterly for Exercise and Sport, 71,* 171–181.

McIntyre, N., Coleman, D., Boag, A. and Cuskelly, G. (1992). Understanding Masters sports participation: involvement, motives and benefits. *ACHPER National Journal, 138,* 4–8.

Maehr, M. L. and Kleiber, D. A. (1981). The graying of achievement motivation. *American Psychologist, 36,* 787–793.

Medic, N., Starkes, J. L., Young, B. W. and Weir, P. L. (2006a). Motivation for sport and goal orientations in Masters athletes: do Masters swimmers differ from Masters runners? *Journal of Sport & Exercise Psychology, 28,* S132.

Medic, N., Starkes, J. L., Young, B. W. and Weir, P. L. (2006b). Testing the Sport Commitment Model with Masters runners. *Journal of Sport & Exercise Psychology, 28,* S132.

Medic, N., Starkes, J. L., Young, B. W., Weir, P. L. and Giajnorio, A. (2004). *Motivational orientation of Masters athletes: comparison to young adult athletes.* Presented at the meeting of the Canadian Society for Psychomotor Learning and Sport Psychology, Saskatoon, SK.

Medic, N., Starkes, J. L., Young, B. W., Weir, P. L. and Giajnorio, A. (2005a). *Masters athletes' motivation to train and compete: first order themes.* Presented at the meeting of the International Society of Sport Psychology, Sydney, Australia.

Medic, N., Starkes, J. L., Young, B. W., Weir, P. L. and Giajnorio, A. (2005b). *Multifaceted analyses of Masters athletes' motives to continue training and competition.* Presented at the meeting of the International Society of Sport Psychology, Sydney, Australia.

Medic, N., Starkes, J. L., Young, B. W., Weir, P. L. and Giajnorio, A. (2005c). *Influence of the coach and training group on Masters athletes' motivation for sport.* Presented at the meeting of the International Society of Sport Psychology, Sydney, Australia.

Newton, M. and Fry, M. D. (1998). Senior Olympians' achievement goals and motivational responses. *Journal of Aging and Physical Activity, 6,* 256–270.

Ogles, B. M. and Masters, K. S. (2000). Older vs. Younger male marathon runners: participative motives and training habits. *Journal of Sport Behaviour, 23,* 130–143.

Ogles, B. M. and Masters, K. S. (2003). A typology of marathon runners based on cluster analysis of motivations. *Journal of Sport Behaviour, 26,* 69–85.

Ogles, B. M., Masters, K. S. and Richardson, S. A. (1995). Obligatory running and gender: an analysis of participative motives and training habits. *International Journal of Sport Psychology, 26,* 233–248.

Piamonte, M. and Young, B. W. (2009). *Examining social support networks of competitive Masters swimmers*. Presented at the annual meeting of the Eastern Canadian Symposium for Sport and Exercise Psychology, Toronto, ON.

Rudman, W. J. (1989). Age and involvement in sport and physical activity. *Sociology of Sport Journal, 6*, 228–246.

Sallis, J. F., Bauman, A. and Pratt, M. (1998). Environmental and policy interventions to promote physical activity. *American Journal of Preventative Medicine, 15*, 379–397.

Scanlan, T. K., Russell, D. G., Beals, K. P. and Scanlan, L. A. (2003). Project on elite athlete commitment (PEAK): II. A direct test and expansion of the Sport Commitment Model with elite amateur sportsmen. *Journal of Sport and Exercise Psychology, 25*, 377–401.

Shaw, K. L., Ostrow, A. and Beckstead, J. (2005). Motivation and the Senior athlete: an examination of the psychometric properties of the Sport Motivation Scale. *Topics in Geriatric Rehabilitation, 21*, 206–214.

Starkes, J. L., Weir, P. L., Singh, P., Hodges, N. J. and Kerr, T. (1999). Aging and the retention of sport expertise. *International Journal of Sport Psychology, 30*, 283–301.

Steinberg, G., Grieve, F. G. and Glass, B. (2000). Achievement goals across the lifespan. *Journal of Sport Behaviour, 23*, 298–306.

Summers, J. J., Machin, V. J. and Sargent, G. I. (1983). Psychosocial factors related to marathon running. *Journal of Sport Psychology, 5*, 314–331.

Tantrum, M. and Hodge, K. (1993). Motives for participating in Masters swimming. *New Zealand Journal of Health, Physical Education and Recreation, 26*, 3–7.

Toepell, A. R., Guilmette, A. M. and Brooks, S. (2004). Women in Masters rowing: exploring healthy aging. *Women's Health and Urban Life Journal, 5*, 74–95.

Weir, P. L., Kerr, T., Hodges, N. J., McKay, S. M. and Starkes, J. L. (2002). Master swimmers: how are they different from younger elite swimmers? An examination of practice and performance patterns. *Journal of Aging and Physical Activity, 10*, 41–63.

Wilson, P. M., Rodgers, W. M., Carpenter, P. J., Hall, C., Hardy, J. and Fraser, S. N. (2004). The relationship between commitment and exercise behaviour. *Psychology of Sport and Exercise, 5*, 405–421.

Yair, G. (1992). What keeps them running? The 'circle of commitment' of long distance runners. *Leisure Studies, 11*, 257–270.

Young, B. W. and Medic, N. (2011). Examining social influences on the sport commitment of Masters swimmers. *Psychology of Sport and Exercise, 12*, 168–175.

Young, B. W. and Starkes, J. L. (2005). Career-span analyses of track performance: longitudinal data present a more optimistic view of age-related performance decline. *Experimental Aging Research, 31*, 1–22.

Young, B. W., Medic, N., Weir, P. L. and Starkes, J. L. (2008b). Explaining performance in elite middle-aged runners: contributions from age, ongoing and past training factors. *Journal of Sport and Exercise Psychology, 30*, 1–20.

Young, B. W., Medic, N., Cameron, S., Theberge, I. and Latham, C. (2009). *Exploring perceived barriers to sport involvement amongst Ontario Senior Games participants*. Presented at the annual meeting of the Canadian Society for Psychomotor Learning and Sport Psychology, Toronto, ON.

Young, B. W., Medic, N., Piamonte, M., Wigglesworth, J. and Grove, J. R. (2008a). *Examining the determinants of sport commitment in competitive Masters swimmers*. Presented at the annual meeting of the Canadian Society for Psychomotor Learning and Sport Psychology, Canmore, AB.

11 What predicts exercise participation of older adults?

Maarten Stiggelbout and
Marijke Hopman-Rock

Introduction

Regular participation in exercise has been associated with a variety of health benefits. It is often seen as an important way to counteract age-related decline of body functions. Several physical functions such as strength and endurance can be improved by an increased amount of physical activity and factors like overweight and high blood pressure could be prevented or treated (Nelson *et al.*, 2007). Physical inactivity is an independent risk factor which may ameliorate several chronic diseases which often occur in the elderly, like coronary heart disease, diabetes mellitus type II, osteoporosis, osteoarthritis and cancer.

The Public Health guidelines for health enhancing physical activity (HEPA) state that 'all adults should participate in 30 minutes of moderate intensive physical activity during preferably all – but at least five – days of the week' (ACSM, 1998a; Bauman, 2006; Kemper *et al.*, 2000; Pate *et al.*, 1995). These guidelines are also applicable to older adults (Nelson *et al.*, 2007). Previously, it was believed that only high intensity physical activity would have a beneficial effect on health status. However, moderate intensity activities, like walking and cycling, are also intensive enough to enhance health. After the age of 65 years, there is a significant decrease in compliance to the HEPA guidelines, and this gets worse with age (Ooijendijk *et al.*, 2007). It is important to counteract this decrease in physical activity in older adults and to establish maintenance in participation in physical activity, as the health benefits diminish quite soon after stopping (ACSM, 1998b).

Determinant and correlation studies have found that several factors are important for older adults to participate in an exercise programme. An overview has been given by Stiggelbout (2008):

- Personal factors: age, gender, socio-economic class, working or not, (past) exercise behaviour.
- Social and cultural factors: influence of a treating physician, social support of friends and family.
- Environmental factors: type of, location of, and quality of physical activities, travel time, physical environment with sufficient opportunities to be physically active (e.g. parks, walking trails, bicycle lanes, physical activity clubs for older adults) and low costs.

When specifically focusing on sports and exercise participation, two aspects are of importance, namely entry in an exercise programme and maintenance in sport and exercise activities.

To study people's transition from a (partly) sedentary lifestyle to a more physically active lifestyle, the transtheoretical model is often applied (Prochaska and DiClemente, 1983). 'Stages of change' constitute the central organising construct of the original transtheoretical model. Prochaska and DiClemente (1983) suggest that individuals engaging in a new behaviour move in an orderly progression through the stages of precontemplation (not intending to make changes); contemplation (considering a change); preparation (making small changes); action (actively engaging in the new behaviour); and maintenance (sustaining the change over time). In the 1990s, Marcus and Owen (1992) modified the original stages of change construct and processes of change to describe behavioural change with respect to physical activity behaviour.

TNO Quality of Life (Leiden, the Netherlands) carried out a study concerning the correlates associated with voluntary entry of older adults in specific exercise programmes and their motivations for these choices (Stiggelbout *et al.*, 2008). Knowledge of these correlates and motivations are of importance when advising other older adults who are considering entering an exercise programme. We will briefly describe the study, which aimed at exploring these correlates and motivations.

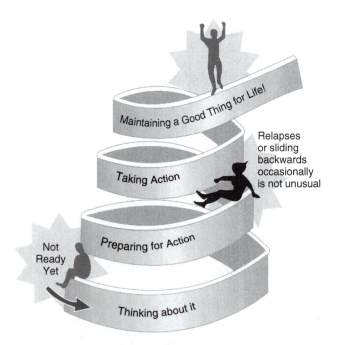

Figure 11.1 Stages of change in adding physical activity into your life.

Source: www.medicinenet.com/exercise_and_activity/page5.htm).

Although considerable effort has been put into promoting exercise programmes to increase levels of physical activity, less attention has been paid to ensuring that people continue to participate in these programmes. In the exercise promotion literature, six months is often accepted as the time frame for behaviour change to become imbedded (Prochaska and DiClemente, 1983) and so we preliminarily accepted this time frame as relevant to maintenance of exercise participation. The second part of the TNO study aimed to seek out the determinants of exercise maintenance.

Research questions and methods

The research questions were:

- What are predictors of voluntary entry (enrolment and actual participation) in ten different Dutch exercise programmes for older adults?
- What are predictors of maintenance in these exercise programmes?

We carried out a prospective cohort study with baseline (at the individual start of the exercise programme) and follow-up measurements (six months after the start as determined by the expected time frame).

In collaboration with several experts in the field, ten different forms of exercise programme were identified as being representative of the exercise programmes available to older individuals in the Netherlands, namely: More Exercise for Seniors Gymnastics (MBvO); organised sports in sports clubs (specifically, athletics, badminton, cycling, gymnastics, skating and table tennis); FysioSport (i.e. a fitness programme delivered by physical therapists/sports physical therapists); Exercise for Heart Patients (HIB); and Walking for sports (referred to as Walking in this chapter). These exercise programmes are supported by national organisations, which facilitated data collection and participant recruitment. Local organisations were approached through their national body and clubs or groups which were known to encourage participation by older adults were recruited.

Over a period of 15 months, all new members of these clubs or groups were asked to participate in the study. Inclusion criteria were (1) age older than 50 years and (2) not being a member of an organised sports club/group immediately prior to the study. The participants gave their written informed consent before joining the study. They completed a baseline questionnaire when they started the exercise programme. Non-responders received a reminder after three weeks. After six months, all participants who had finally returned the first questionnaire received a second questionnaire. Non-responders to the second questionnaire received a reminder after three weeks.

Drop-out in this study was defined as 'no longer participating in the specific organised exercise programme, according to the opinion of the respondent'.

Results and discussion

The initial study population consisted of 2,020 participants. After six months, 1,725 participants remained. The non-response rate was 15 per cent, mainly due to illness, or moving to another city.

Predictors of entry in an exercise programme

There were several interesting demographical issues identified. MBvO-gym attracted relatively older participants (mean age = 67.7 years), followed by gymnastics (63.2 years). The participants of athletics were relatively younger (54.8 years). There were exercise programmes with mainly female participants, such as MBvO-gym (85.7 per cent), Walking (85.6 per cent) and gymnastics (73.9 per cent), and with specifically male dominated exercise programmes, like cycling (87.1 per cent), table tennis (82.9 per cent) and HIB (76.8 per cent). Participants with high education levels enrolled in athletics while a lower level of education was associated with MBvO enrolment. Most participants lived in a multi-story building and more older adults who lived in a service apartment enrolled in MBvO, compared to the other programmes.

Overall compliance to the HEPA guidelines in the study population at baseline was 34.6 per cent. This is relatively low. In the total Dutch older adult population compliance to HEPA guidelines was 46 per cent (Hildebrandt *et al.*, 2004). This indicates our study did attract the lower active older adult population.

There were differences between the exercise programmes regarding compliance to the guidelines. In gymnastics, over 41 per cent of the participants reported to comply with the guidelines, while most other activity programmes reported below 40 per cent, with badminton as low as 28 per cent. These results show that even among active older adults, it remains of importance to pay attention to promoting the message of healthy exercise. In addition to their initial exercise or sports participation, these older adults may be stimulated to become active daily for at least 30 minutes of moderate exercise.

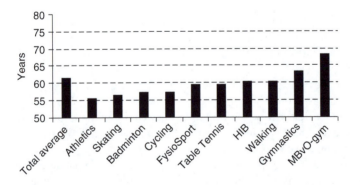

Figure 11.2 Age of participants in the ten different types of exercise programmes (in years; n = 2,020).

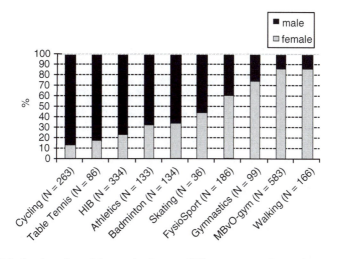

Figure 11.3 Gender of participants in the ten different types of exercise programmes (n = 2,020).

Only a few adults over 70 years of age participated in organised exercise programmes in our study; whenever they did participate, it was associated with MBvO activities. The younger seniors tended to participate in organised sports activities (especially athletics, skating, cycling and badminton), which follows the literature which states that as people age, they tend to change from sports to other (often less competitive) exercise formats (Visser *et al.*, 1997). It is also known that there is a general decrease in participation in physical activity with increasing age (King *et al.*, 1992; Ooijendijk *et al.*, 2002). The most popular activities among seniors are cycling, walking, swimming and gardening (Ooijendijk *et al.*, 2002). The study of Stiggelbout (2008) suggests that in older adults, MBvO tended to be the most popular exercise programme. More than 300,000 seniors participate in MBvO programmes on a weekly basis (Kroes and De Greef, 2000).

Vigorous activity levels and sports activities are generally lower among women than men. When lower and moderate intensity levels are included, the sex differences in activity levels between women and men diminish or even disappear (King *et al.*, 1992).

Predictors of maintenance of exercise participation

In the TNO Quality of Life study, Stiggelbout *et al.* (2008) reported an average drop-out incidence of 0.15 after six months of participation. In the general population, the average drop-out from exercise programmes is about 0.50 during the first six months. This difference in drop-out may partly be explained because we focused on organised exercise.

According to McAuley and Courneya (1993), maintaining participation in exercise programmes is determined by attitude, social influence, self-efficacy and intention. Attitude, social influence and self-efficacy are considered to be prime targets for intervention, because they affect an individual's intention to be physically active and ultimately his or her physical activity patterns. Consistent with this, we found that both attitude and self-efficacy were independent predictors of the intention to continue participation, which in turn was a predictor of actual maintenance of exercise participation. Some background variables (being married, in paid employment and female sex) were also significant independent predictors of the intention to continue participation in the exercise programme.

Aside from these determinants, several additional factors to predict maintenance were also found. For example, the perceived quality of the exercise programme was a predictor of maintenance. For this reason, an instrument should be developed to monitor the quality of exercise programmes, with a view to preventing people from dropping out because of 'poor' programmes. Because a positive attitude towards exercise participation at baseline was a predictor of maintenance, it may be worthwhile to highlight the positive effects of exercise participation to potential and new participants, in order to improve their attitude and indirectly decrease drop-out.

Both the occurrence and duration of lapses were predictors of maintenance of exercise participation. Analysis of the variables that predicted the occurrence of lapses revealed there to be a higher chance of lapses when there were more risk situations and when participants had a lower self-efficacy. There was a lower chance of lapses occurring when the level of education was higher, when the vitality score was higher and when there was less reported pain. Thus, although one might expect health to predict maintenance of exercise participation, it was found to have an indirect influence, by affecting the likelihood of lapses. Not only did more risk situations predict the occurrence of lapses, but a smaller number of risk situations were also an independent predictor of maintenance of exercise participation.

The Relapse Prevention Theory of Marlatt and Gordon (1985) includes the identification of situations that are high-risk situations for lapses and training in problem solving to deal with risk situations. In a study of the effectiveness of relapse prevention training on maintenance of exercise participation, Marcus and Stanton (1993) found that while their programme did not appear to promote continued participation, it decreased the number of lapses. Belisle *et al.* (1987) reported a small but consistent effect of the relapse training programme on maintenance of exercise participation. Thus, relapse prevention training appears to be a cost-effective means to increase maintenance of exercise participation. However, Belisle *et al.* (1987) studied younger adults, and it would be necessary to carry out a similar study with older adults. Such a programme may be beneficial for older individuals because it was found that lapses and a lower number of risk situations were important predictors of continued participation.

References

ACSM (American College of Sports Medicine) (1998a). American College of Sports Medicine Position Stand. Exercise and physical activity for older adults. *Medicine and Science in Sports and Exercise*, 30, 992–1008.

ACSM (American College of Sports Medicine) (1998b). American College of Sports Medicine Position Stand. The recommended quantity and quality of exercise for developing and maintaining cardiorespiratory and muscular fitness, and flexibility in healthy adults. *Medicine and Science in Sports and Exercise, 30*, 975–991.

Bauman, A. (2006). Physical activity and exercise programmes. In C. Bouchard, S. N. Blair and W. L. Haskell (Eds), *Physical activity and health*. Dallas: Human Kinetics.

Belisle, M., Roskies, E. and Levesque, J. M. (1987). Improving adherence to physical activity. *Health Psychology, 6*, 159–172.

Hildebrandt, V. H., Ooijendijk, W. T. M., Stiggelbout, M. and Hopman-Rock, M. (2004). *Trendrapport Bewegen en Gezondheid 2002–2003*. Hoofddorp/Leiden, the Netherlands: TNO.

Kemper, H. C. G., Ooijendijk, W. T. M. and Stiggelbout, M. (2000). De Nederlandse Gezonde Beweeg Norm. *Tijdschrift voor Sociale Gezondheidszorg, 78*, 180–183.

King, A. C., Blair, S. N., Bild, D. E. and Dishman, R. K. (1992). Determinants of physical activity and interventions in adults. *Medicine and Science in Sports and Exercise, 24*, 221–S236.

Kroes, G. and De Greef, M. H. G. (2000). National initiatives for the promotion of physical activity for older persons in the Netherlands. *Journal of Aging and Physical Activity, 8*, 431–435.

McAuley, E. and Courneya, K. S. (1993). Adherence to exercise and physical activity as health-promoting behaviours: attitudinal and self-efficacy influences. *Applied & Preventive Psychology, 2*, 65–77.

Marcus, B. H. and Owen, N. (1992). Motivational readiness, self-efficacy and decision-making for exercise. *Journal Applied Social Psychology, 22*, 3–16.

Marcus, B. H. and Stanton, A. L. (1993). Evaluation of relapse prevention and reinforcement interventions to promote exercise adherence in sedentary females. *Research Quarterly for Exercise and Sport, 64*, 447–452.

Marlatt, G. A. and Gordon, J. R. (1985). *Relapse prevention: maintenance in treatment of addictive disorders*. New York: Guildford Press.

Nelson, M. E., Rejeski, W. J. and Blair, S. N. (2007). Physical activity and public health in older adults: recommendation from the American College of Sports Medicine and the American Heart Association. *Medicine & Science in Sports & Exercise, 39*(8), 1435–1445.

Ooijendijk, W. T. M., Hildebrandt, V. H. and Hopman-Rock, M. (Eds). (2007). *Trendrapport Bewegen en Gezondheid 2004–2005*. Leiden: TNO Quality of Life.

Ooijendijk, W. T. M., Hildebrandt, V. H. and Stiggelbout, M. (2002). Lichamelijke activiteit in Nederland in 2000. In W. T. M. Ooijendijk, V. H. Hildebrandt and M. Stiggelbout (Eds), *Trendrapport Bewegen en Gezondheid 2000–2001*. Hoofddorp/Leiden: TNO Arbeid/TNO Preventie en Gezondheid.

Pate, R. R., Pratt, M., Blair, S. N., Haskell, W. L., Macera, C. A., Bouchard, C., Buchner, D., Ettinger, W., Heath, G. W., King, A. C., Kriska, A., Leon, A. S., Marcus, B. H., Morris, J., Paffenbarger Jr., R. S., Patrick, K., Pollock, M. L., Rippe, J. M., Sallis, J. and Wilmore, J. H. (1995). Physical activity and public health. A recommendation from the Centers for Disease Control and Prevention and the American College of Sports Medicine. *Journal of the American Medical Association, 273*, 402–407.

Prochaska, J. O. and DiClemente, C. C. (1983). Stages and process of self change of smoking: toward an integrative model of change. *Journal of Consulting and Clinical Psychology, 51*, 390–395.

Stiggelbout, M. (2008). *More exercise for seniors: opportunities and challenges*. Amster-dam: Body@Work VUMC TNO. Thesis; ISBN 978-90-5986-258-6. Retrieved 4 January 2011, from http://dare.ubvu.vu.nl/bitstream/1871/12905/5/7506.pdf.

Stiggelbout, M., Hopman-Rock, M. and van Mechelen, W. (2008). Entry correlates, and motivations of older adults participating in organised exercise programmes. *Journal of Aging and Physical Activity*, *16*, 342–354.

Visser, M., Launer, L. J., Deurenberg, P. and Deeg, D. J. H. (1997). Total and sports activity in older men and women: relation with body fat distribution. *American Journal of Epidemiology*, *145*, 752–761.

12 Energising lives and the value of physical activity for older adults

Len Almond

Introduction

The relationship between physical activity and older adults is complicated. Functional decline and the association of medical conditions with advancing age make it difficult for many older adults to comprehend the value of being active. In the same way, many practitioners find it difficult to convince older adults that they can benefit significantly from being more active on a daily basis.

In this chapter, a positive approach to the promotion of purposeful physical pursuits will be presented, together with an account of why older adults do not value physical activity. This will be followed by an outline of a range of promotions that have been undertaken in the United Kingdom (UK) and what has been achieved in promoting the physical activity message. Finally, it will be proposed that an understanding of how to engage with older adults is a productive route for practitioners to pursue.

Background

We are often told that regular exercise is important and the Chief Medical Officer in England (Department of Health, 2004) has provided substantial evidence that exercise is good for all of us, especially older adults, and can bring significant health benefits and enhance well-being. But is this advice taken up by the general population? From the 2007 and 2008 Health Surveys for England (Craig and Shelton, 2008; Craig *et al.*, 2009) it is quite clear, because the figures are so low, that very few people, especially older adults (beyond 55 years) value exercise. Table 12.1 illustrates quite clearly how little exercise was undertaken by older adults in 2008. Between the two surveys, there has been a very slight increase in levels of physical activity in some older adults, but there has been no change in participation by adults aged 75 and above, yet adults in this age bracket could benefit substantially from undertaking some exercise.

The costs of physical inactivity to the English health service are substantial. Allender *et al.* (2007) estimate £1.06 billion per annum, with most of this cost associated with older adults. Only a small proportion of people who are inactive, however, can claim that a medical condition limits their participation in physical

Table 12.1 Percentage of people who do not do sufficient physical activity (Craig *et al.*, 2009)

	Men	Women
55–64 years	65%	73%
65–74 years	79%	84%
75+	92%	96%

activity. This means that much of the health cost is caused by lifestyle choices, a lack of commitment to regular physical activity or a lack of awareness of the importance of being active.

People over the age of 55 represent the most sedentary segment of the adult population (Sport England, 2006a). Sedentary behaviour, such as long spells of sitting,[1] combined with low levels of physical activity, contribute significantly to a major decline in functional capacity among older people, which in turn can lead to limitations in everyday life.

For older adults, this situation is made worse by a steady decline in muscle mass and strength, endurance, bone density and flexibility, which are all 'lost' at a rate of about 10 per cent per decade after the age of 30 (Rennie, 2009). Muscle power (the speed with which a muscle is used) is lost at an even faster rate of about 30 per cent per decade which means that many older adults will find it difficult to rise from a chair unaided (Skelton *et al.*, 1994). As a consequence of this significant decline, 31 per cent of women over 70 are unable to walk 400 metres (Allender *et al.*, 2008). In effect, this means that their world is restricted to a radius of approximately 200 metres around their home. This has major implications for adults who can be prone to isolation and therefore loneliness, which has a major impact on social care costs (Abate *et al.*, 2007).

The combined effect of inactivity, long spells of sedentary behaviour and the gradual decline in muscle strength and muscle mass generates for many people an *inactivity impairment* that constrains their quality of living, leading to a loss of independence and reduced opportunities to participate in the community. When one examines the evidence of functional decline associated with ageing, together with an *inactivity impairment*, it signifies the need to place a much higher priority on the importance of promoting regular physical activity for all older people. This impoverished situation is preventable, yet so little is being done to address it: it is simply not recognised as a priority.

The previous argument relates to all older adults, but adults near to retirement age are just as vulnerable, especially those with a history of doing very little physical activity. The move towards longer working lives (working beyond current retirement age) and concern over the productivity of workers raises questions about workability, particularly post-55 years of age. An ageing workforce presents a problem that needs to be recognised by all employers as well as employees.

Workability and capacity to lead a productive working life depends on the level of regular physical activity to which people have made a commitment, and their maintenance of functional ability. The active person is far more likely to be more productive and healthy than an inactive employee (Medibank Private, 2007). However, workability also depends on the level of functioning impairments (poor quality sleep, sedentary lifestyle as well as anxiety and depression), which combine to reduce a person's workability. Individuals' capacity for physical activity (even though they may have a stable medical condition) and their commitment to being active on a regular basis are the main contributors to enhancing workability and enabling them to enjoy the benefits of a longer working life, as well as contributing to the quality of their leisure time. All employers need to be aware of the value of regular physical activity for the workforce (Boorman, 2009) and how it contributes to enhancing workability and productivity. In the same way, all older employees need to be aware of the significance of regular physical activity in enhancing their quality of living, their health and well-being status, as well as enabling their capacity to raise productivity levels.

In recent years, substantial progress has been made in clarifying how much and what kind of physical activity is needed to maintain functional ability and reduce the risk of developing debilitating conditions that hinder the quality of daily life and one's health. A number of countries have provided guidance for professionals to ensure informed practice as well as messages and tips for the general public. In the United Kingdom, Australia, Canada and United States of America, comprehensive guidelines are available, which highlight the need for flexibility in how the minimum requirements can be achieved (US Department of Health and Human Services, 2008). Instead of just one message to aim for 30 minutes of moderate physical activity on at least five days per week, there is now a more flexible message to aim for 150 minutes of physical activity per week, which provides scope for a variety of ways to achieve this minimum weekly target, including vigorous exercise, light activity and different combinations of frequency and duration. A number of adults in their sixties and early seventies are able to engage in vigorous exercise whereas others can only sustain a walking pace. Thus, the flexibility of the new messages and guidance enables the professional working with older adults of differing abilities to design programmes that accommodate diverse needs.

The new guidelines also focus on the need to recognise the value of activities that promote muscle strength and, for those at risk of falls, balance training is recommended. However, the new international guidelines have highlighted a major shift in thinking. There is a new recommendation to limit the amount of sedentary behaviour because there is robust evidence that demonstrates the dangers that prolonged spells of sitting can have on people's lives, their health and well-being (Hamilton *et al.*, 2008; Owen *et al.*, 2009). In the case of older adults, this represents a major problem that is not being addressed. The guidelines make a very important point by proposing that the risks of inactivity far exceed the risks that can arise for some people when undertaking physical activity.

Why do older adults not do sufficient exercise?

There have been a considerable number of research reports, particularly in psychology, which have explored the determinants of inactivity patterns or why people are unwilling to participate regularly in physical activity. However, despite this research, there are some very basic issues that need to be addressed. The work of the British Heart Foundation National Centre for Physical Activity and Health (BHFNC) with older adults has involved a wide range of seminars throughout the UK and a number of key issues have emerged. Three issues dominate.

For most adults, 30 minutes of physical activity represents only 2 per cent of their day, yet the majority of adults will spend a significant amount of their day sitting in front of a screen (television, computer or games console). Estimates vary between 14 and 21 per cent of their day. In the sample derived from BHFNC seminar responses, it was 16.3 per cent. Thus, 'Not having enough time' is not an adequate explanation for low levels of physical activity. It is simply that adults do not recognise daily physical activity as a priority in their lives. When one examines how often people are physically active at weekends, this position is reinforced; adults and children are less active at weekends than working days or school days. This position is similar with older adults, even though their free time is considerably more. Compared with weekdays, all adults are less active at weekends when theoretically they have more time. Thus, the first issue is that engaging in purposeful physical pursuits is a low priority in the lives of most people. Social marketing techniques need to recognise this position and investigate how this can be addressed.

The first issue is reinforced when listening to discussions with many adults where they express the view that they have great difficulty in understanding the physical activity message and what they need to do. There is good evidence for this point of view with only 3 per cent of male and 7 per cent of female older adults (55–64 age range) knowing what the current physical activity recommendations were (Craig and Shelton, 2008). Focus groups with older adults aged 55–65 during the British Heart Foundation media campaign, '30 a day', in 2008, reported very little understanding of what is entailed in 30 minutes of moderate activity on five or more days a week. The media compounds the problem by citing different research projects that appear to contradict each other. As a result, the picture for many adults is confusing.

The second issue is compounded by the diversity of the population called 'older adults'. This is particularly important, because the older adult could be a very active 55-year-old woman, a 68-year-old man exercising daily with two medical conditions, a person who has never exercised for 40 years, an active 95-year-old woman living independently or a very frail 80-year-old man; the range is extensive. It is little wonder that older adults express confusion when there is this level of diversity. Much more detailed and personalised guidance is required to take account of the diversity of the older adult population – a 'catch-all' policy is inadequate.

In 2008, in response to this issue, the BHFNC launched a consultation document, and held a series of regional seminars where they explored this issue in greater depth. This resulted in a new guidance document, *30 MINS a day: policy blueprint for increasing physical activity levels in the over 50s* (BHFNC, 2009) that provided more comprehensive and informed advice for all professionals working with older adults. The Chief Medical Officer for England will launch new physical activity guidelines for the whole life-course in 2011.

A third issue was identified in a report commissioned by BHF to explore attitudes of older adults to physical activity in preparation for the BHF Older People media campaign (unpublished document for BHF-30 a Day, 2008). One disturbing point emerged that 62 per cent of the sample reported that they would not be motivated to exercise, even if their life depended on it. This report illustrates what a complex problem we are dealing with, in trying to convince people that regular physical activity has value. For older adults, their age and the presence of some limiting medical conditions, together with a sense of fatalism, are often cited as reasons why they cannot undertake sufficient exercise on a daily basis (Sport England, 2006b).

When one considers these three issues, it would appear that we have failed to demonstrate that physical activity can be a powerful force in promoting well-being, enabling people to flourish and enrich their lives.

How can these issues be addressed?

The promotion of physical activity is often justified on the grounds that it can reduce the risks of people acquiring specific medical conditions or delaying the onset of functional decline. This prevention agenda also sees physical activity as a way of reducing the costs of ill-health. This argument appears to have little power in persuading people to become more active and therefore a different, more positive perspective needs to be adopted.

There is a powerful case for promoting the idea that more people should be more active more often. The Chief Medical Officers' report (Department of Health, 2004) and more recently Be Active Be Healthy, a plan for getting the nation moving (Department of Health, 2009), provide evidence to demonstrate the effective role physical activity can play in the treatment of specific medical conditions and identify the major economic benefits of getting the nation to be more active.

However, in an analysis of documents that promote physical activity and health, it is usual to associate physical activity with two roles: (1) therapy and treatment of specific medical conditions; and (2) prevention. Engagement in physical activity can reduce the risks for acquiring specific medical conditions as well as functional decline in older adults. Physical activity is seen as an instrumental tool to support therapy (treatment) programmes. Of course, this is valuable and primary care teams need to ensure that effective programmes are in place. However, this approach alone is inadequate and decision-makers need to highlight the role of a preventative agenda for physical activity.

For example, in terms of older adults, the prevention agenda is advocated on the grounds that it will:

- reduce the risk for specific medical conditions associated with older adults;
- delay functional decline;
- delay dependency;
- prevent the complications of immobility.

Thus, the justification for the promotion of regular physical activity in strategy documents highlights the economic cost of inactivity and the need for a prevention action plan. However, there is a major problem with the prevention agenda because it tends to be associated with a negative message: 'if you don't exercise regularly you put yourself at risk of acquiring a number of medical conditions, which could reduce your life expectancy and constrain your ability to maintain your health at an optimal level and influence your wellbeing'. In the same way, 'if you don't exercise you (an older adult) will be at risk of substantial functional decline'. People are warned of the dangers of lifestyle choices that can cause ill-health and reduction in quality of living. Thus, promoting more physical activity will reduce the risk of specific conditions that impinge on well-being and once again save health services considerable sums of money.

It is quite clear that current approaches to the promotion of physical activity have failed because large numbers of people have not been convinced that they need to take up exercise on a regular basis. How should this be approached? The presentation of the prevention agenda may be the problem because it is clearly more important to halt or delay the development of specific conditions than wait until people have developed a condition. One way to approach this problem is to formulate a more positive message associated with being active, together with a different image of purposeful physical pursuits. There is a need for a more positive message that reaches individual people, engages their interest and stimulates action instead of an association with negative messages.

One starting point is to build on the evidence emerging from a series of 34 focus groups (Sport England, 2007) with sedentary adults, who had joined a workplace programme to encourage people to become more physically active in a wide variety of activities and who had maintained their commitment over a whole year. 'I have more energy now' was the main reason that most participants gave for making a commitment to being active and completing the programme. This is a significant point because the participants associated their new vitality and having more energy with being active on a regular basis. This is also a powerful argument and needs to be recognised because it may be the lead that stimulates people to see 'being active' as a much higher priority in their lives. It is also particularly pertinent in the case of older adults because they often comment that they don't have much energy. It represents an important start for a new message with a positive perspective for the promotion of purposeful physical pursuits. We need to use the idea that purposeful physical pursuits can energise lives, enabling people to feel that they have more vitality and dynamism.

In the development of the Moving More Often programme older adults' feelings were taken into account (Laventure, 2004). In discussions with older adults who were asked 'what would make life better?' the following three points were highlighted. They would like to:

- get out more;
- talk with someone regularly; and
- do something.

Central to these three points is the capability to move but a stimulus is needed for action. In one project, the results of this study formed the basis for action by community nurses who identified people (usually women) living independently but who rarely left their house or flat and experienced isolation. The nurses were able to encourage the older adults to start walking to local shops to meet people and talk. This led to more walking on a regular basis on walks led by experienced staff, who encouraged the social side of meeting and walking as a group. Some of the older adults who gained confidence and increased their stamina and mobility were then encouraged to try other physical pursuits that enriched their social life and improved the quality of their lives. Once again, regular walking enabled the participants to claim that they had more energy and more vitality.

This project illustrates another positive message; that of enriching lives. The idea of enriching lives through engaging in physical pursuits, such as walking, supported by a social context, represents a powerful reason for introducing a whole range of purposeful physical activities to both young and old. However, we need to emphasise that enriching lives is about widening perspectives, extending one's horizons of what one is capable of doing, acquiring confidence, achieving a sense of success and feeling good about one's achievements. This was achieved in the project with community nurses but it was also the social context that reinforced the commitment to being active because it extended social contacts and built new social networks. These are important factors for older adults.

In a more positive perspective, the value of the message 'purposeful physical pursuits' can be seen as one that builds a well-being resource and enables people to flourish in three ways:

- energises lives;
- enriches lives; and
- support by a social context in which there is a wealth of social contacts.

If we are to persuade more people to be more active more of the time, we need to ensure that the positive benefits are associated with having more energy and a feeling of enhanced vitality. This may help older adults (as well as people of all ages) to recognise that regular purposeful physical pursuits can be important for one's well-being. The health benefits of this commitment will naturally accrue and the prevention agenda will be addressed with no extra resources or cost. These points are important because a more positive and personal message can present purposeful physical pursuits in a different light since the activity levels of older adults are exceptionally low. In the place of a more traditional view that regular physical activity can reduce the risks of particular medical conditions, we need to replace it with a focus on the central role that physical activity can play in energising lives and enabling people to live life to the full, whatever their age. In this way, the health benefits of regular physical activity can be achieved and we will have addressed the prevention agenda in the process.

In addition, we can help the general public to understand that even people with medical conditions can exercise safely and recognise that the risks of inactivity and sedentary behaviour can be more serious than the risks of exercising.

Promoting purposeful physical pursuits with older adults

The British Heart Foundation National Centre for Physical Activity and Health (www.bhfactive.org.uk) developed a range of initiatives to promote physical activity for older adults. Under the direction of Bob Laventure (a consultant for the BHFNC) a number of regional training seminars were conducted to enable professionals in different fields to capture the imagination of older adults and stimulate more purposeful physical pursuits to energise and enrich their lives. The training seminars also identified the need to provide professionals with a pedagogy of practice that enabled them to engage productively with older adults. A number of these initiatives are outlined below.

In the first instance, an 'Active for Later Life' resource was created to provide a 'one stop' source of information and reference for professional staff in the field (Laventure, 2003a). This comprehensive resource provided detailed guidance, together with a range of briefing papers covering the whole field. It was supported by series of regional seminars to guide participants through the material.

At the same time, a peer mentoring resource 'Someone Like Me' was developed to encourage older adults to help other older adults, to stimulate interest in being active and to provide a support to those who found it difficult to maintain a commitment (Laventure, 2003b). It was felt that older adults needed people of their own age to supplement the role of physical activity professionals. Older adults who attended the training courses had the opportunity to learn the skills of engaging with their peers and promoting physical activity. In this context, the mentors learned how to adopt an educational role and use a pedagogy that enabled them to reach out to people, engage with them and enable them to gain the confidence to be more active, more often. However, there was recognition that this was not enough. Many of the mentors and their peers were of a certain age and the people who needed most help in becoming active were being neglected.

To solve this problem, a programme called 'Moving More Often' was developed to enable staff in care homes, sheltered accommodation and community hubs to provide purposeful physical pursuits to encourage residents and other interested older adults to be more active (Laventure, 2004). A number of different modules to cater for different needs and interests were developed:

- Games People Play
- Walk with Me
- Out and About
- Just Me
- Dance with Me
- Gardening and allotments
- Action rhymes and songs
- Tai Chi
- Electronic games that encourage being active (e.g. Wii).

Training was provided so that staff in different settings could deliver a range of modules to suit their needs, preferences and the availability of resources. The evaluation of different schemes indicated that the modules raised a great deal of interest and increased participation rates considerably when there were enthusiastic staff. However, they also identified the considerable problems that care settings experience in devising ways of encouraging physical activity on a regular basis, such as space, available resources, reaching all residents and having enthusiastic staff with confidence to get older adults interested. There was considerable reluctance from many residents who simply didn't want to participate. These issues are being tackled in a new wave of developments but it has to be recognised that we need to sell the idea first to managers of care settings if we are to reach the majority of older adults.

In Wales and Yorkshire, two areas have gone beyond 'Moving More Often' and introduced the idea of a Care Homes Olympic festival, which has been called an OlympAge. In an OlympAge, men and women residents from different care homes come together to take part in a festival to experience a wide range of purposeful physical pursuits. The festivals have generated considerable interest, including media attention, and attracted acclaim from different sources due to the obvious enjoyment and the physical abilities of the participants. In one instance, each care setting was asked to make its own flag which was paraded in front of a large audience in the same way that Olympic athletes do.

This idea has spread more widely as physical activity and health professionals, together with care setting staff, recognise the value of such events. Many people would see this as a genuine legacy from the 2012 Olympics if each town and city in the UK promoted a Care Homes OlympAge prior to the Olympic Games. This would be a real achievement and provide a significant image of just what older adults are capable of. It would represent a very powerful media message. However, there is a long way to go before we can encourage all care homes to see physical activity as a way of enriching and energising lives.

These initiatives have been supported by two campaigns. The British Heart Foundation (BHF) launched a media campaign called 30 a Day. A range of media opportunities including television advertisements, radio programmes, large billboard posters, leaflets and booklets were widely distributed across the country. They raised considerable interest and the posters aroused substantial reaction and controversy that generated even more publicity. It was the first time that such a campaign had been held and it was widely regarded as a great success.

In order to support Older People's Day (1 October 2010), a promotion coordinated by the Department of Work and Pensions was instigated. The BHFNC contributed to the campaign by writing a comprehensive set of guidelines for promoting purposeful physical pursuits with older adults. In this new resource, guidelines were developed for professionals working with older adults outlining how much physical activity was needed for older adults to maintain health and enhance their well-being, how programmes could be developed to suit different needs and examples of evidence-based interventions with older adults. Advice was also provided on how to communicate positive messages about purposeful physical pursuits.

Pedagogy

In addition to promoting a positive message about the values of being active, there is one factor that is rarely addressed; the skills and empathy of the practitioner working with older adults. Older adults need to relate to the practitioner and feel confident that they are safe and in good hands. These skills represent a pedagogy of engagement – engaging productively with older adults. Thus, pedagogy needs to be seen in terms of the art and science of engaging with people for productive learning or productive relationships. A pedagogy of engagement is central to the art of health promotion and working with people of all ages, especially if the practitioner is trying to convince older adults to love being active and to help them to make a commitment.

The following items are seen as crucial skills to ensure successful engagement:

• reach out to older adults;
• establish a connection with individual adults that enables a relationship to prosper;
• engage with them productively with enthusiasm and empathy;
• draw them out with challenges that excite, engage their interest and allow them to develop with confidence; and
• stretch their capabilities, interests and love of being active.

The skills outlined above represent a set of core competences, not simply technical competences because the practitioners need to apply them in context and with an understanding of the older adults with whom they are working. These technical competences need appropriate practice, critical reflection, refinement and a recognition that they are striving to learn how to engage with people to improve their competence and success.

Conclusion

Finally, to be successful in ensuring that all older adults have the opportunity to engage in purposeful physical pursuits to enhance the quality of their lives and make an impact on their well-being, we need to make a convincing and comprehensive evidence-based case to national decision-makers. This advocacy needs to go beyond the National Coalition for Active Ageing, supported by the BHF National Centre for Physical Activity and Health. They have led attempts to promote a range of initiatives for professionals working with older adults, but more work needs to be done. The main priority is to develop a comprehensive working document that highlights the economic value of promoting physical activity and make comparisons with other lifestyle initiatives to demonstrate that physical activity is undervalued and needs to be taken much more seriously. Relevant central government departments need to be presented with convincing evidence of its value and potential uses in health policy for older adults.

Local authorities need to have available a comprehensive evidence-based framework of essential services for physical activity promotion that caters for the diversity of needs amongst older adults. Such a framework can become a guide to good practice and if it is closely associated with a strong economic case for deci-sion- and/or policy-makers, local authorities can make a significant impact on the lives of older adults.

Note

1. Sitting for two hours is seen as a risk factor for a number of medical problems (Owen *et al.*, 2009; Hamilton *et al.*, 2008).

References

Abate, M., Di Iorio, A., Di Renzo, D., Paganelli, R., Saggini, R. and Abate, G. (2007). Frailty in the elderly: the physical dimension. *Eura Medicophys*, *43*, 407–415.

Allender, S., Hutchinson, L. A. and Foster, C. (2008). Life-change events and participation in physical activity: a systematic review. *Health Promotion International*, *23*, 160–172.

Allender, S., Foster, C., Scarborough, P. and Rayner, M. (2007). The burden of physical activity-related ill health in the UK. *Journal of Epidemiological Community Health*, *61*, 344–348.

Boorman, S. (2009). *NHS health and well-being: final report*. Department of Health.

BHFNC (2009). *30 MINS a day: policy blueprint for increasing physical activity levels in the over 50s*. Retrieved from www.bhfactive.org.uk/older-adults/currentprojects. html#guidelines.

Craig, R. and Shelton, N. (2008). *Health survey for England – 2007: vol 1 healthy lifestyles, knowledge, attitudes and behaviour*. NHS Information Centre.

Craig, R., Mindell, J. and Hirani, V. (2009). *Health survey for England – 2008: vol 1 physi-cal activity and fitness*. NHS Information Centre.

Department of Health (2004). *Chief Medical Officer's report: at least five a week: evidence on the impact of physical activity and its relationship to health*. London: HMSO.

Department of Health (2009). *Be active, be healthy: a plan for getting the nation moving*. London: DH Publications.

Hamilton, M. T., Healy, G. N., Dunstan, D. W., Zderic, T. W. and Owen, N. (2008). Too little exercise and too much sitting: inactivity physiology and the need for new recom-mendations on sedentary behaviour. *Current Cardiovascular Risk Reports*, *2*, 292–298.

Laventure, R. M. E. (2003a). *Active for later life. British Heart Foundation tool kit for promoting physical activity with older adults*. British Heart Foundation National Centre for Physical Activity and Health, Loughborough University.

Laventure, R. M. E. (2003b). *'Some like me!' – senior peer mentoring and physical activity – a guide to practice*. British Heart Foundation National Centre for Physical Activity and Health, Loughborough University.

Laventure, R. M. E. (2004). *'Moving more often'*. British Heart Foundation National Centre for Physical Activity and Health, Loughborough University.

Medibank Private (2007). *Sick at work. The cost of presenteeism to your business and the economy.* Retrieved from www.medibank.com.au/Client/Documents/Pdfs/sick_at_work.pdf.

Owen, N., Bauman, A. and Brown, W. (2009). Too much sitting: a novel and important predictor of chronic disease risk? *British Journal of Sports Medicine*, 43, 81–83.

Rennie, M. J. (2009). Anabolic resistance: the effects of aging, sexual dimorphism, and immobilization on human muscle protein turnover. *Applied Physiology, Nutrition and Metabolism, 34*(3), 377–381.

Skelton, D. A., Greigh, C. A., Davies, J. M. and Young, A. (1994). Strength, power and related functional ability of healthy people aged 65–89 years. *Age and Ageing, 23*, 371–377.

Sport England (2006a). *Active people survey 2.* London: Sport England.

Sport England (2006b). Understanding participation in sport: what determines sport participation among recently retired people? London: Sport England.

Sport England (2007). *Evaluation of the £1 million challenge.* Manchester: North West Sport England Region.

U.S. Department of Health and Human Services (2008). *Physical activity guidelines for Americans.*

Index